Welcome to the *EVERYTHING*® series!

These handy, accessible books give you all you need to tackle a difficult project, gain a new hobby, comprehend a fascinating topic, prepare for an exam, or even brush up on something you learned back in school but have since forgotten.

You can read an *EVERYTHING*® book from cover-to-cover or just pick out the information you want from our four useful boxes: e-facts, e-ssentials, e-alerts, and e-questions. We literally give you everything you need to know on the subject, but throw in a lot of fun stuff along the way, too.

We now have well over 100 *EVERYTHING*® books in print, spanning such wide-ranging topics as weddings, pregnancy, wine, learning guitar, one-pot cooking, managing people, and so much more. When you're done reading them all, you can finally say you know *EVERYTHING*®!

FACTS

Important sound bytes
of information

SSENTIALS

Quick handy tips

ALERT

Urgent warnings

QUESTIONS?

Solutions to
common problems

Dear Reader,

Although they have been around since the thirteenth century, candles are making a modern-day comeback. Not only do bring light to darkness, but they have the power to alter moods, add warmth to a room, or bring a sense of celebration to any occasion.

If you love candles, making them at home is a great way to have an ample supply on hand all the time without spending a fortune. But in addition to the cost benefits, home candlemaking is a fun and entertaining way to spend an afternoon, whether you're by yourself or with friends. All you need to get started are a few basic materials, some instructions, and a sense of creativity. Making candles yourself also gives you the opportunity to be an artist, adding personal and unique touches to your creations.

In this book, I've shared some of my favorite candles to make, as well as some fascinating bits of history about the craft. I hope that it will inspire you to create your own beautiful and unique candles.

Happy candlemaking!

M.J. Abadie

THE
EVERYTHING
CANDLEMAKING
BOOK

Create homemade candles in
house-warming colors, interesting
shapes, and appealing scents

M.J. Abadie

Adams Media Corporation
Avon, Massachusetts

EDITORIAL
Publishing Director: Gary M. Krebs
Managing Editor: Kate McBride
Copy Chief: Laura MacLaughlin
Acquisitions Editor: Allison Carpenter Yoder
Development Editor: Sue Ducharme

PRODUCTION
Production Director: Susan Beale
Production Manager: Michelle Roy Kelly
Series Designer: Daria Perreault
Layout and Graphics: Arlene Apone,
Paul Beatrice, Brooke Camfield,
Colleen Cunningham, Daria Perreault,
Frank Rivera

An Everything® Series Book.
Everything® and everything.com® are registered trademarks of F+W Publications, Inc.

Published by Adams Media, an F+W Publications Company
57 Littlefield Street, Avon, MA 02322, U.S.A.
www.adamsmedia.com

ISBN: 1-58062-623-8
Printed in the United States of America.

J I H G F E D C B

Library of Congress Cataloging-in-Publication Data
Abadie, M.J. (Marie-Jeanne)
   The Everything candlemaking book : set the perfect mood with
homemade candles in housewarming colors, interesting shapes, and
appealing scents / by M.J. Abadie
      p.   cm. — (Everything series)
   ISBN 1-58062-623-8
   1. Candlemaking. I. Title. II. Series.
TT896.5 .A23 2002
745.593'32—dc21   2001053951

This publication is designed to provide accurate and authoritative information with regard to the subject matter covered. It is sold with the understanding that the publisher is not engaged in rendering legal, accounting, or other professional advice. If legal advice or other expert assistance is required, the services of a competent professional person should be sought.
   —From a *Declaration of Principles* jointly adopted by a Committee of the
American Bar Association and a Committee of Publishers and Associations

Cover illustrations by Barry Littmann.
Interior illustrations by Kathie Kelleher.
Interior photographs by Jagdish Agarwal, Dinodia Photo Library, *www.dinodia.com.*

This book is available at quantity discounts for bulk purchases.
For information, call 1-800-872-5627.

Visit the entire Everything® series at everything.com

Dedication

To Jimmi Rushing in
appreciation of her genuine
and generous support

and *in memoriam* to
the Princess Mushkin
January 3, 1987–
November 3, 2000.

Contents

ACKNOWLEDGMENTS xi

CHAPTER 1 *The History of*
Candlemaking 1

Candle Renaissance 2
The Earliest Traces of Candlelight . . . 3
Who Made the First Candle? 4
The Development of Rushlights 5
Nothing New under the Sun 7
The Advent of Modern
        Candlemaking 8
Candle Streetlights 9
The First Candle Molds 9
All the World's a Stage 10
Fire Without Matches 11
Revolutionary Developments 12
Illuminating Gas 14
From Past to Present 15

CHAPTER 2 *Candles in the New World* . . 17

The Colonial Period 18
Burn That Fat 20

Superior Spermaceti 21
Pioneer Candlemaking 23
Wick Development 24
Introduction of Stearin 25
Made in the U.S.A. 26
A Flip of the Switch 26
A Modern Romance 27
Candlemaking As a Natural Art 28

CHAPTER 3 *Candlemaking As*
a Sacred Art 29

Marvelous Mythology 30
Candles in Christianity 33
Jewish Candle Symbolism 35
Let There Be Light 36
Sacred Candlelight 39
Making Candle Magic 41
Everyday Rituals 43
Candle-Gazing Meditation 45
Ritual Candle Sets As Gifts 46
Mind-Calming Visualization
        with Candles 46
Healing with Candles 48

CHAPTER 4 *Candles—All You Need to Know* 49

Candle Industry Facts 50
Industry Directory Available 51
The Lost Art of Burning
 Candles Properly 52
How to Put Candles Out
 Correctly 53
Storing Candles 53
Basic Methods 54
Candle Shapes 56
The Significance of Candle Colors . . 58
Keep a Notebook! 59

CHAPTER 5 *How to Get Started* 61

Candle Terminology 62
Wax 101 63
Minding Your Beeswax 65
All about Paraffin 68
Suppliers 69
Recycle Your Wax 70
Wicks 70
Wick Priming 73
Burn Rate 74
How to Avoid the Draft 74
Fire Retardant Is Better 75
Candlemaking Equipment 76
Miscellaneous Equipment 81
Safety First 86
A Clean Workplace Is a
 Safe Workplace 88
The Do's and Don'ts
 of Candlemaking 90
What to Wear 91

CHAPTER 6 *Handmade Rolled and Poured Candles* 93

Roll Your Own 94
Making Your Own Wax Sheets 95
Start Rolling! 97
How to Make a Diagonal
 Rolled Candle 100
Making a Square-Shaped
 Rolled Candle 101
Homemade Birthday Candles 101
May I Pour You a Candle? 102
Advantages of Additives for
 Paraffin Wax 103
Stirring the Pot 104
Making Container Candles 105
Selecting Containers 106
How to Make a Container Candle . . 109
Making a Candle of Many Colors . . 113

CHAPTER 7 *Molded Candles* 115

Using Disposable Molds 116
Molds, Molds, Molds 116
Molding Terminology 117
Molded Candle Basics 118
The Molding Process 119
Finishing the Candle 124
Automatic Wicking 127
Technical Assistance Online 128
The Craft of Moldmaking 128
Moldmaking Step by Step 129
Two-Piece Moldmaking 132
Making a Latex Mold: A Step-by-
 Step Guide 134
Complex Molded Shapes 136
Plaster Bandage Molds 137

CHAPTER 8 *Dipped Candles* 139

Dip Your Wick 140
The Skinny on Dipping 142
Take the Plunge 144
Troubleshooting 150
Dipping in Quantity 154
Dipping for Kids 101 155
Candle-Burning Safety 157
Good News about Wax Removal . . . 157
Create a Pure Beeswax
    Dipped Candle 158
Overdipping: Another Kind of Dip . . 160
Method for Overdipping Candles . . . 161

CHAPTER 9 *Introducing Unusual
    Candles* 165

A Most Unusual Candle! 166
Creative Contemporary
    Candlemaking 167
Danish Tapers 167
Cutout Tapers 168
Birthday Candles 169
Making Wax Matches 170
Making Glow-Through Candles 171
Hand-Molded Candles 172
Unusual Rolled Beeswax Candles . . 174
Beaded Candles 174
Surface Mottling 175
Unusual Molds 176
Unusual Candles Made with
    Large Molds 177
Multiwick Candles 177
Dripped Dipped Candles 180

CHAPTER 10 *Shape, Color,
    and Fragrance* 181

Infinite Variety 182
Blending Waxes for Molding 183
Basically Interesting 184
Identical Twins 186
Improvise 187
Using Color and Fragrance 188
Delightful Shades 189
Colorants at Home 191
Mix and Match 192
Blending Basic Colors 193
Making Sense of Scents 196
All About Essential Oils 198
Herbal Scents 204

CHAPTER 11 *Advanced Creative
    Methods* 205

Making Braided Tapers 206
Twisted Tapers 208
Winding Waxed Wicks 208
Making Spiraled Tapers 210
Advanced Creative Techniques
    with Color 210

CHAPTER 12 *Holidays and Special
    Occasions* 213

Gift-Giving 214
Yule Rules! 215
Hearts and Candles 216
Spring! 218
The Fourth of July 219
Halloween Candles 220

Making Candles for Thanksgiving . . 221
New Baby 222
Romantic Weddings 223
Birthdays 224
Candle Centerpieces for
    Special Occasions 225

CHAPTER 13 **Surface Techniques for**
    Decorating Candles **227**

Candle-Painting 228
Stenciling Candles 229
Other Surface Decorations 232
Making Textured Candles 232
Adding Texture to Finished Candles   234
Carved Candles 235
Surface Decorating Methods 237
Mixing Methods 239

CHAPTER 14 **Appliquéd and**
    Inlaid Candles **241**

Using Pressed Flowers and Grasses . . 242
Wax Appliqué Method 244
Waxing Real Flowers 244
Openwork Appliqué 245
Inlays 245
Inlay with Dried Fruits 247

CHAPTER 15 **Making Decorative**
    Shapes with Molds **249**

Build It Yourself 250
Copycat Molds 252
Casting Candles 253
Casting Sand Candles 254

CHAPTER 16 **Decorative Candleholders**
    and Containers **259**

Candleholders Galore! 260
Shimmering Glassware 261
Wax Will Bowl You Over 262
Nature's Bounty 263
Punched-Tin Holders 265
Potted Candles 266

CHAPTER 17 **Novelty Candles** **267**

The Novelty Challenge 268
Floating Candles 268
Making Floating Flowers 270
By the Beautiful Sea 272
Whipped Wax 273

APPENDIX A **Quick and Easy**
    Molded Candle **275**

APPENDIX B **Quick and Easy**
    Seashell Candle **277**

APPENDIX C **Quick and Easy**
    Sand Candle **279**

INDEX **281**

Acknowledgments

First, I would like to thank my dear friend, Jimmi Rushing, M.L.S., of Stephen F. Austin State University—master researcher and Internet wizard—for her invaluable help in ferreting out much of the information about candles and their fascinating history included herein. In truth, I could not have written this book without her talent for locating information.

Next, my gratitude goes to the many candle crafters who have so generously shared their knowledge through their writings. Of these, special mention goes to the following wonderful and inspiring resources, whose books I highly recommend:

Betty Oppenheimer, author of *The Candlemaker's Companion*; Sue Spear, author of *Candlemaking in a Weekend*; David Constable, author of *Candlemaking: Creative Designs and Techniques*; and Gloria Nicol, author of *Candles: Illuminating Ideas for Creative Candlemaking and Enchanting Displays*.

My appreciation goes also to Chris Santini, who was always there to say an encouraging word; to Anne Sellaro, my agent, for her continuing support of all my work; to Dr. John Torres, whose chiropractic expertise kept me functioning when tension took over; to my nephew Paul Abadie, for cheering me on; to Glen and Yvonne Grey, for their sturdy friendship through all weathers; and to Dr. Bruce Cox, my wonderful veterinarian, and his caring and compassionate staff, for seeing me through the death of my beloved companion cat of twelve years, Mushie, who returned to the great goddess Bast on November 3, 2000.

CHAPTER 1
The History of Candlemaking

The candle has never ceased to fascinate human beings, despite the development of the electric light bulb. Perhaps that is because a candle produces fire as well as light, and fire is essential to human life. After all, a light bulb is merely a fire trying to burn in a vacuum. But a candle offers the real thing: fire you can see, heat you can feel, aromas to smell.

Candle Renaissance

Candles hark back to a time when they were a vital component of life. In this day of ever expanding forms of technological advance, the humble candle is undergoing an amazing renaissance. Its magic never really died, however. It merely went underground during the time when people were so fascinated with the mechanical and manufactured products of their own nimble brains.

My own sense of the amazing interest in and use of candles, both commercially available and more so made by both professional handcrafters and ordinary home candlemakers, is that it is a reaction against the alienating experience of all that is technological and, therefore, soulless. As an exemplar of the soul, the candle provides something that switching on the electric lights can never offer.

Perhaps this is why candles are so valued as mood-altering tools—you can create a wide range of moods with candles that are totally drug-free! You can use candles to match a mood, whether reflective or festive, or to change a mood—from ho-hum to romantic and exciting.

So, hail to the candle and to its burgeoning return to our daily lives.

Fascinating Flames

Why does the candle continue to fascinate us all? I am reminded of an old saying: "The gods gave humans cats so they could stroke the tiger." In some ways, a candle is like a cat—a domestic version of a great force.

Fire—the essence of the candle—was believed to be one of the four elements basic to life on earth, and it is an element fraught with mystery. We gaze into the flames of the fireplace and see all sorts of inner dimensions within ourselves, or we project shapes from our imaginations onto the dancing, leaping flames. Fire fascinates us, whatever its form. We are irresistibly drawn to its magic and mystery.

True, many people still think of candles as something to be used only on holidays such as Christmas or for fancy dinner parties, but more and more of us are finding that we enjoy candles every day. We might light a candle while we are soaking in a tub to relax after a long stressful day, because its gentle flame will enhance our sense of relaxation. Or, we might set a couple of long slender tapers on the dining table, even if the menu is meatloaf, to make dinner more than a humdrum meal. Candles make us linger over our food, they encourage conversation, and they bring people together in their soft glow.

The Earliest Traces of Candlelight

The use of candles and improvements in candlemaking have paralleled human ascent from the Stone Age. We do not have much accurate detail about the use of candles in ancient times. However, references to candles and candlelighting have been found that date as far back as 3,000 B.C. Most of these clues have been discovered in Egypt and the island of Crete in Greece. For instance, clay candleholders dating from the fourth century B.C. have been found at archaeological sites in Egypt.

FACTS

Although highly prized today and throughout history, beeswax was not found to be useful for candlemaking in Europe until the Middle Ages. However, beeswax candles have been found in the tombs of the Egyptian rulers dating back to circa 3000 B.C. They were made much as rolled beeswax candles are today—usually conical in shape (tapered) and with a reed for a wick.

The tomb of Tutankhamen was discovered and opened in 1922 by the team of English Egyptologists Howard Carter (1873–1939) and George Carnavon, the fifth earl of Carnavon (1826–1923), during their explorations of the Valley of the Kings (1906–1923). The death of the Earl of Carnavon so soon after the opening of King Tutankhamen's tomb, and under peculiar circumstances, led credence to the famous "curse" which is supposed to attach to all persons and objects related to the tomb. The discovery of a bronze candleholder in the tomb led to crediting the ancient Egyptians for being the first to develop candles.

Candles are also mentioned in Biblical writings, as early as the tenth century B.C. But although candles appear in the Bible several times, there is no information on how or of what they were made.

Who Made the First Candle?

Although we have no historical record of the first candles used by humans, the oldest actual candle fragment ever found was unearthed by archaeologists near Avignon, France. The fragment has been dated to the first century A.D. It is the Romans who have been given credit for developing the wick candle. These Roman wick candles were used for lighting travelers on their way, illuminating homes and public places, and for burning at night in the temples and public places, especially those used for worship to Roman gods, though we know that the Romans also made use of torches, both for exterior and interior lighting. However, our knowledge of candles such as we know them today dates only to the European Middle Ages.

FACTS

Most people gathered around the light provided by an open fire at night until the invention of oil lamps, or rushlights, which were the first primitive candles. With portable light, people could venture abroad to forage or hunt, or to nearby villages to trade or visit.

Necessity Is the Mother of Invention

There is an old saying that necessity is the mother of invention, and as we have seen, early candles were the product of inventiveness in response to necessity—long before electricity made such needs obsolete for much of the world (except, of course, in times of power outages, when we again must rely on candles, just like our ancestors!). We do not know for sure who invented the candle—there's not enough scientific evidence for proof—but we do know that the ancient Egyptians used rushlights for light. Rushlights were made by dipping grasses or reeds in melted tallow. Such "rush dips" were described by the Roman historian

Pliny, and they had been quite common to countryfolk living in the villages of northern and central Europe until quite recently.

The Development of Rushlights

Rushlights or "rush dips" differ from modern candles because they are made without wicks. These first candle-like lights were probably made from stones or rocks that contained natural depressions. Animal fat would be put in the cup-like shape and a rush (a straw-like plant material) was pressed into the fat and lighted. In time, people learned to press oil out of fruits, nuts, and plants. For instance, in warmer climates such as Italy, olive oil was generally used.

Another development was the extraction of oil from marine life. (See the description of candlefish in Chapter 2.) People began to craft lamps to hold the fat or oil and its rush, or wick. These were made of soft natural stone, like soapstone, or out of clay, beautifully made and decorated. In those days, people considered fire to be sacred and treated its containers with respect, devoting care to their making.

FACTS

Archaeologists have found lamps in nearly every dig. Ancient lamps have a small reservoir for the oil and a lip into which the wick was placed. Some were made of hard precious stone, such as quartz, serpentine, and lapis lazuli, suggesting that the candle's use was highly regarded.

Rushes, which could be found in abundance, could be peeled of their outer bark. The inside pith is a soft and absorbent fibrous material from which an excellent wick can be obtained. (In a pinch, if you were lost in the woods and had some fat or oil from your outdoor cooked meal, you could make your own rushlight.) The technique involved peeling the rush while leaving a strip of the outer bark attached so it would stand upright. Then, the rush was dipped into hot animal fat and cooled. This makes a rudimentary candle. By dipping the same rush into fat several times, you have quite a long-burning candle. A rushlight 15 inches long will burn for half an hour. Several of them will provide enough light to read by. For general illumination, they can be set upright—stuck in the ground or supported otherwise.

A wonderful thing about rushlights was that they were cost-free. Anyone who butchered a pig or a sheep (and nearly everyone did) had plenty of fat available to make them. Even the poorest people could scrounge some rancid fat. They were smoky and smelly—but who cared?

Improvements Continue

The simple rushlights used by earlier people gradually evolved into a rather sophisticated (by the standards of the time) form of rushlight. As always, humans have experienced with the plant forms they found in their environment and turned them to various uses, including medicine and household conveniences, as well as for shelter and transportation.

Rushlight holders

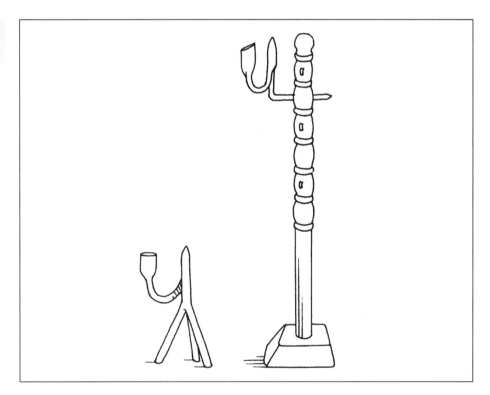

Nothing New under the Sun

The annals of ancient Ireland record candles "as thick as a man's body and the length of a hero's spear." These massive candles—probably made by the process of dipping peeled rushes into melted tallow thousands of times—were crude but effective means of lighting. They were customarily burned all night outside the tents of warrior kings on campaign.

There is evidence that early Chinese and Japanese people made candles with wax derived from insects (perhaps bees: we don't know for sure because in Europe beeswax was not discovered as useful for candlemaking until the Middle Ages) and the seeds of the tallow-tree. These vegetable waxes were molded in paper tubes—a method we can make use of today with the cardboard rolls around which toilet tissue and paper towels are wound! The old adage that "There's nothing new under the sun" may indeed be true!

FACTS

Candles for timekeeping have been recorded from the ninth century. They had twelve divisions marked on them, and each candle burned for twenty-four hours. These candles were in use until only about fifty years ago to measure the duration of a work shift in coal mines.

Most early candles were made of animal fat, but in India, where the use of animal fat was outlawed for religious reasons (the Hindus are primarily vegetarians), wax skimmed from boiling cinnamon was the basis of tapers made for use in Indian temples. Today, we scent candles with cinnamon for the pleasant odor without being aware of the history of this common (now—not then!) flavoring agent, which is actually the bark of a tree.

First Dipping Candles

Candles were also used in the great halls of medieval times—apparently in great number, for those halls were dark and dank and badly in need both of light and cheer. These candles were made by simply dipping a rush wick into fat and letting the fat cool. This dipping process could be repeated indefinitely and is the basis for the modern method of dipping candles.

Prior to the nineteenth century, there were three kinds of animal fat used in candlemaking—all called "tallow"—beef fat from cows, pork fat from pigs (very white), and mutton (or lamb) fat from sheep. Of these, mutton fat was thought superior: it burned longer, smoked little, and was not as smelly. Pork fat, though a nice white, produced a thick smoke and a foul stench. Luckily, today we have odor-free waxes and perfumes and scents to make candles smell nice. But back then, one had to put up with the unpleasant smell of animal fat burning. Lucky people had mutton fat; poor people settled for pig fat, the smelliest.

The Advent of Modern Candlemaking

Candlemaking as we know it began in the thirteenth century when itinerant chandlers (as candlemakers were called then), traveled from town to town and door to door. So in demand were their services that in Paris alone a tax list of 1292 named seventy-one chandlers. The chandlers set up their candlemaking equipment and dipped tapers for their clients, who provided the material. In both Paris and England, wax chandlers and tallow chandlers formed guilds. The English Tallow Chandlers were incorporated in 1462 and they regulated trade in candles made from animal fat, made for the common folk. Those who worked with wax were the upper crust of candlemakers and made a lot more money because only the wealthy could afford wax. So prized were wax candles that the home that had them set them proudly in pewter or silver holders.

Although beeswax had probably been recognized for centuries as a material for making candles, it is extremely difficult to handle. Therefore, until the invention of candle molds and stearin (1820s), all beeswax candles had to be made by hand, which was a time-consuming and laborious process. Yet, only beeswax candles were used in churches and monastery chapels.

Because churches and monasteries of the period were great users of candles, monasteries had extensive candlemaking facilities on their properties. Candlemaking, like cooking and gardening, was one of the common works carried on in these institutions. One writer has speculated that monks' reputation for being always cheerful came not from spiritual development but from the drinking of mead, a byproduct of the honey left over from the making of beeswax candles. No doubt the danger of getting stung by a bee had its compensations.

So valued was beeswax, and so expensive, that Catholics in the Middle Ages were permitted to use beeswax to pay their tithes to the Church! And since the Church's candles *had* to be made of beeswax, by papal decree, this was an important source of the precious substance for Church use.

FACTS

Canon law of the Roman Catholic Church declared that the church's beeswax candles must contain not less than 5l percent beeswax. The balance can be a vegetable or mineral wax, but never tallow. Candles for specific rites must contain either l00 percent or two-thirds beeswax. For this reason, the Catholic Church has been the largest consumer of candles made of beeswax—the most expensive of all waxes and the most difficult to manipulate, especially in olden times—throughout the world.

Candle Streetlights

From the l400s on, candle lanterns were used to light streets at night. The town crier, whose job it was to attend the candles, would call out the hour, "Ten o'clock and all's well," to advise the populace the streetlights revealed no threat to their safety. Before these candle streetlights were invented and installed, people stayed indoors after dark for fear of assault, robbery, or attack. Only the brave, the aristocracy (who could afford candlelit carriages and servants to carry lighted candles ahead of them if they walked), and the criminally intent went out.

The First Candle Molds

The first use of molds for candlemaking of which we are aware was in fifteenth century, in Paris, which was a center of wax chandlering at the time. In fact, the Parisian wax chandlers were the first to form their own guild.

However, these wooden candle molds could only be used to make tallow candles. Beeswax, when melted, is very sticky, and it couldn't be got out of the molds. Therefore, beeswax candles, made only for churches and the homes of the rich, continued to be made totally by hand. This labor-intensive process added much to the already expensive raw material. Even today, beeswax candles are expensive to purchase, which is a good reason to make your own!

FACTS

Candle-molding machinery has been improved since it was developed in the nineteenth century. Rows of molds in a metal tank are alternately heated and cooled. After the molds are cooled, the candles are ejected by pistons. Spools of wicking material from the bottom of the machine are threaded through the pistons, by which they are inserted into the candle molds. As the cooled candles come out of the machine, the wicks are trimmed to proper length. Voilà!

All the World's a Stage

Candles weren't just for churches, homes, and the outdoors. During the sixteenth century in Italy, theatrical performances—pageants and tableaux and musical events—began to be held indoors. These events were sponsored by the Italian aristocracy. Palladio's indoor theater in Italy used the common everyday light sources, including tallow candles. In England at the end of the sixteenth century, winter performances of Shakespeare's plays were performed in the enclosed Blackfriars Theatre, which was lighted mainly by candles.

Early Footlights

The earliest known definite description of stagelighting is by Joseph Furtenbach (1628), of Sienna. He describes the use of oil lamps and candles set in a row along the front edge of the stage, out of the audience's sight. Tallow candles were the common source of this light. Old prints show them affixed to crude hoop-shaped chandeliers (a word, incidentally, derived from "chandler," or candlemaker). These could be hoisted aloft on pulleys from where they hung in lighted but dripping and smelly splendor. Theater designers applied gold decorations to the interior spaces to catch the reflections and make them glitter, thus giving us the contemporary non-word "glitterati" to describe theater and movie celebrities.

FACTS

In 1545, the Italian architect, Serlio, wrote a treatise in which he discussed the creation of lighting effects for the theater. One of his recommendations was to place candles behind flasks filled with colored water.

The Drury Lane Theatre

In Britain's famous Drury Lane Theatre, David Garrick masked the candle-footlights with screens in 1765. By 1784, when Richard Brinsley Sheridan was its manager, the Drury Lane's candle-lighting system was completely invisible to the audience, hidden by now familiar wings and borders.

Fire Without Matches

Today we are so accustomed not only to common matches, but to cigarette lighters both in our pockets and in our vehicles—and sophisticated gas cartridge barbecue lighters—that it's hard for us to imagine how people lit fires or candles without them. Of course, we've all heard of twirling a stick on a stone to strike a spark (hard-core wilderness students learn this technique), but what did the common folk do before the invention of matches?

The prevalent method was repeatedly striking steel against flint (a hard shale rock). Every home had a tinderbox, containing a steel striker, some flint, and tinder—a cotton rag, straw, or wood.

It took approximately 3 minutes to strike a light using the tinderbox method. This was not a job for the impatient. And if the tinder was damp, it took much longer. Sometimes, in wet weather—common in England—it wouldn't strike at all. One can imagine the frustration on a cold morning!

Got a Match?

The invention of sulfur matches was a great boon, and getting the tinder to light became a much easier job. The moment a spark hit the tinder, it was used to ignite the sulfur match. Later on, the discovery of sulfur matches that could be ignited by friction—the kind of matches we still use today—caused the old tinderbox to become outmoded.

Revolutionary Developments

The state of candlemaking changed little until the Industrial Revolution period, roughly from 1750 to 1850, during which striking changes in the economic structure of the world took place. Voyages of exploration in the fifteenth and sixteenth centuries paved the way for worldwide commerce. Capitalism appeared as early as the seventeenth century.

The developments brought about by the Industrial Revolution economically and socially had great effects on chandlery, or candlemaking. The renaissance of candle crafting occurred during the first half of the nineteenth century when candle molding machines were invented.

The year 1825 saw the invention of the braided wick by a Frenchman named Cambaceres. The braided wick solved the problem of wicks that burned unevenly and had to be "snuffed," or trimmed, while alight. With one thread in a braided wick tighter than the others, the wick can trim itself as it burns. This was a major improvement, which meant that candles produced with braided wicks were more efficient (a non-braided wick had to be trimmed frequently—as often as every thirty minutes). Even so, candles were still made by the same old time-consuming, labor-intensive handmade methods, and candlemakers were still limited in the number of candles they could produce in a day's work.

Then, in 1834, Joseph Morgan invented a machine that could produce molded candles at the rate of about 1,500 per hour. This machine could wick continuously. The new ability to mass-produce candles changed the lives of everyone. For the first time, candles became an affordable commodity available to almost everyone.

That same year, another important innovation was introduced—the "mordanting" process. This was a major breakthrough in candlemaking. Mordanting—soaking the wick material in an acid-like solution—causes the burned end of the wick to curl at a 90° angle *away from the pool of melted wax*, outside of the flame zone, where it turns to ash.

FACTS

Back in the bad old days of whaling when that supremely useful animal was hunted almost to extinction for its oils and spermaceti, stearic acid was refined from whale oil. Today, thankfully, it is made from palm tree nuts so that no animals are sacrificed in its manufacture.

In 1850, commercially manufactured paraffin was introduced, providing a welcome alternative to tallow (animal fat). And when the chemist Michel Eugène Chevreul discovered that tallow was not one substance, but a composition of two fatty acids—stearic acid and oleic acid—he invented a new substance known as *stearin*. Added to paraffin, stearin produced a harder, opaque, longer-burning candle.

It was this breakthrough that transformed candlemaking into what we know today. Factory-made cheap commercial candles became available to the general public and effectively ended the tremendous effort of making candles by hand.

By 1854 paraffin and stearin were being combined to create stronger, longer-burning candles of the type with which we are familiar. Some combination of the two is still the basic candlemaking stock. Today's home candlemaker regularly uses a combination of paraffin and stearin.

FACTS

The only other substance that was used to make comparable candles was spermaceti, from the cachalot (sperm whale). Spermaceti was utilized in candle production during the 1800s when the whaling business was at its height, but it was expensive, and not in common use. Highly desirable because it did not smoke or smell, it was a luxury for the rich.

Illuminating Gas

The advent of gaslight early in the 1800s was the first major advance in artificial lighting for centuries. It was a Scottish engineer, William Murdock, who developed a practical method of distilling gas from coal for the purpose of illumination.

The advantages of gaslight over candlelight were recognized immediately and exploited quickly. Despite the initial costs, entrepreneurial industrialists were able to foresee the future, for even without a chimney an open gas jet flame gave a much brighter light than candles or oil lamps. Also, there was the advantage of control. By varying the inflow of gas a smooth increase or decrease of light could be effected from a central point. This discovery became the precursor of the modern central heating systems.

Still, there were definite disadvantages to using gas for lighting: it was hot, gave off offensive (and often dangerous) fumes, and having an open flame indoors was a serious fire hazard. Therefore, a protective code was established mandating guards, screens, and glass chimneys.

Gas stations and city gas mains were not installed until 1850, so candles remained the primary source of illumination for most people. Even after city mains were bringing gas to urban dwellers' homes, the rural folk still depended on candlelight. It was only in 1890, after the introduction of electric lighting, that the incandescent gas mantle was developed. This invention greatly improved the quality of gaslight—made it whiter and brighter—but it did not remove the hazards of fire.

Theatrical Review

The first successful adaptation of gas lighting for the stage was at the Lyceum Theatre in London, in 1803, by a German, Frederick Winson. In the United States, the Chestnut Street Opera House in Philadelphia installed a gas lighting system in 1816, supplying its own gas by installing a gas generator on the premises.

In the Limelight

If you thought the phrase of being "in the limelight" was a figurative one for getting attention, you didn't know about Thomas Drummond. He was a British engineer who invented limelight in 1816, although it did not come into general use until thirty years later. Limelight is produced by directing a sharp point of oxyhydrogen flame against a cylindrical block of lime. The tiny area of lime becomes incandescent, emitting a brilliant white light that is soft and mellow. Limelight was particularly suited to theatrical use because of its intensity. A mirrored reflector allowed it to be directed onto the stage to illuminate and follow individual performers as they moved—hence the present meaning of the term, used when speaking of somebody who is getting attention.

From Past to Present

Rathborne's, founded in Dublin in 1488, is the world's oldest candle manufacturer in continuous existence. Established when knights did battle in armor, towns were walled, and cloistered monasteries dotted the landscape, Rathborne's "lit the way through the dark Middle Ages of Irish and European history." For more than 500 years Rathborne candles have been illuminating the daily events of human life. As Europe was experiencing "the shining era of Renaissance splendor, the time of Leonardo da Vinci, Michelangelo, and Raphael, the Rathborne family business in Winetavern Street in the heart of the ancient walled city of Dublin was flourishing and prospering."

Henry VIII ordered the closing of all Irish monasteries—a main source of candles—in 1537, but Rathborne's went right on, winning the contract for lighting Dublin and becoming closely identified with the ancient Fraternity of St. George, the Guild of Tallow Chandlers, Soap Boilers, and Wax Light Makers. In 1600, Rathborne's moved across the Liffey River from Wintavern Street to Stoneybatter.

Time passed, with its wars, famine, pestilence, rebellion, and revolutions, but Rathborne's endured. In 1912, while the rumblings of World War I were being felt, Henry Burnley Rathborne turned the ancient firm into a private company. Thirteen years later, the company consolidated its operations under one roof in its former warehouse on East Wall Road, where Rathborne's Candles is located this day.

Finally, in 1966, Rathborne's merged with Lalors, making their factory the largest supplier of church candles in the country. Using modern candlemaking techniques and equipment, Rathborne's produces millions of candles each year. Thousands of beeswax candles are still handcrafted at Rathborne's by master chandlers using the age-old technique of dipping, with wicks hanging from iron hoops. If you visit Rathborne's factory, you can see many of the old cast-iron candlemaking machines that stretch back to a past of great antiquity.

CHAPTER 2
Candles in the New World

Candlemaking today is naturally an offshoot of the entire history of human candlemaking and its evolution from the earliest of times to the present. There are no real differences between candles made in the distant past and those made today, except for the techniques and processes, such as mass production. Let's examine how the process of candlemaking has been modified throughout the history of our country.

The Colonial Period

The first known candles in America go back as far as the first century A.D. when Native Americans fished for "candlefish." This fish is so oily that it could be used as a candle. To that purpose, candlefish was dried, then stuck on a stick and lighted.

When the European settlers began arriving in America, they found they had to be resourceful in order to survive in the New World. In the southwestern United States, early missionaries boiled bark from the Cerio tree, which produced a wax-like substance that they skimmed and used for making candles. They may also have used the desert shrub jojoba, which yields a useful wax. What goes around comes around—and jojoba is now much in demand for "natural" candles, and is also being used in cosmetics.

In New England, settlers who needed to survive those cold dark New England winters also became quite skilled at making their own candles. Native Americans taught them how to extract wax from bayberries, berries of the beach shrub *Myrica carolinensis* native to New England. This wax could be used to make candles. Today, bayberry candles are a rarity because of the expense of making them—it takes 1½ quarts of bayberries to make a single 8-inch taper!

SSENTIALS   Pure bayberry candles are making a comeback both in home candlemaking and in the mail-order catalogs which sell old-fashioned products, such as the *Vermont Country Store*, and upscale mail-order catalogs such as *Smith & Hawken*.

Consider this quote when you think about the importance of candles to the settlers: "In the tropics the sun rises at six in the morning and sets at six in the evening and that's that. There is very little twilight. As you go further north or south of the equator, the differential between winter and summer daylight hours increases until you reach those unfortunate latitudes where the sun never sets all summer or rises all winter. To spend a winter in such a place without [candle] light would surely drive you mad."—*The Forgotten Household Crafts*, John Seymour

In the Household

A Colonial housewife was a hard worker indeed. Her many chores included making candles for the family's use from animal fat, which she collected diligently in pottery crocks all year long. When the time came to make candles, she rendered the often-rancid fat and made "taller tips" by repeatedly dipping wicks into the hot tallow and allowing it to cool between dips. This is the exact same method used today for dipped candles (except that we have the advantage of using wax, often sweetly scented, instead of the smoky, smelly tallow).

 **SSENTIALS** For a wonderful and well-written look at the various crafts practiced by the men of Colonial America, take a look at *Colonial Craftsmen and the Beginnings of American Industry*, written and illustrated by Edwin Tunis (World Publishing).

Some well-to-do households owned tin molds capable of casting a dozen candles simultaneously. This was an enormous advantage over the dip-and-cool method. The itinerant chandler included in his equipment large molds that could cast as many as six dozen candles. Though his presence was malodorous, he had the advantage of being able to cast a year's supply of candles for a family in one operation. He strung the candles up with the tow-linen wick provided by the mistress, melted down the hard fat, and in the course of a day's casting relieved the household of much onerous labor. A welcome offshoot of his work was the making of soap, which was the softer fat boiled with lye and then cooled.

A Stinky Business

Although chandlers were unwelcome as neighbors (for theirs was a greasy and stinky trade), they were vital to the well-being of their communities, especially as society became more complex and sophisticated than in the early colonial days. The importance of candlemaking in early American economy cannot be overemphasized, for it formed the basis of an entire industry, which grew as the society advanced and the population increased.

One of the more famous chandlers (thanks to his son) was Josiah Franklin, Benjamin Franklin's father. Originally a dyer in England, Josiah switched to candlemaking, becoming a "tallow-chandler and sope-boiler" when he came to Boston, where his old trade did not pay well enough to support his family. Perhaps candlemaking was more lucrative because plainly dressed Bostonians disdained clothes of bright colors and had no need for dyers.

By the eighteenth century, the word "chandler" was in competition with the word "grocer" to indicate a shopkeeper. In those days, there were different types of chandlers—the terms "tallow chandler," "wax chandler," and "ship chandler" were in common use. Interestingly, the term "ship chandler" survives to this day, and refers to a retailer of specific goods. In the 1760s, a group of candlemakers—who did not make soap as did the less-respected tallow chandlers—chose to call themselves "candlers." However, the term did not stick, and today it is used to designate a person who tests eggs (by holding the egg up to a candle flame and looking inside). Prior to 1750, wax chandlers made their finest candles from beeswax, or from bayberry wax.

Burn That Fat

Today's cheap candles are made of paraffin, a petroleum byproduct discovered during the early years of the twentieth century. By then the cattle industry was in full development and tallow came from beeves rather than (as formerly) sheep or pigs. A bull butchered for meat provided enough fat to make twenty-six dozen candles. And when the entrepreneurial Yankee ship captains carried hides to the colonies for the shoemakers, they also brought along the fat from the animals.

Unlike today's simple wax-melting procedure, the chandler of old didn't merely melt the fat. He processed it by rendering it in boiling water. This allowed the fibrous material to rise to the surface, from where it was skimmed off, just as one skims scum from a pot of meat broth today. The vessels used were called "trying pots," and the term "to try out" (meaning "to render fat") is still used in some areas of the United States. These trying pots were made of copper, battered out by the local coppersmith. When making dipped candles, the chandler ladled the hot fat into another vat of rectangular shape for pre-cooling prior to dipping. This was because hot tallow left a thin layer on a dipped wick; worse, it could melt the earlier dipped layers. Conversely, if the tallow cooled too much it made lumpy layers. When that happened, a fire had to be built up under the pot to reheat the tallow, not an easy job.

An Old Recipe for Lard Candles

Take 12 pounds lard, 1 pound saltpeter, 1 pound alum. Pulverize and mix the saltpeter and alum; dissolve the compound in a gill of boiling water; pour the compound into the lard before it is quite melted. Stir the whole until it boils, and skim off what rises. Let it simmer until the water is all boiled out, or until it ceases to throw off steam. Pour off the lard as soon as it is done, and clean the boiler while it is hot. If the candles are to be run in a mould, you may commence at once, but if to be dipped, let the lard cool first and cake. Then treat as you would tallow.*

Superior Spermaceti

American whaling ships often brought in cachalots, or sperm whales, and it was soon discovered that the fatty solid substance called "spermaceti" (erroneously thought to be the whale's sperm, hence the term "spermaceti" and the name "sperm whale") could be used to produce splendid candles. In fact, spermaceti was the best candle material known to that time. Candles made from it gave a brilliant light, burned evenly, and never dripped: a miracle! The reason they did not drip was because the flame burned without melting the wax into the usual liquid pool. So treasured were these candles that a candlemaker could sell them at extremely high prices—and therefore make a good profit, limited only by the supply of sperm oil he could garner. Since even in the poorest of times, there were always people with sufficient funds to afford such luxuries as the spermaceti candles, whaling became a lucrative trade.

* Nettie, Terre Haute, Indiana. *The Home & Farm Manual, A Pictorial Encyclopedia of Farm, Garden, Household, Architectural, Legal, Medical, and Social Information.* Jonathan Periam (Greenwich House).

By mid-century, chandlers were using all the spermaceti they could buy from the whalers, which made the whale one of the most fiercely hunted creatures on earth. As we now know, the whalers became so efficient—and the demand for their catch was so great—that once it was discovered that spermaceti made such splendid candles, the whale population was hunted nearly to extinction.

Spermaceti candles are the basis of the Standard International Candle unit of light intensity on which incandescent light bulbs were based when they were invented. A Standard International Candle unit is the intensity of light an incandescent bulb matches alongside the light from a $1/6$ pound spermaceti candle burning at a rate of 120 grams per hour.

FACTS

Ambergris, a fatty substance formed in the sperm whale's intestinal tract, was the most precious material whale hunters sought. Prized by perfumers, it was found floating in the ocean when whales were in the area. Although in the fresh state it is black and has an unpleasant odor, after exposure to sun and sea and air, it is transformed to a pleasant-smelling mass, yellow or gray in color. One wonders who discovered its properties for use in fragrances!

The First Commercial Spermaceti Factory

Obediah Brown, of the entrepreneurial family of Rhode Island Browns, opened the first spermaceti candle works in 1753. That year alone his company made three hundred barrels of spermaceti candles. Brown and his brother Nicolas became the moving force behind the United Company of Spermaceti Candlers, which was responsible for parceling out the supply of spermaceti oil, which was limited despite the avaricious whaling industry's most stringent efforts. And, they always got the biggest share. The association kept its trade secrets close to its vest—so closely guarded, in fact, that Nantucket, into whose ports came more whales than at Naragansett, only learned how to make the candles in 1772.

Pioneer Candlemaking

Pioneer candlemakers followed in the footsteps of the candlemaking techniques practiced during the Colonial era. In the pioneer states of Kentucky, Ohio, Indiana, and Illinois, the women had brought their knowledge of candlemaking to the frontier. All suet and fat were conserved most carefully and candlemaking was an important and vital household chore. Every housewife made a supply of candles in the fall. Candle rods, each with a row of wicks attached, were repeatedly dipped into big iron kettles of boiling water and melted tallow. It was all-day, back-breaking, smelly, unpleasant "women's work." To make the wicks, women could either buy cotton twist, or use the silky down from milkweed pods.

Historical candle-making

Later, the tallow was mixed with powdered gum camphor. Finer candles with scent were made with wax from the bayberry or wax myrtle. These inventive women even achieved decorative effects by layering wax dyed with the red juice of pokeberries, made green from wild nettles, or yellow from alder bark, as well as other natural dyestuffs.

How were wicks made?
The earliest settlers used wicks made of linen, spun from flax, which they grew. Or, if they had no other materials available, they used pith from plants. However, spun cotton made the most serviceable wicks.

Wick Development

Samuel Slater (1768–1835) was an industrialist born in Derbyshire, England. He was apprenticed to the partner of Richard Arkwright, who invented cotton-spinning machinery. Slater familiarized himself with Arkwright's machines and those of James Hargreaves and Samuel Crompton before embarking for America in 1789. Once on these shores, he contracted with the firm of Almy & Brown of Providence, Rhode Island, to reproduce for them Arkwright's cotton-spinning machinery. In 1793, Slater established a factory in Pawtucket, named Almy, Brown & Slater.

Samuel Slater is regarded as the founder of the American cotton industry. Thanks to him, cotton mills began to spin material for candlewicks and sold it rolled into balls. A young male apprentice cut lengths of about 20 inches on a sharp-bladed measuring cutter—much like the office paper cutter we know. The lengths intended for dipping were hung in sets of two over 3 feet–long rods, called "broaches," that lay parallel on a wooden frame. Separated by a space of about three inches, the boy then twisted the two strands together. This required both skill and dexterity, for first the boy tightened the twist the spinner had made in the yarn and then had to twist the strands in the opposite direction, like a rope. Made that way, they would "hold their lay," as was said of a well-made wick.

Production of Dipped Candles

A professional dipper used a number of broaches (racks) at the same time. Suspending them over the tallow vat, he was able to dip all the wicks into the fat simultaneously and evenly. This process allowed him to, with a helper, dip and cool as many as 500 candles per day.

As the candles thickened with repeated dippings, they developed the irregular shape of a "taper." When each candle had been dipped enough times to accumulate enough tallow to weigh approximately ¼ pound, the candles were removed from the broaches and packed in barrels. The loop of the wick remained, making pairs.

To set up wicks for molding, the apprentice performed the same doubling and twisting process as for wicks for dipping. But he also had to poke each wick through the mold's top and draw it out the bottom where there was a small hole.

Introduction of Stearin

In the United States, candles remained the main light source until well after the Civil War. By the early nineteenth century, a new way of extracting a substance called "stearin" from animal fat was developed. When mixed with the fat, stearin produced a candle that smoked less and gave a clearer light. Almost simultaneously, snuffing (that is, the need to trim the wick of the burning candle regularly) became obsolete with the invention of braided wicks. These curled out of the flame as it consumed its fuel, eliminating the need to trim the wick as the candle burned.

Here is how a housewife recommends a vegetable-based substitute for stearin: Take the common prickly pear and boil or fry it in the tallow, without water, for half an hour, then strain and mould. I use about six average-size leaves to the pint of tallow (by weight 1 pound of leaves to 4 pounds of tallow), splitting them up fine. They make the tallow as hard as stearin, and do not injure its burning qualities in the least.
  —Mrs. E.L.O., Waco, Texas. From *The Home & Farm Manual*

Made in the U.S.A.

Most of the candles used in this country are made in Syracuse, New York, where the candlemaking industry was founded in 1855 by Francis X. Baumer. This German from Bavaria located his manufactory in Syracuse, and other Americans of German descent soon followed him. Using ingenious machinery, these now very large companies make about 3,500 different kinds of candles for a great variety of uses. They import mineral waxes from Utah, Germany, Poland, and Spain; carnauba wax comes from Brazil. China provides a wax created by insects feeding on trees.

They also make candles from bayberry wax. In Syracuse's large Merchandise Mart, there are fascinating displays of candles in a stunning variety of shapes, sizes, and colors.

FACTS

In the Chicago region, there are two small candle plants that make candles for religious purposes only. By canon law candles used in certain rituals of the Roman Catholic Church must contain not less than 51 percent beeswax; some must be 100 percent beeswax. Those for Greek Orthodox Churches are composed entirely of paraffin. One size is 3 inches in diameter and 6 feet tall!

A Flip of the Switch

Then came electricity, and candlemaking became an almost obsolete occupation, both for the professional wax chandler and the housewife (who no doubt gave thanks to be relieved of this harsh and unpleasant chore which was always "women's work").

However, the electricity we take for granted today, in almost every corner of the United States, wasn't always available in rural areas, only in cities. It wasn't until 1933 when the U.S. Congress created the Tennessee Valley Authority that rural areas in the South had a reliable supply of electricity, from hydroelectric plants that produced cheap power.

A Modern Romance

Today, of course, machines and factories produce most commercial candles, but even though handcrafting is largely a thing of the past—except for the hobbyist or craftsperson—the candlemaking *process* is pretty much the same as it was.

FACTS

Domestic candle manufacturers have a long tradition of making high-quality, long-lasting, and safe candles. At this time, candlemaking is not regulated by law. However, the National Candle Association members are working with the American Society for Testing and Materials (ASTM) to establish and implement voluntary standards for American-made candles.

Improved technology has allowed us to enjoy beautifully colored and heavenly scented candles, using new additives such as dyes and essential oils. Most modern candles are made of paraffin (with stearin added), but with our prosperous times there's now a renewed demand for beeswax candles, which are undergoing a surge in popularity among those who can afford them.

SSENTIALS

No safety information is required on candle labeling. However, most U.S. candle manufacturers voluntarily place safety and use instructions on their candles. Wax sold for home candlemaking is labeled as to its content, i.e., paraffin, stearic acid, beeswax, etc.

The developments in the mass production of candles mean that today candles can be made or purchased in wide variety of sizes and shapes, and in a broad spectrum of colors. Choose from elegant tapers tinted every color of the rainbow and quite a few more besides, to match your fancy or your decorating scheme for a party, or scented mood-enhancing candles perfumed with essentials oils specific to many purposes, including healing. The home candlemaker can create these "intentional use" candles him- or herself, but they are also widely available at shops and mail-order catalogs that specialize in spiritual and/or healing products.

Candles are safe when burned properly and responsibly: They should always be attended; and kept out of the reach of children and pets, and away from drafts or flammable objects. Wicks should be kept trimmed. The flame should be extinguished properly. Finally, you should always follow the manufacturer's instructions.

Candlemaking As a Natural Art

With all of these candles readily available, one might imagine that the craft of handmade candles would be a thing of the past. Not so! Some designers still create beautiful and original hand-crafted candles for sale and, more importantly, many people are now choosing candlemaking as a rewarding hobby, often for its spiritual aspect.

Electricity has replaced candles as our main source of light—but they are still important to us (especially when the power fails!). We now use candles mostly for decoration on festive occasions, or to dress up our dinner table. We appreciate candles for the sense of calm they create, and we respond to candlelight in religious ceremonies. In today's technology-driven world with its ever more hectic pace, candles bring us rest and respite by providing a general mood of warmth and relaxation—and enhancing romantic moments.

CHAPTER 3

Candlemaking As a Sacred Art

There are many sacred arts, but the making and keeping of fire is among the first in importance to humanity. Without fire for heat, light, cooking, and keeping away predatory animals, humans would long ago have perished. Even today, in this ultra-modern, Internet-connected world, there are still areas where artificial light is provided not by a great power plant, but by a simple candle.

Marvelous Mythology

In times of old, the ancient Greeks thought so highly of fire that they provided us with a marvelous myth about how people got hold of this precious stuff, which was originally reserved only for the gods' use.

You may have heard the story of Prometheus, the Greek titan (titans were lesser divinities than the gods of Olympus such as Zeus) who stole fire from the gods and gave it to humans. It's a wonderful rendition of the wonder and power of fire, and every little candle is a repetition of that wonder and power in its own small way, just as the tiniest ray of sunlight is part of the great ball of intense burning fire in the sky we call the sun, without which there would be no life on earth.

According to the Promethean myth, Prometheus was fond of humans and had argued their case when one of the gods wanted to destroy them for being too clever and talented. To help the humans, Prometheus sneaked up the backstairs of Olympus, so to speak (with the help of the goddess Athena), and lighted a torch at the fiery chariot of the Sun. He then carried the fire down to humanity, protected in the pithy hollow of a giant fennel stalk. Extinguishing the original torch, he departed quietly, unseen and undiscovered, leaving the glowing coal behind and thus giving fire to humankind.

FACTS

It is thought that the legend of Prometheus's enchainment may have been the result of a giant snowman-shaped frost protrusion recumbent on Mount Caucasus, over which many vultures flew. Prometheus is also related to another fire god, Hephaestus, a lame blacksmith who fashioned the thunderbolts of lightening Zeus threw around when he was annoyed or angry. And to this day Greek islanders still carry fire from one place to another in the pith of a giant fennel plant.

So angry were the Olympic gods when they discovered that Prometheus had pulled off this trick that Zeus decided to punish him. Prometheus was chained naked to a rock in the Caucasian mountains.

All day, a hungry vulture tore at his liver, causing excruciating pain, to which there was no end because every night (when Prometheus was exposed to cruel frost and cold) his liver regenerated itself. And so the next day the process began all over again.

Fortunately, eventually Prometheus was rescued by the centaur, Chiron, the teacher of Apollo (who drove the chariot of the Sun across the sky on its daily rounds). Known as "the wounded healer," Chiron was half horse and half man (the bottom half was the horse). He sustained a wound in his thigh that would not heal, giving him horrible pain. And since he was immortal (a demi-god) he could not die from his wound. So he arranged with Zeus to give up his immortality—a great sacrifice—and take Prometheus's place. Prometheus was released, and Chiron was able to die and feel no more pain. According to another myth, however, Prometheus was rescued by Hercules.

Not only did Prometheus steal the gods' fire and give it to us humans, he also taught us architecture, astronomy, mathematics, navigation, medicine, metallurgy, and other useful arts. The Promethean myth is the theme of the ancient Greek dramatist Aeschylus's *Prometheus Bound*. The English poet Percy Bysshe Shelley (1792–1822) was inspired by this legend to write his famous poem *Prometheus Unbound* (1820), which expounds on the theme of humankind's deliverance.

Hestia, Goddess of Fire and the Hearth

The Greeks honored fire with the goddess Hestia, who was known as the goddess of the hearth and temple. She was also known as a wise woman and a maiden aunt.

One of the three great Virgin Goddesses, along with Artemis and Athena, Hestia was in charge of the fire that burned on a round hearth at Olympus. Hestia was thought to be presented in the living flame at the center of every home, temple, and city. As Roman hearths were round, Hestia's symbol was a circle, which is also the symbol for our Sun (astrologically speaking). Therefore, temples dedicated to her were circular in shape.

No home or temple was considered to be properly sanctified until Hestia had officially entered it—by way of fire ceremonies specifically for that purpose. Once Hestia was installed, both homes and temples were considered to be holy places. Her presence insured the sacred fire that provided not only illumination, warmth, and heat for cooking food, but also the feeling of a living spiritual presence.

Unlike the other two virgin goddesses, Athena (the goddess of wisdom and a protectress of cities) and Artemis (also known as "Lady of the Beasts," and whose turf was the wilderness), Hestia never strayed from the hearthside. She always remained inside homes and temples dedicated to her, protecting the sacred fire of the hearth. In this respect, she is related to the astrological sign of Virgo, which deals with the details of daily life. Represented by the Virgin Goddess with a sheaf of grain, Virgo relates to daily work and service, such as keeping the hearth going, cooking food, and housekeeping. Tending to the details of keeping house can be a meditative experience for those inclined to relish it as a meaningful activity vital to life rather than a meaningless, repetitive chore that has to be done—usually by women! With Hestia, the details of keeping a home are equivalent to a spiritual meditation.

The Vestal Tradition

The Romans called Hestia *Vesta* and kept a special temple in Rome in her honor where "vestal virgins" tended an eternal flame that could not be allowed to go out. This perpetual fire was central to Roman life and the girls chosen to serve it (Virgo is also the sign of service!) were especially proud of their important task. Beginning between the ages of six and ten, they served for thirty years and had no contact with men.

Tradition had it that if a girl could blow on a dying flame and make it rekindle, she was a proper "virgin," which meant that she was of an independent spirit and able to get along quite well by herself without a man to lean on, rather than sexual abstinence. Her suitability to serve the sacred flame was symbolized by her ability to blow on the holy fire without its being extinguished, for symbolically, breath was equivalent to spirit.

Candles in Christianity

It is quite possible that the early Christians in Rome copied the sacred fire of Vesta's temple as they set up and elaborated the ceremonies of their new religion. In Christianity, the candle represents the seven gifts of the holy spirit, which are: counsel, knowledge, peace, piety, strength, understanding, and wisdom. It also is considered a symbol of Christ's dual nature, part human, part divine. The earliest evidence of a continuous light burning before a tabernacle is from the early thirteenth century, when the bishop of Worcester declared that "a lamp must burn day and night before the Eucharist." Candles in churches served a more mundane purpose as well—that of illuminating the dark, dank churches that were often made out of stone, and for lighting functions celebrated at night.

Catholic Rituals Involving Candles

From baptisms to the blessing of an elderly person through the Anointing of the Sick, the use of candles by Catholics has been a vital aspect of the liturgy and the sacraments since the Church's earliest years.

FACTS

For mystical reasons, the Church prescribes that the candles used at Mass and at other liturgical functions be made of beeswax [because] the pure wax extracted by bees from flowers symbolizes the pure flesh of Christ received from His virgin Mother, the wick signifies the soul of Christ, and the flame represents His divinity. Although the two latter properties are found in all kinds of candles, the first is proper of beeswax candles only.

—*Catholic Encyclopedia*: *Altar Candles*

Candles were used for the Lucenarium, the second-century ceremonial light for evening prayer, which was the precursor to the Paschal Candle. Candles were also held aloft during funeral processions. During the third century, they were burned at the tombs of the dead—especially those who died as martyrs. During the fourth and fifth centuries, sacred images, especially of the Virgin Mary, always had candles burning before them, as did the tombs that held relics of saints.

Candles in the Catholic Mass

Candles were not used at Mass until the seventh century, when they were carried by monks and priests in the procession to the altar; carried for the Gospel; and placed around the altar during the Mass. But it was not until the eleventh century that candles were put on the altar itself. Paintings from the medieval period show the Mass in progress without candles on the altar. Beginning with the thirteenth century, it was essential for the parish clerk, an assistant priest, or an altar boy to hold up a lighted candle when the officiating priest elevated the host before the congregation. In Catholic churches today, there are always banks of votive candles in red glass cups which a worshipper can light after dropping a few coins in a collection box.

Advent Prayer

Several religious feasts have candles as their primary sacramental, not merely as an adjunct. The most important of these is Advent, which is marked by the lighting of a wreath with four candles. After the candles are lighted, this prayer is recited:

We pray, then, that the
Richness of God's blessing
Rest upon this Advent wreath,
Upon our home and upon each of us
As we light this candle
In the name of the Father,
And of the Son,
And of the Holy Spirit.
Amen.

The Candle as the Soul

The burning candle is a common symbol of the soul of the individual, of the relationship between the spiritual (the flame) and the material (the wax). The flame is representative of the soul's eternal nature (as is the sun) and the wax is symbolic of the material body, which is consumed by the flame as age consumes the physical body. Thus, the candle as it burns down is symbolically compared to the transitory nature of human life.

Jewish Candle Symbolism

Candles are also incorporated into the religious services in Judaism. Before the destruction of the Temple in Jerusalem, the menorah, a seven-branched ceremonial candlestick, was lighted ritually by the temple priests. The seven branches of the Jewish menorah symbolize the seven planets, the seven heavens, the seven days making up the week, the seven archangels, and, by extension, the seven "Ages of Man."

The Jewish Shabbat Ceremony

ESSENTIALS

The correct time to light the Shabbat candles is 18 minutes before sunset every Friday evening. Young girls should light before this time. A married woman customarily lights two candles. An unmarried girl should light one candle in deference to her mother.

According to Chabad House in Austin, Texas, the lighting of the Jewish Shabbat (or Sabbath) candles is "something that inspires you, offers hope and provides peace. It's something that bestows the blessing of light to illuminate the world above you.

"Look back to biblical times, to Sarah, our matriarch, whose miraculous lamp gave light to her husband Avraham [Abraham], her son Yitzchak [Isaac], from Shabbat to Shabbat. Refer to Rivkah [Rebecca] who, after Sarah, blessed the Shabbat lamp from the time she was only three years old. It is this 3,700 year-old tradition which Jewish women remember and observe in welcoming the Shabbat Queen. It is this mitzvah that rekindles the Divine spark in every Jewish being."

Let There Be Light

There is a well-known saying, "It's better to light one candle than to curse the darkness." Light and darkness have always been considered in fundamental terms, especially before artificial light was invented. Try to imagine going abroad at night where there is absolutely no artificial light. Nothing at all but stars and the moon—if she is showing her light. This happened to me once, on a trip to Portugal's Algarve, where there was no electricity whatsoever except for that which was generator-driven. Donkey carts were the usual mode of transportation for the local farmers, and they carried oil lanterns swinging from the postern. Even so, they were hard to see.

Night was so black that—quite literally—you could not see your hand in front of your face. My traveling companion and I had to hold hands when we went outside our villa just to know where each of us was! On moonless nights, the darkness was so total we could not see what was on the ground beneath our feet, or each other—even when we were holding hands!

This was an amazing experience for me. For the first time I saw the sky as I imagine the first astronomers, who were also astrologers (as am I), must have seen it. No wonder they were so fascinated by the movements of the stars and planets! There was nothing to obstruct their view of the sheer magnificence of a sky so totally filled with the bright twinkling pricks of diamonds on black velvet. Few of us today, especially those in urban areas, have seen this amazing view, which is right over our heads. It's really hard for us to appreciate the fundamental difference between light and darkness.

However, these inescapable terms in the description of anything in life or literature, whether used literally or metaphorically, still speak to our imaginations. When we speak of the "dark side of the moon," or the dark side of someone's character, we know exactly what is meant.

The Candle As a Symbol of Virtue

Light is traditionally linked with goodness and with all that is desirable in life—knowledge, justice, truth, hope, virtue. Darkness inevitably refers to what we hate or fear—death, despair, evil, ignorance, deception, deceit. Our traditional Western religious traditions reinforce this handy division of opposites, which are actually only two halves of the same whole. For example, when the entire universe lay in darkness, the first thing God did was to create light (Gen. 1:3). The supposition here is that light is a precondition to creation of any kind. The Bible is rife with such references: The Lord is our light and salvation (Ps. 271:1); Christ is "the light of men" (Matt. 1:4); and so on. Jesus is frequently quoted as referring to himself as "the light of the world: he that followeth me shall not walk in darkness, but shall have the light of life" (John 8:12). Paul repeats the message in different words: "ye are all the children of light, and the children of the day; we are not of the night, nor of darkness" (1 Thess. 5:5). Though we may today have distanced ourselves from the literalness of biblical imagery and terminology, it is still true that we revere light—just look at an American city from an airplane coming in for a landing! The whole planet is one great Christmas tree when seen from above. And what is a candle if not light? I doubt there is not a soul you know who does not have at least a small supply of candles for emergency purposes, should the electricity go out!

And when it does—as it did recently in my area during an ice storm for two days—how appropriate that famous Shakespeare quotation becomes, "How far that little candle throws his beams!" And how grateful we must be that *our* candlemaking is a delightful and "fun" hobby, done for pleasure and entertainment rather than a vitally necessary but unpleasant and difficult task! Let us not forget that we are involved in a sacred art—that of making fire and giving light—whenever we get out our candlemaking pots and wax, colors and scents, molds and decorations. Candlemaking takes us closer to the gods than we realize.

The Candle As a Symbol of Old Age

The face of an aged person is often compared to a candle. In "The Old Woman," author Joseph Campbell (1897–1944) compares the subtle beauty and serenity of "an aged face" to a votive candle (then used primarily in churches). His comparison may have been taken from a phrase in the Apocrypha (Ecclesiastes 26:22): "As the clear light upon holy candlesticks, so is the beauty of the face in ripe age." And William Shakespeare often used the burning down candle as a symbol of aging and death: "Out, out, brief candle!" (from *Macbeth*; act 5, scene 5); "Here burns my candle out, ay, here it dies, / Which, while it lasted, gave King Henry light . . ." (from *3 Henry VI*; act 2; scene 6).

Literary References to Candles and Light

The English poet John Milton opens his Book 3 of *Paradise Lost*: "Hail, holy Light, offspring of heaven first-born!" And Dante concludes *The Divine Comedy* with a stirring vision of "the Highest Light" (*Paradiso* 33:50). By contrast, darkness is awfulness itself, it inhabits the Inferno. In *Pilgrim's Progress*, the English poet John Bunyan uses the symbol of the burning candle to remind his readers of the transitory nature of human existence and uses this connection to instruct on the value of a virtuous life:

Matt: Why doth the fire fasten upon the candlewick?
Prud: To shew that unless Grace doth kindle upon the heart, there
    will be no true Light of Life in us.
Matt: Why is the wick, and tallow, and all spent, to maintain the
    light of the candle?
Prud: To shew that Body and Soul, and all should be at the
    service of, and spend themselves to maintain in good
    condition, that Grace of God in us.

The fading candle as a symbol of old age often appears in Elizabethan sources. The following is taken from the *Zodiakus Vitae*, a versified teaching text used in the classrooms of Elizabethan England:

. . . A fiery spirit doth raine,
Which quickenth every living thing, in world which doth remaine.
This heat doth lively moisture feede, as flame of Candle bright, . . .
At length it makes an end and stayes, when spent is all the heate,
Which fading, body fades: as shews in them whose yeares are great.

Candles have also inspired many a modern poet. For instance, in his poem "The Wicket Old Man" W. B. Yeats (1865–1939) refers to the "candle-end" as an image of old age.

Many of us pray, meditate, and use other forms of communion with our higher selves for spiritual purposes. Candles can be especially prepared for these special ritual uses.

Sacred Candlelight

There are many ways you can use your handmade candles as a sacred art. For example, you can create a sacred space in your home to go to whenever the world is too much with you—to refresh your spiritual energies for the tasks ahead, to rest, to meditate, to reflect, to be silent and alone. Your handmade candles can be the perfect accompaniment for such a sacred space where you can use them to put you in touch with your most peaceful center. By surrounding yourself with candlelight from candles of your own making, you connect with your inner self in a deep and significant way. To further personalize the candles you might use on such occasions, you can choose different colors and scents to accommodate specific spiritual needs and purposes. (We'll give you more information on the specifics later on. The significance of color in candles is discussed in detail in Chapter 4. Study the meanings of the various colors before you make special candles for ritual purposes.)

Creating Daily Life Rituals with Candlemaking

Ask yourself these questions:

- What rituals do I use for ordinary everyday life? These may include how you prepare yourself for bed, for work, for dinner, for play or recreation.
- What rituals do I observe as part of my spiritual practice? These may include churchgoing or any worshipful practice carried on through an outside or public forum, or purely private activity such as doing yoga, meditating, or praying.

- Am I fully aware of my private rituals?
- What do the rituals I use mean to me?
- What connections do I make through ritual?
- Do I want to include more rituals in my everyday activities?
- Does ritual serve to satisfy a need in me?
- Would I enjoy designing my own rituals for myself and my family?
- How can I integrate my candlemaking into my ritual observances?

Make a list of how you now use candles in ritual, and then add all the ways you can think of to use them more.

Using Candles in Ritual

Here are some suggestions for incorporating rituals using candles into your daily life:

- Create a welcoming ritual for any new possession, especially an important one, by making a candle in its honor. Burn the candle every day for a week and say a blessing while the candle burns.
- Create a disposing ritual to "bury the dead"—things in your household that broke or that you need to give up for any reason—by making a special candle to honor them and their past usefulness. Japanese Buddhists observe "Needle Memorial Day," to honor all the needles that have been "killed in action," or worn out, during the year. As you dispose of such an object, burn the candle while you give thanks to the object for its service.
- Make a candle to prepare you for each day's work. Light it and while it burns, bless your workspace and all the equipment it contains. Thank them for being a part of your life and work.
- Make a special candle to honor a visit to any site that is spiritually meaningful, such as a cemetery, a local or national memorial site, or a natural setting that appeals to you spiritually. Make a pilgrimage to the site and burn the candle there. (Always take due caution with fire and be sure to extinguish your candle properly after each use.)
- Invite others to participate with you in creating candles for a ritual to honor common space, such as a park or playground.

- Make special candles to celebrate earth's seasons. Burn the candles on the spring and fall equinoxes and on the summer and winter solstices.
- Make moon candles for the phases of the moon, and especially the new moon and full moon, to ritually honor the earth and her moon.
- Discover your own moon sign and make a special white candle to burn on the days the moon occupies the same sign in which it appeared at your birth.

ESSENTIALS

Free astrological charts are available on the Web at *www.astro.com*. Select atlas and time zone server and follow instructions to enter place of birth, date, and time. Choose Placidus and western geocentric (tropical). Be sure to press the "update time zone" button prior to viewing your chart.

Making Candle Magic

From olden times, people have relied on candles for all kinds of rituals, both religious and magical. Candle magic is one of the most important ways in which candles have been used, and continue to be used. According to Raven Grimassi's *Encyclopedia of Wicca and Witchcraft*, "candle magick is the use of candles to perform spells or other works of magick. In candle magick the candles are anointed with oil and magickally charged for a specific purpose. Colored candles are used to symbolize the nature of the desired outcome. Examples of this symbolism are red for passion, green for gain, black for binding, yellow for motivation, blue for calming, and brown for grounding." (See "The Significance of Candle Colors," p. 58.)

Although candle magic can be a complicated affair, it need not daunt those wanting to try this ancient form of candle use. Below are some simplified steps for you to try.

The first step is the selection of the proper color of candle. Select a color of candle that is suited to your purposes or aims. This step is of primary importance.

Thoroughly clean the candle you have selected. Ideally, you should make a candle for the purpose you have in mind, and while making it concentrate on its eventual use. If this isn't feasible, try to use a freshly made candle. However, if you choose to use one that has been used previously, you must clean it in order to remove the vibrations left by the last use (unless you keep a specific set of candles for different purposes and always use the same one for the same purpose). To cleanse the candle (especially if it is a store-bought one), soak a tissue or soft cloth in rubbing alcohol and gently wipe the candle from its base to the top. Then polish it with a clean cloth. If your candle is in a container, wipe the container with the alcohol-soaked cloth and dry it well (remember, alcohol is flammable).

QUESTIONS?

How did candle magic originate?
Candle magick evolved from the old lunar cults where torches were lit to invoke the Moon Goddess. The lit candle symbolizes the presence of the Moon Goddess, who is the Enchantress, Mistress of Magick. All acts of magick performed in the glow of her flame are empowered by the momentum of the Past.
—*Encyclopedia of Wicca and Witchcraft*

Now, dedicate your candle to the purpose for which you have designated it. To do this, you can simply say a prayer invoking the higher powers to help you. Or, you can carve symbols into the wax exterior—for instance, astrological glyphs or rune figures—with a sharp tool such as an awl or an icepick. For prosperity, a dollar sign is appropriate. Concentrate on your purpose while you carve. Another method is to use a verbal incantation, preferably chanted softly. Affirmations work very well for this method.

Next, oil your candle. You can use essential oils meant for specific aims—such as peace, love, tranquility, money, health, healing, etc. (These can be purchased at health food stores or metaphysical shops.) Dipping your fingers in the oil, gently rub it into the entire candle surface: for attracting something you want, oil from top to bottom; for getting rid of something you don't want, from bottom to top. Say affirmations while you oil and concentrate on your goal.

Finally, spray or sprinkle your candle with pure water. You can enhance this by using "color water" to match your candle, which is water stored in a colored bottle and left in the sun for several hours. Set candle aside until ready for use.

Decide how long you are going to burn your candle: some spells suggest burning a candle for several days (or nights) in a row if the goal is important or difficult to achieve. You can either use a large candle or several small ones, burning one per day (or night). If you use several candles, prepare each one in the same fashion.

Once you have made and consecrated a candle, reserve it for that purpose only. Don't use a prosperity candle for love magic spells, for example. And always handle your prepared candle with care and respect; after use, put it away in a wrapping for future use. And always remember the Wiccan Rule, "Good to all; harm to none."

Everyday Rituals

Make a candle to burn during any activity you want to "spiritualize," from performing household chores to getting the car ready for a journey. If you have school-age children, make a new candle to burn on the first day of school each year. Take a "spiritual break" every day by lighting a particular candle made for a particular purpose. (Also see "Candle-Gazing Meditation" later in this chapter.) You might even want to make a different candle for each day of the week to connect with the significance of that day. (For example, Monday is Moon Day.) Turn your personal hygiene and grooming into a candlelit ritual to honor your body. Use different colors and scents for different bodily attentions.

If you keep a spiritual journal, create a candle to burn while you are writing in it. (For more information on keeping a spiritual journal, consult my book *Awaken to Your Spiritual Self*, Chapter 9, "Keeping a Spiritual Journal," p. 167.)

Your Sacred Space

Your sacred space is for silence and solitude. You should have at least a small area of your home for this purpose. Whatever space you designate as sacred should be well tended, with an array of handmade candles readily available for your intentions when you utilize your sacred space. Some general topics are listed below, but they are only guidelines: You will undoubtedly create your own intentional subjects and make your candles in order to serve your specific purposes. For example, there might be a wedding coming up in your family. You could make a special candle to bless that union and light it on your altar in your sacred space while you offer a blessing prayer for the couple to be married.

A Candle for Each Occasion

Here are some examples of special-purpose candles you can make:

Peace—An invitation to bring serenity to the center of your being

Love—To open your heart for giving and receiving

Happiness—To enhance your playful nature

Thankfulness—To appreciate more of life's gifts already yours

Healing—To help resolve conditions of illness, physical imbalance, and/or emotional difficulties

Home—To bring tranquility to your living quarters and make your home a safe haven

Abundance—To increase the flow of all good things into your life, including money and material goods as well as goodwill and blessings from on high

Passion—To bring pleasure and learn to be more fully alive

Protection—To ease mind and body with a feeling of being safe and sound

Wisdom—To learn to see with the heart as well as think with the mind, and awaken the spiritual self through inner insights

Courage—To move beyond fear and into strength with the ability to face the unknown

New Beginnings—To create a fresh start and inspire positive feelings about change. (Feel free to add your own intentions to this list of intentional-use candlemaking.)

Tips for Creating Your Sacred Space

Set aside a space in your home that you will designate as sacred. Make this space a place where you can practice silence and solitude. Make your sacred space comfortable and calm, and advise family members that when you are in your sanctuary you are not to be disturbed. Treat your sacred space with respect. Keep out anything that will profane your intentions there. Collect objects that help you to feel your spiritual energy, that connect you to your Higher Self. These objects can be "found" items or ones you have acquired or created, such as candles. They might include rocks and crystals, flowers, driftwood, twigs or tree branches, pine cones, candles, incense, aroma oil, and a special chair, pillow, or floormat.

Candle-Gazing Meditation

Meditating will help you develop your power of discipline and concentration, both skills that are prominent in the lives of successful people. Candle gazing is an excellent meditation method that will teach you concentration. It will also accustom you to the practice of sitting quietly and focusing on your inner world, letting go of the distractions of the outer world. To perform this exercise, place a lighted candle at eye level, about 2 feet from where you are sitting. Focusing your gaze on the candle's flame, simply watch it constantly. Try not to blink, but do not *force* yourself to keep your eyes open. Keep watching the candle flame for several minutes. If your gaze wanders, gently return it to the flame. Stay aware of your thoughts, but don't attempt to control them.

SSENTIALS

Lavender is a well-known stress reliever. Make a lavender colored and scented pillar candle and burn it while you are soaking in the bath. Some lavender bath salts will intensify the relaxation experience. Use of a lavender candle delivers a potent dose of aromatherapy to your senses.

Ritual Candle Sets As Gifts

Bring a touch of the sacred to the gifts you give. Here are some ideas:

- *Happy Home Candle Set*—This set makes a wonderful gift for someone who has just moved to a new house.
- *Romantic Love Candle Set*—Give this set of candles, using *Passion, Happiness,* and *Love* intentional-use candles, to someone you know who is involved in a new romance, or would like to get involved. It's a great positive encouragement.
- *New Beginnings Candle Set*—This is a wonderful gift for anyone going through a transition period in life—be it a marriage or a divorce, puberty or menopause, moving to a different location or taking a new job. It is also appropriate to give this set to a person who is stuck in a rut and wants to initiate change in his or her life. Be sure to include *Abundance, Wisdom,* and *New Beginnings* candles.
- *Good Health Candle Set*—Making candles for someone who is ill is a thoughtful get-well gesture.
- *Anniversary Gift*—Make the same candle each year as a wedding anniversary or birthday gift for someone you love, thereby creating a lovely tradition that is much appreciated!

Mind-Calming Visualization with Candles

When you are feeling anxious about anything, you can calm yourself with the following visualization, done in a quiet space. Surround yourself with the appropriate handmade candles and light them one by one before beginning.

Become quiet and let the peace of your candlelit space sink deeply into your inner mind and spirit. Then, visualize a natural setting. It can be a place you love to visit, or a place you have seen in a magazine picture or a TV travelogue, or an imaginary place.

You might take a walk through snowy woods, hike up a mountain pass, take a leisurely break by the side of a cool lake, or go to the beach at whatever time of year you like best. The idea is to pick something you find calming and soothing. The light from your handmade candles will enhance this process immeasurably.

You might try imagining sitting by a lake in spring when the wildflowers are just beginning to bloom. Visualize yourself walking down a country road to the shore of the lake, enjoying the fresh yet warm spring air with its breeze that hints of nature's renewal. Allow yourself to feel invigorated and relaxed. Feel the warmth of the spring sun on your shoulders. You might take off your jacket and turn up your face to the sun's gentle warmth, which adumbrates the summer to come.

When you reach the lake's shore, find a comfortable spot to sit and relax. Enjoy the feel of the grass beneath you, inhale the scent of the wildflowers, watch the lake waters swelling gently, listen to the birds chirping, see the myriad forms of life all about you exhibiting nature's annual renewal of herself.

Take off your shoes and dabble you feet in the water, feeling its refreshing coolness. Perhaps a small fish nibbles at your bare toes and tickles you. Watch a pair of mating ducks land on the lake and see the water birds soaring overhead in the clear blue sky. Feel at one with the scene. Notice how the water catches the sun's light and see the reflection of a passing cloud on its placid surface.

Take your time to enjoy this place, letting all your worries and tensions slip away until you feel utterly calm.

After finishing this healing meditation, carefully begin to extinguish your candles, one by one, in the same order in which you lit them originally.

When using candles for meditation, remember that contemplative silence is necessary for the spiritual journey—and there is no better method of doing this than gazing deep into the mysterious flame of a candle. You can use candles in all sorts of meditations. For more meditations I have developed, see my books *Awaken to Your Spiritual Self*, *Your Psychic Potential*, and *Healing Mind, Body, Spirit*. These are excellent guidelines for those of you who want to meditate more or develop meditations of your own.

Healing with Candles

You can also do a healing meditation with your own homemade candles. As you make the candles, keep your mind focused on who or what is to be healed—a person, a situation, a relationship, a pet, a quarrel, a local environmental problem. After you have done the healing meditation, put out the candle or candles you have used, and do not use them for any other purpose. When extinguishing each candle, strongly visualize that the therapeutic flame has healed what was being treated. Don't blow the candle out with your breath—use a snuffer or a piece of foil, or if you are using pillar candles, push the wick gently down into the pool of melted wax with a spoon.

CHAPTER 4

Candles—All You Need to Know

The word "candle" comes from *candela*, meaning "a light or torch," and also from the Latin *candere*, a verb translated as "to shine or be bright." In this chapter, you'll learn more about candles and how to use them correctly, before we embark on the exciting journey of making your own "bright torches."

Candle Industry Facts

U.S. candle consumer retail sales for 2001 are projected at over $2.3 billion, not including candle accessories. Since the early 1990s, the industry has averaged a growth rate of 10–15 percent annually. In recent years, this growth has doubled. There are more than 300 known commercial, religious, and institutional manufacturers of candles in the United States, as well as many small craft producers for local, noncommercial use.

Candles are sold principally in three types of retail outlets: department stores, specialty and gift shops, and mass merchandisers, including drugstore chains, supermarkets, and discount stores. The U.S. market is typically separated into seasonal (Christmas, holiday) business at roughly 35 percent, and nonseasonal business at about 65 percent.

QUESTIONS?

What is the National Candle Association?
The National Candle Association is the major trade association representing candle manufacturers and suppliers in the United States. Founded in 1974, NCA acts as the collective voice for the candle industry to promote the safe use and enjoyment of candles.

Typically, a major U.S. candle manufacturer will offer 1,000 to 2,000 varieties of candles in its product line. Types of candles manufactured in the United States include: tapers, straight-sided dinner candles, columns, pillars, votives, wax-filled containers, and novelties. Many of these come in different sizes and fragrances, and all come in a range of colors. Candles can range in retail price from approximately 50 cents for a votive candle to around $75.00 for a large column candle, although a specialty candle could cost as much as $200.

Candle shipments increase substantially during the third quarter of the year because of the seasonal nature of candle sales during the end-of-year holiday celebrations (Christmas, Hanukkah, Kwanzaa), since candles play a large role at this time of year—they are used for religious purposes, and as gifts and decorations.

Candle industry research findings indicate that the most important factors affecting candle sales are color, shape, and scent. Fragrance is the most important element when it comes to selecting candles for the home. Candles are used in seven out of ten American households. A majority of consumers burn candles for less than three hours per occasion, between one and three times per week, with about half of them burning one to two candles at a time. And here is another interesting finding: Candle manufacturers' surveys show that 96 percent of all candles purchased are bought by women. For more information on candle manufacturing statistics, contact National Candle Association, 1030 15th Street, Suite 870, Washington, D.C. 20005; *www.candles.org.*

Industry Directory Available

The *National Candle Association Directory of Members,* which includes manufacturer and supplier members, is published annually by the National Candle Association. Listings include company background information, contacts, plant locations, and descriptions of candles manufactured or products and services offered. Supplier members are also indexed by product.

Note: To find out more information, including price and payment options, or to order the directory, visit *www.candles.org.* Or, if you do not have Internet access, you can write to the NCA and obtain an order form by mail at: National Candle Association, 1030 15th Street, NW, Suite 870, Washington, DC 20005. The directory is a valuable addition to the library of anyone seriously interested in pursuing candlemaking as a hobby or for arts and crafts teachers and others involved in making candles or teaching about candlemaking.

Technical Papers Available

The National Candle Association offers a wide range of papers for purchase. These papers have been presented at past Association spring and fall meetings and cover a variety of topics. For complete details you can call NCA at (202) 393-2210.

The Lost Art of Burning Candles Properly

Many people buy candles, light them, and that's it. But if you go to the trouble of making your own candles, you should learn the principles of burning them correctly to get the best effects from your work.

A well-made candle burns evenly with a smokeless flame if you follow these basic rules:

1. Your handmade candle should be a day old before use.
2. Do not burn your candles in a draft or breeze.
3. Before lighting the candle, trim the wick to ½".

Bear in mind that even the best-made candles can drip. The best way to avoid dripping is to keep the burning candle out of drafts and to keep the wick trimmed. Observe the flame. If it flickers, there is a draft affecting it. The flame should be absolutely still and shaped like a teardrop. If candle wax drips on your tablecloth, here's what to do: rub the cloth between your hands until most wax flakes fall off (do this over a covered surface or in the yard). Then iron the cloth between several sheets of paper toweling or brown craft paper, which will absorb the melted wax.

ESSENTIALS

To avoid candle wax dripping on your table or table cloth, use decorative mats or leaves—banana leaves work well—to prevent a mess. Alternatively, place candles on plates or in shallow bowls, or on hard nonflammable and washable surfaces, such as a cutting board. Add decorations.

If you have a smoking candle, that is a signal that the candle is not getting enough oxygen to feed its flame. The fire in the fireplace needs a proper supply of oxygen, and so does a candle. Don't burn candles without adequate ventilation, such as in a small, closed room. Not only will the candle fail to receive sufficient oxygen, but you will use up oxygen that you need to breathe. This is important for asthma sufferers or those with chronic respiratory conditions.

SSENTIALS

Observe your burning candles to determine their combustion qualities. A well-made candle will have a 1–2" flame that burns steadily and does not flicker. A good performing wick will bend 90° or remain straight. The melted wax should pool around the wick without spilling or guttering the wick.

How to Put Candles Out Correctly

It is best not to simply blow the candle out. You may get soot in your eye or in your lungs. Using a snuffer made for the purpose is ideal, but you can also pinch it out with wet fingers, if you are quick about it. Another way to put out the candle flame is to stick two fingers out sideways, so you can't see the flame, about an inch in front of the flame, then blow hard directly at your fingers. The flow of air will jump over your fingers, hit the flame, and put it out. Alternatively, you can turn a soup spoon over the flame until it is extinguished.

For candles you plan to light again at another time, snuff the candle rather than blowing it out.

Extinguishing Large Diameter Candles

The best way to put out a container candle, a refillable candle, or any large-diameter candle with a large well of melted wax in the center is to simply push the wick down into the molten wax with a match stick, burned end down. You can also use a pencil or a metal skewer, or the handle end of a spoon. Push the wick into the hot wax, which will extinguish it, and then lift it out of the wax so you can trim it for relighting. If any bits of burned wick get into the pool of wax, just fish them out with your utensil.

Storing Candles

The best place to store your candles is in a wooden box (such as a cigar box) or a closet or drawer. Don't store candles in the refrigerator.

When the weather gets hot, find a cool place for them, such as the basement. Keep your candles out of the sunlight—otherwise, colors may fade. So when you burn candles outdoors after dark, make sure to take them back inside with you after they are distinguished. Otherwise, they will soften and become unusable (except for remelting) under the next day's burning sun.

 **SSENTIALS** Although it is not advisable to store candles in the fridge, you can give them a longer burn time by putting them in it for a few hours before you plan to use them. This will harden the wax (especially in summer or hot climates), making the candles burn longer.

Basic Methods

There are seven basic methods of making candles, whether by hand or commercially. Familiarize yourself with these terms and you'll be on the way to fluent "candlespeak."

Rolled—An excellent method for the home candlemaker, this consists of merely rolling a sheet of wax around a wick. It's a good method for novelty candles as well as ordinary shapes such as tapers and pillars. The beauty of this way of making candles is that you don't have to melt the wax.

Poured—This is a method favored by home candlemakers, and is, along with dipping, the easiest one to use in a small space such as your kitchen. This very old-fashioned method consists of pouring the melted wax in layers over the wick until the size you wish is reached.

Cast and Molded—This type of candle is made by pouring the liquefied wax into a mold or shape. Candle molds can be purchased, improvised from what's on hand (empty cans, muffin tins, etc.), or created (such as a roll of corrugated cardboard taped together into a cylinder or other shape).

Milk cartons of all sizes make great molds. So do sea shells and sand. A garage sale is a great source for things that can be used as molds—anything made of metal or hard plastic (the kind that doesn't melt). Rubber and latex are good materials for making your own molds.

Dipped—Candles that are dipped are made by simply dipping the wick over and over again into the pot of liquid wax, letting it drip-dry between layers. You can dip candles to any thickness you prefer. The term "taper" comes from dipped candles, for they naturally form a tapered shape while being dipped and dripped. A simple rack for drying dipped candles can be made by fixing a small dowel or other round stick on two holders. Dipping frames can also be purchased.

If you're handy with woodworking, you can easily make your own dipping frame by boring or cutting a small circular hole in each of two upright boards, supported by a horizontal board, with the dowel or bar inserted in the holes. You can make it as tall or as short as you want.

Drawn—This method is very old but still in use today. To make drawn candles, you literally draw a very long wick through the liquid wax. This is a good way to make small diameter candles such as birthday candles. It is also used to make "wax matches," or long waxed wicks that are used for lighting multiple candles.

In earlier times, special lamps existed to hold a wound length of drawn candle, which as it burned down unwound itself. This simple, easy method let the candlemaker produce a long-burning candle with a minimum expense of wax, as the wick did not need to be thickly coated.

Pressed—Not for the home candlemaker, this is a commercial method of recent development. The hot wax is atomized onto a cooling drum, during which process it forms small beads that are compressed (pressed) into molds. The "pressing" binds together the small beads into a candle form. From a commercial standpoint, the advantage is that pressing is quicker—because the wax is already cool, the candles can be removed from their molds without the waiting time needed for ordinary hot-wax poured candles.

Extruded—Generally used by commercial candlemakers, this method requires a machine that pushes the wax out through a template, or different templates, rather like a cookie "gun" presses out dough. Once the wax is extruded, the long candle can be cut to any size desired, short or tall. Extruded candles require strict control of the wax's heating and cooling so that the wax retains the proper shape as it is extruded through the die, or template.

In this chapter, the delights of handmade rolled and poured candles are explored.

Candle Shapes

Candles are commonly identified by their shape—tapers, pillars, etc. Let's review a list of the most common shapes used in candlemaking today.

Container—A container candle is set in the shape of the mold in which it is made by pouring.

Pillar—A popular candle shape, the pillar is a thick candle (usually 3–4" in diameter). If the pillar is 3" in diameter and 6" tall, it is called a "three by six," and so on. Most pillars are cylindrical, but they can be made in any shape—oval, hexagonal, square, etc. Commercial pillar candles come in standard sizes, but you can make a pillar candle any size or shape you choose.

Novelty—This term refers to odd-shaped, usually colored candles that are made by pouring and/or molding and then sculpting or shaping. Novelty candles are practically unlimited in their possibilities—from bananas to snow balls and beyond. They let you get as creative as you desire.

Tapers—As the name implies, these are tapered candles that most of us think of first when we think "candle." The most common candle shape—often found on the dinner table during festivities—tapers are expressly made to fit into a candleholder of some sort, whether for a single candle or for multiple candles. Tapers are made by dipping (the most common method), pouring into a mold, or by rolling, and are generally sized to fit standard candleholders, between $1/2$" and $7/8$" in diameter at the base. Exceptions are the so-called Danish tapers which are smaller and shorter than regular tapers: $1/4$" in diameter at the base. Birthday candles are also designated tapers ($3/16$" is standard, but the home candlemaker can vary the size to suit herself—I personally like a larger, thicker birthday candle as they stay put in the cake better than the store-bought size).

Tealight—Used to keep chafing dishes warm or to fit some novelty candleholders (I have a fat, hollow pink salt candleholder that takes a tealight and gives off a lovely rose-colored glow from within.). Tealights are similar to votives, but they are much smaller, flat cylinders usually only $1/2$" high and $1\frac{1}{2}$" in diameter.

Votive—The term *votive* comes from the Latin for "to vow"; votive candles were originally used in church to light in front of an icon or a sculpture of a saint while asking for intercession. In church, they are generally placed on a multiple rack holder and are often in little red glass cups. In recent years, this type of candle has become very popular to be lit at home as well, especially as scented candles of different colors. Votives are cylinders 2–3" high, ordinarily $1\frac{1}{2}$" in diameter. Again, the home candlemaker can vary the size—and shape—of votives as he or she pleases. As the votive burns, it melts in its container and uses itself as fuel, so you get a longer burn-time than if you set the votive candle on a plate or other flat surface. Votives are designated by the length of burn-time: ten-hour, fifteen-hour, etc. You can check the burn-time of your handmade votives by burning one down while watching the clock.

ESSENTIALS

Votives are especially useful in small spaces, such as bathrooms, or on home altars. You can use them singly or in groups to get the desired effect. If you color your votives, it's best to use a clear glass holder. Scent them for special purposes.

The Significance of Candle Colors

Candles of different colors have always been used for different purposes, whether mundane or spiritual. We set the Christmas table with red and green candles to represent and harmonize with the holiday season, and burn white candles at Easter. Metaphysicans use candles of different colors to achieve the desired results.

Here are some general ideas on what each color represents, and how a candle of that color might best be used.

White—Self-protection; purity; sincerity; truth; peace; purification; innocence; moon magic; increased spirituality

Red—South; fire (element); energy; strength; health; vitality; courage; power and willpower; passion; enthusiasm; overcoming obstacles

Yellow—East; air (element); intellectual progress; creativity; education and learning enhancement; mental renewal; harmony

Blue (dark)—West; water (element); psychic development and protection; fidelity; meditation; inspiration; truth; dreams

Blue (light)—Tranquility; healing; patience; happiness; intuition; antidepression; domestic harmony; peace; safe travel

Green—North; earth (element); money; growth; gardening; earth magic; herb and nature magic; luck; prosperity; healing; balance

Lime—Reconciliation of disputes; healing discord; overcoming anger; negating jealousy; facing danger bravely; optimism

Orange—Stimulation; attraction and the attraction principle; encouragement; mind-clearing; good luck; opportunity

Purple—Spirituality; intuition; spirit communications; angels; occult developments; idealism; higher powers; honor

Pink—Love and romance; feminine power; affection; healing the heart; togetherness; better relationships; friendship

Lavender—Spiritual development; divination; blessings from the other world; psychic intuition; emotional calmness

Violet—Self-development; spiritual guidance; intuitive growth; creative work; clairvoyance; mental calm

Magenta—Spiritual healing; soul work; quick changes; exorcism rituals; high vibration. Magenta is best when combined with other colors

Indigo—Meditation; balancing karma; spirit contact; antidefamation; meeting spirit guides; learning ancient wisdom

Gray—Contact with the Other World; quest of vision; out-of-body travel; cancellation rituals; overcoming doubt; non-nature spirits

Black—Endings; closure; death; overcoming negativity; end discord or confusion; banishing rituals; releasing

Silver—The Goddess; lunar magical work; psychic protection against negative forces; astral travel; meditation; money

Gold—The God; solar principle; physical stamina; mental development; good health; fortunate circumstances; wealth

Keep a Notebook!

Think of making candles as a learning process. Even experienced candlemakers are always learning from both their successes and their failures. And, even though you may think you'll *never forget that disaster*, you won't remember the details. The solution is to write everything down immediately after your candlemaking session. Note the wax formula you used. Specify the type of wick. Fill in every single step you took along the way. Keep a record of your moldmaking and exactly how you did each one. Indicate the results, good or bad, any problems you encountered, and what solutions (if any) you found.

A loose-leaf notebook is a good choice, one that you can insert dividers into. Make a section on each type of candle you make—container, molded, dipped, etc. Then, use a separate page for each candlemaking session. Date the page and note any other pertinent information. One day you might wonder just how you made that wonderful candle, but chances are you won't remember. In our hectic lives, it's often difficult to remember what happened yesterday, let along a few weeks, or months, ago.

Keep careful notes of anything unusual that you do—if you made a two-part mold, for example. List the materials you used, with comments about how they worked for that model. You can't jot down too many details, and it's best if you get your notes recorded as soon as possible after your candlemaking session. Even a day or two later you may not remember exactly what percentage of what you used—of wax additives, colorants, scents, and the like. You may want to duplicate a scent that turned out differently than you expected—if you know exactly what perfumes you used, and in what proportion, you'll be able to duplicate it. Otherwise, it will be hit or miss next time around. The same applies to color. One candlemaker recounts how she achieved a beautiful color by sheer accident. She wanted a particular scent, and she used an herb that she thought would do the trick. However, it turned out that the resulting candle was not fragrant at all—but it was tinted a great color! So, take this advice and follow it even when you're making your very first candle.

ESSENTIALS

When making a large batch of candles, from whatever formula you have chosen, always *test, test, test*. Make a small batch of wax with color and scent, for one or two candles, perhaps using different wicks. Allow to harden and test-burn before making a quantity.

CHAPTER 5
How to Get Started

From necessary labor, candlemaking has evolved into an art practiced by creative people who enjoy learning new skills. Once you learn these basic skills, detailed in the pages that follow, you will be able to make candles of all shapes, sizes, and designs, and let your imagination take flight.

Candle Terminology

Before we begin, let's review the various types of candles and some common candlemaking terms that you should know. The following definitions have been provided by the National Candle Association.

Candle: One or more combustible wicks supported by a material that constitutes a fuel, which is solid, semi-solid, or quasi-rigid at room temperature (68–80° Fahrenheit or 20–26° Celsius). Candles can contain additives, which are used for stability, color, fragrance, or to modify the burning characteristics of the wax base. The combined function of these is to sustain a light-producing flame.

Candle Accessory: An object, such as a candleholder or tray, designed for use with a candle or candles.

Filled Candle: Also called a container candle, this is a candle produced and used within the same vessel, or container. Many containers can be refilled and reused.

Freestanding Candle: This term refers to a rigid candle (a pillar-shaped, column-shaped, or novelty candle in the shape of a figure). Freestanding candles are safest when placed on a heat-resistant, nonflammable surface, such as a plate or metal pan, or special candle accessory made for the purpose.

Taper Candle: A taper candle is a slender candle, usually 10"–12" in height, intended to be supported by a candle accessory, usually a candlestick made of glass, crystal, or metal, with a well in the center that matches the circumference of the candle's base. Purchased taper candles come in standard sizes to fit standard candlesticks.

Tealight Candle: A cylindrical filled candle produced with a diameter and height of approximately 1.5" (38 mm) and 0.75" (19 mm), respectively. Tealight candles are commonly used as food warmers, but they can also serve as fillers for candle shells and small receptacles.

Votive Candle: A candle produced for use inside a candle accessory, usually a standard votive candleholder, which is a cylindrical vessel (ordinarily made of glass) of the same size as the votive candle. Votives can also be placed on a hard, nonflammable surface like freestanding candles. They are nice to use in groups of a single color or in several colors to match a particular décor or seasonal theme.

Votive Holder: A small open vessel designed to hold a votive candle while it is burning. The votive holder must be capable of containing the melted candle wax.

Wax: A solid or semi-solid material consisting of a mixture of hydrocarbons and/or hydrocarbon derivatives.

Wax Candle: A candle that contains petroleum wax, vegetable wax, animal wax, or insect wax as the primary fuel.

Wick: A string-like object that delivers fuel to a flame through the process of capillary, or wicking, action.

Wax 101

When one thinks of making candles, the first thing that comes to mind is wax. Although in times past candles were made of tallow (animal fat), those days are long gone. Modern candles are all made of wax, and the home candlemaker relies on wax exclusively, or along with various additives. Therefore, we begin our discussion of what you need to get started with wax, the basis to modern candlemaking.

What exactly is wax? It is, put simply, what your candle burns for fuel. As the wick burns, the candle wax melts and is "wicked" into the flame to feed its fire. Although other types of wax exist (as you'll see), most candles these days are made of beeswax or paraffin, or a combination of the two.

Making Merry with Bayberry

As we have already seen, in colonial times candles were sometimes made of bayberries. The Pilgrims found bayberry bushes growing along the shores of Cape Cod Bay, and that's how they got their name.

Bayberry wax is still available today; it is extracted from the berries by boiling them. When boiled, the abundant wax in the bayberries floats to the top of the water, from where it can be skimmed off and used for making candles.

FACTS

In addition to bayberry, candelilla and carnauba are plants that produce wax. Candelilla is a reed-like, scaly native of northern Mexico and southern Texas, while carnauba is a fan-leaved palm native to Brazil. Mostly used in wood and leather finishing and polishing, these vegetable-based waxes are expensive and brittle, with a high melting point. Their use in candlemaking is limited: they can be used to harden a soft wax (such as paraffin) by raising the melting point of the mixture.

Although we associate bayberry candles with New England, these bushes are found as far north as Nova Scotia and as far south as the Carolinas. In fact, they can be found as far west as upstate New York.

Bayberry Lowdown

Today, most candles sold as "bayberry" are actually made of paraffin that has been scented with the spicy odor we associate with bayberry. True bayberry wax is naturally a lovely sage green color and already scented by nature. Real bayberry wax is expensive, and can be difficult to find, although if you are fortunate enough to have bayberry bushes in your area you can collect your own and make you own bayberry wax. To make your own bayberry wax for candles, you'd need ten to fifteen pounds of berries—for a pound of wax! A pound of wax would be enough to make about five or six pairs of tapers by the dipping method, or several small molded candles. First, you have to boil the berries, and then filter out the skins, seeds, and other impurities. If this is impracticable, and you want to use bayberry wax, there are specialty candlemaking-supply houses that sell it. (See the list of suppliers on p. 69.)

Minding Your Beeswax

Instead of dirt and poison we have rather chosen to fill our
hives with honey and wax; thus furnishing mankind with
the two noblest of things, which are sweetness and light.
—Jonathan Swift, *The Battle of the Books*

Beeswax is the most elegant of the waxes available for candlemaking.
Just as silkworms are famous for making fine silk, bees make excellent
wax. The bees are essential to life's natural processes, for they pollinate
plants, including those that provide us with food.

As everyone knows, beeswax is produced by bees as a byproduct
of their honeymaking. It is actually a secretion that they use to create
the combs where the honey is stored and where the larvae are
incubated. Though it may seem odd than an insect can manufacture
wax in its system and then secrete it for building purposes, this is
simply another of nature's miracles by which we are continually awed
and astounded.

Amazingly, these little creatures not only make the wax and exude it,
they shape it into perfect hexagonal shapes that are the tiny boxes that
make up a honeycomb's structure. Each tiny hexagon has angles that are
so accurately made, their margin of error is a mere 3 or 4 degrees from
the average, an architectural marvel that results in the perfect use of
space. This structure is so cleverly engineered that 1 pound of hive wax
holds 22 pounds of honey, which is the optimal weight for the comb. Not
only that, but bees all over the world, of whatever country or type, create
hexagons out of their wax in the same structural proportions! Add to this
capability their indispensable function of pollinating trees, fruits, flowers,
and vegetables, and you'll never swat a bee again!

Beeswax, because it is permeated with honey during its preharvest
life, naturally has a wonderful, sweet fragrance. Its odor will vary
depending on what the bees are feeding on—which might be wildflowers,
clover, avocados, or various herbs. Unrefined beeswax in the natural state
has a golden yellow to brownish or reddish-brown color. It also contains
plant parts and bits of the bees themselves.

Harvesting and purifying pure beeswax is a time-consuming, difficult process, so it is not surprising that beeswax is far more expensive than paraffin. However, one of its advantages is that it is long-lasting. Most pure beeswax is used in church candles, where it has been a standard for hundreds of years. (My father used to buy our candles for use at the dinner table from the local Catholic cathedral to which our family belonged; he believed that pure beeswax candles were the only permissible candles for the home.)

FACTS

Beeswax ranges from pale yellow to darkest brown in color, according to the age and food supply of the bees. The raw wax smells of honey and has a taste reminiscent of balsamic vinegar. In the natural state, beeswax is soft to brittle. Technically, it has a specific gravity of about 0.95 and a melting point of about 140° Fahrenheit (60° Celsius). It consists primarily of free cerotic acid and myricin (myricyl palmitate) along with some high-carbon paraffins.

Beeswax is indeed lovely when it burns: It creates a warm, golden glow that nothing else can match, and the sweet honeyed smell permeates the house and the people's hair and garments. However, for budgetary purposes, beeswax can be combined with paraffin to make candles that will be long-lasting yet less expensive.

From Comb to Candle

The average bee consumes between 6 and 10 pounds of nectar (honey) to make each pound of the wax it secretes in small flakes from glands on the underside of its abdomen. After the beekeeper removes the honey from the honeycomb, the honey is melted and strained to remove impurities. Some artisan honeys are sold unfiltered and may have bits of wax in them. The waxy residue is pressed to obtain the beeswax. Honeybees that live in the United States and the Western World produce a distinctive wax that is somewhat different from wax obtained from the bees of East Asia.

After purifying, the beeswax is poured into molds to harden into blocks for commercial sale. Some beeswax is bleached to make a white product, but the natural honey color is much preferred by those who appreciate the qualities of beeswax.

FACTS

Long ago, candlemaking was such an arduous affair, requiring careful and long attention to many details, that gossipy women—who apparently had time to take off from their domestic duties, including making beeswax candles—were sharply told to, "Mind your own beeswax."

Versatile Beeswax

Insoluble in water, beeswax can be dissolved in such substances as carbon tetrachloride, chloroform, or warm ether. Because it is soluble in these chemicals, it is used as an ingredient in the manufacture of furniture and floor waxes, leather dressings, waxed paper, inks, and cosmetics.

Befriend a Beehive

Sheets of beeswax were originally invented by beekeepers. These were, and are, used (in their natural color only) to line the beehives. This wax liner gives the bees a firm foundation on which to build the honeycomb. Thus, the beekeepers call beeswax sheets "brood foundation." Beeswax candles can be made from foundation sheets. If you have a friendly neighborhood beekeeper, you might obtain them that way.

SSENTIALS

Store beeswax sheets at room temperature. When exposed to excessive cold, they can become brittle and crack, making the sheets unusable for rolled candles; excessive heat can melt beeswax. Don't leave it in a closed car trunk in summer.

All about Paraffin

Since pure beeswax is a rare commodity and pure beeswax candles are so expensive, most beeswax candles available on the market today are mixed with paraffin, a byproduct of the refining process that turns crude oil into motor oil on the way to becoming gasoline.

In the oil-refining process in which paraffin is produced, crude oil is heated from the bottom of a pipe still (a tall pipe), and as it heats, it separates according to the temperature it reaches: heavy oil at the bottom; then light lubricating oil; next, fuel oil; and, lastly, gasoline. At the top, it becomes hydrocarbon gas. Waxes produced from the light lubricating oil are further processed by chilling, sweating, and additional distillation, based on the various melting points. Afterward, the waxes are refined further through hydrogenation, which allows them to end up with quite specific chemical properties.

Paraffin Wax

Paraffin waxes used for candlemaking are classified by their melting points: low, medium, and high. In general, most homemade candles need to be melted to 125–150° Fahrenheit.

Never buy grocery-store paraffin to use in candlemaking—it is not the same as paraffin wax used to make candles. It has a lower melting point and does not harden sufficiently to make a candle stand up straight.

Some paraffin wax comes with stearin already mixed in, usually 10 percent. Alternatively, you can buy stearin separately and mix it into the paraffin to suit your needs. Stearin, or stearic acid, is added to paraffin to make it harder and to increase opacity.

Paraffin waxes can be used without additives, but they burn much faster and are less opaque. However, paraffin wax used alone gives a lovely translucent quality to the candle, an advantage that can make up for the shorter burning time of the wax.

Choose Your Paraffin

Paraffin is normally sold by suppliers and craft shops in 11-pound slabs; the next standard size up is a 55-pound case. Depending on your needs—that is, how many candles you want to make—you may want to bypass your local craft shop and go to a wholesaler for your paraffin wax, thus saving money and having more options available. Don't hesitate to contact your supplier for additional information. (See "Suppliers" below.)

You can buy paraffin wax in pellets or powered form, which is easier to measure or weigh, and easier to handle. However, bulk is cheaper. The best way to break up the 11-pound slabs is to put one into a heavy-duty disposable trash bag and drop it from shoulder height to the floor.

SSENTIALS Wax purchased from candlemaking suppliers, or from craft stores, are labeled with the melting point range and the use for which they are intended. Do not use paraffin waxes in any way contrary to the label instructions and guidelines.

Suppliers

Wax is heavy and costly to ship. Therefore, it is economical to have a local supplier. Your craft shop is the place to start. However, if it cannot fill your needs, ask the manager for the names and addresses of local wholesale suppliers who sell to individuals. Also check your yellow pages. Here are some regional suppliers:

Northwest
Barker Candle Supplies
(800) 543-0601

South
Earth Guild
(800) 327-8448
www.earthguild.com

Midwest
The CandleMaker
(888) 251-4618
www.thecandlemaker.com

Northeast
The Candle Mill
(800) 772-3759

West Coast
Yaley Enterprises Inc.
(877) 365-5212
www.yaley.com

Recycle Your Wax

You can save money and help protect the environment by recycling old wax, including cheese coverings and sealing wax. Save all your candle ends, as well as any scraps left over from making candles, and store them either in zippered plastic bags (away from heat) or in an airtight tin such as the type in which Christmas cookies are sold. Also, chip or scrape or melt the dregs of votive cups and save them as well. And, of course, any failed homemade candles with which you weren't satisfied can be reused to make new, successful candles. You can remelt everything (keeping colors separate, if necessary). Strain melted candle ends through a fine sieve or cheesecloth to remove burned bits.

You can separate your candle scraps by color if you like, or throw the whole bunch in together—if you are in the mood to experiment, melting different candle colors together can be the way to go. A yellow cheese coating mixed with a green deodorant candle might give a nice lime color. Be sure to save all of the wax that gets spilled during your candlemaking efforts—a putty knife kept handy is a good tool for scraping spills up. When melting different colored leftovers together, if you don't like the result you can dilute it with new wax to lighten it, or add dye to darken it. As always, your imagination rules the day.

SSENTIALS If you are looking for pure vegetable wax to make kosher candles, you will have to find a special supplier because all-vegetable waxes and/or additives such as stearic acid are rarely available at craft shops. Read labels carefully: wax labeled "vegetable" may not be.

Wicks

If the first component of a candle is wax, it follows that the next is the wick. Indeed, the wick is the heart of the candle, not only in that it lies at the center but also in that it is what determines if a candle will burn, and how well it will do so. One might even make a case that the wick is the single most important part of the candle. In fact, one can make—not a candle—but at least a light with only a wick and some oil. Remember, in earlier times, before candlemaking was discovered and evolved, these puddles of oil with a wick immersed in them, called rushlights, were one of the few sources of illumination indoors after dark.

QUESTIONS?

How are wicks made?
Today's wick is a braided (sometimes cored) bunch of threads, usually made of cotton but sometimes of linen or other fabric. The braided material is then subjected to a process known as "mordanting," which means that it is pickled in a chemical solution that is intended to make it fire-retardant.

Select the Best: Wick, That Is

Choosing the correct wick for your candle is most important. However, it can be difficult to determine precisely what wick is best for a particular candle.

Few people make their own wicks these days. Candlemaking suppliers sell packaged wicks to those who choose to make their own candles. These prepackaged wicks will usually have recommendations printed on the label, such as, "Use this wick for 2"-diameter candles." Unfortunately, although such instructions are a useful guide, they aren't always the complete story. Other considerations besides the candle's diameter must be taken into account, especially the wax, with its various components.

Braided wicks come in a flat type and a square-braided type, in a full range of sizes. The flat-braided type is just like a braid of hair: a three-strand braid made of many tiny threads. Flat-braided wicks are sized according to the number of these small threads, called "plies," in each wick. It follows that the larger the number of plies, the larger the wick. When flat-braided wicks bend while burning, they may get off-center on the oxidation side of the flame.

Square-braided wicks look like square columns with rounded corners. They are available in various sizes and are classified according to different numbering systems. Square-braided wicks are labeled "for use in beeswax candles, also pillars, blocks, and novelties." One writer says that her experience is "that a $\frac{1}{10}$" square-braided wick is roughly equivalent to a 30-ply flat braid," and that square-braided wicks tend to stand straighter and remain centered in the burning candle.

FACTS

Candlemaking suppliers ordinarily classify their wicks by the diameter of the candle:

0–1" = extra small;   2–3" = large;

1–2" = small;   4" or greater = extra large.

Special wicks for container candles are available in small, medium, and large sizes.

A third type of wick is known as *cored*. These wicks are woven around a central core—made of paper, cotton, zinc, or lead—that holds them upright. These are metal-core wicks designed for longer-burning candles. Floating candles require a special floating-candle wick.

Use Your Supplier

In choosing wicks, your supplier is your best friend. In the beginning, follow the instructions that come with your supplies, or that you find in the suppliers' catalogs. As you experiment—especially with waxes other than beeswax and paraffin, or if you use very large containers—you may find that you need further information about wicks and how to use them. Your supplier is usually happy to provide any additional information and help you with troubleshooting if your candle doesn't burn well.

One source reports using primed, all-cotton shoelaces as wicks in very large block candles. However, unless you are trying to recreate a Colonial lifestyle, you are advised to use purchased wicks. The chemicals used for the mordanting process are apparently a closely guarded trade secret.

Wick Sustainers

These are little metal disks that are used to anchor the wick in container candles, votives, and tealights. Wick sustainers are available wherever candlemaking supplies are sold. To use, you push the wick through a small hole in the sustainer and pinch the metal together so that it sits flat on the container base.

Wicking Needles

Wicking needles are made of steel and come in sizes from 4"–10" long. With an elongated hole in one end, they look a lot like darning needles, and you can even use a large darning needle for wicking. You'll need several sizes of this useful tool.

Wick Priming

Prior to use, all wicks need priming. This is a process that saturates the wick with wax in advance of its being placed in the candle mold, or dipped. Priming is done to eliminate air that may have become trapped in the plies of the braid.

Priming the wick

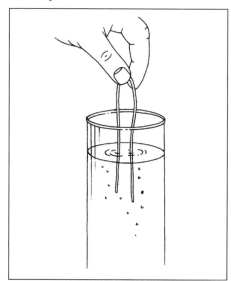

Ordinarily, when you pour the wax over the wick, or dip the wick, the air is forced out naturally. However, as this can't be relied on, it's best to prime the wick before use. This is especially important for molded and novelty candles. To prime the wick, heat some wax to 160° Fahrenheit (using your thermometer to check the temperature). Then, dip the length of wick into the wax. Air bubbles will form as the air escapes. Continue to hold the wick in the wax until you don't see any more air bubbles (this usually takes about five minutes). Remove the wick from the pot of wax and stretch it out. Allow it to cool thoroughly. When completely dry, it will be stiff. At this point, it is ready to use.

Always trim the wick to within ½" of the wax surface before lighting the candle. For larger candles, especially pillars, allow the candle to burn at least two hours before extinguishing to distribute the liquid wax evenly. Don't burn large diameter candles longer than three hours at a time.

To check your wicks, you can do a side-by-side burning comparison. Using the same wax formula and candle diameter with two or more different type wicks in two or more candles, set the finished experimental candles in muffin cups next to each other and light them. Keep notes.

Burn Rate

Burn rate is a term used to determine how well a particular combination of wax and wick is working. It can happen that by altering the wax mixture and using a different wick you can have a longer-burning candle that is therefore less costly.

To find the burn rate, first weigh the candle. Then, burn the candle for a specific length of time; put it out and weigh it again, with any drippings. Unburned wax was not consumed as fuel by the flame.

Burn rate is usually figured in grams. Here's an example: your candle weighs 340 grams. After burning 1 hour, it weighs 40 grams. Therefore, each minute it burned (burn time) consumed 5 grams of wax. Your burn rate is 5 grams per minute.

How to Avoid the Draft

The most well-made candle with the perfect combination of wax and wick will burn poorly and drip if it is subjected to a draft. What a draft does is to create more oxygen on one side of the flame than on the other, causing uneven burning. If your candle is not burning properly, check the air flow and move it to a draft-free location.

Another form of draft is oxygen deprivation—this occurs when a container or large pillar candle has burned down sufficiently so that the hole made by the melted wax's consumption in the flame is so deep that not enough oxygen can get in to feed the fire. This is a common and regular problem with pillar and container candles.

To correct oxygen deprivation in large candles, use paraffin instead of wax or a mixture that produces a soft wax with a lower melting point. Don't burn the candle longer than three hours per session so that the pool of wax can resolidify in between use.

Fire Retardant Is Better

It might seem odd that a wick, which has as its essential characteristic the ability to burn, would be made fire-retardant. But, the idea is that the *fuel* (usually the melted wax) should burn up before the wick does. If the wick were entirely flammable, it would go up in smoke and the candle wouldn't burn at all!

Prior to the invention of the braided wicks, wicks were simply twisted, using whatever fibers were available, including unrefined natural fiber such as hemp. Many natural plant fibers were twisted together to improvise wicks in ancient times.

Twisted wicks were unpredictable—they might fall over into the pool of melted wax and extinguish themselves, and they couldn't be relied upon to curl in a constant manner. With the coming of the braided and mordanted wick, all that changed. Our modern wicks are remarkable in that they bend at exactly 90°!

Why Braided Wicks Burn Best

Braiding plays a vital role in wick preparation. Without it, the wick would not burn properly. Technically, what happens with braiding is that the air space between the braids permits air into the zone of combustion. This makes a better fire (as oxygen is needed for fire to burn). Also, the structure formed by the braid forces the wick to bend as it burns, which in turn removes the wick from the combustion zone into the oxidizing zone, where, due to the mordanting process, it burns slowly and decomposes fully as it burns down, allowing the melted wax to serve its function as fuel for the wick.

When to Snuff Was Not to Dout

Prior to 1850, the long-handled candlesnuffing device with a bell-shaped metal cup on a long handle, used to extinguish the flame of candles, was called a douter, from the expression "to do out (dout) the candle." This item came into use rather late in candle history, after the advent of the braided and mordanted wick.

Prior to that time, a snuffer was a sort of scissors, with a small cup attached to one of the blades. The scissors was used to snip the wick and the little box-like cup caught the trimmings so they didn't spill into the melted wax pool. An experienced person could trim the wick neatly without putting out the flame.

The term "snuff" originally did not refer to putting out the candle, as it now does. It meant trimming the wick, usually to about ½", periodically (while the candle was burning), to prevent excess smoke from forming. A special gadget was used for this purpose.

Candlemaking Equipment

In addition to wax and wicks, making candles at home requires some basic equipment, most of which is neither expensive nor complicated. Your kitchen and your household probably already contain most of the bare essentials. Once you are aware of what you need for candlemaking, you will begin to realize that much of what you have on hand is "just right." Items you don't already possess are easily available and usually inexpensive.

If you choose to use any of your cooking implements and/or pots for making candles at home, dedicate any and all candlemaking equipment to that end only. Not only will you avoid confusion, but you will keep your food safe from contamination from wax, additives, dyes, and the like.

Candlemaking
equipment

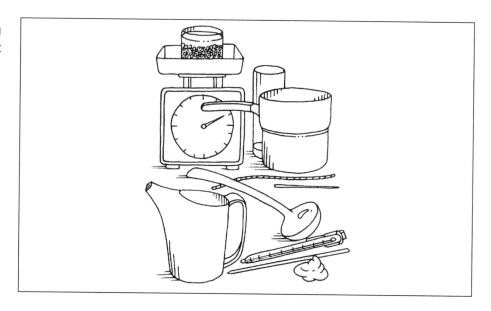

Descriptions follow of everything you will need to make the different types of candles discussed in this book: sheet wax, poured and dipped candles, rolled and novelty candles. Unless you are already an experienced candlemaker, it's important for you to review and thoroughly understand the supplies before you begin to make your own candles. As you'll see, you will need to decide exactly what type of candles you are going to make (you may refer back to the description of the different types of candles in Chapter 4) before you gather the appropriate equipment. For example, if you want to make molded candles, you will need molds of the size and shape you intend the finished candle(s) to have. In later chapters, for your convenience and quick reference the materials and equipment needed to make each type of candle are provided in brief form at the beginning of each set of candlemaking instructions.

ESSENTIALS

Copy the list of materials and equipment needed for each type of candle you regularly make on a card and keep a file of these "recipes" handy in a file box. You can also use cards to make notes to yourself and keep records of your candlemaking experience and results.

Thermometer

Though a small item in your candlemaking equipment collection, your thermometer is vital. You can buy a special wax thermometer or use a candy or other cooking thermometer that covers a scale from 0 to 300° Fahrenheit. It should have a clip so that you can immerse it deep enough into your pot of melting wax to get an accurate reading. *Make sure your thermometer is accurate.* You must always know the precise degree to which your wax has been heated. Even a few degrees hotter than the burning point is a danger. Check your thermometer regularly and discontinue use if it is no longer accurate.

ESSENTIALS

All temperature instructions in this book are given in Fahrenheit. To convert, follow the following formula: For given temperature in $x°$ Fahrenheit, $(x - 32) ÷ 9 × 5 =$ degrees Celsius. Also remember:

1° Celsius = 1.8° Fahrenheit

1° Fahrenheit = .56° Celsius

0° Celsius = 32° Fahrenheit

Melt That Wax

Obviously, a system for melting wax is the primary consideration in candlemaking. There are two methods commonly used: the double-boiler and the concealed element (a slow cooker for example) method. Both systems work equally well as far as the actual melting of the wax is concerned. However, with the concealed element method you are forced to ladle the hot wax either directly into a mold, or transfer it to a pouring tool such as a measuring cup. On the other hand, unless you use an insert to the double-boiler with a handle (such as a large can) the same problem can arise. My suggestion is that you assess your skills at physical coordination before deciding which method to use. If you tend to be a bit of a klutz in the kitchen, by all means use the double-boiler method with a pot that has a sturdy handle. If you can balance and carry four full dinner plates to the table with ease, you are a candidate for the concealed element method, or the handle-less double-boiler system.

ESSENTIALS   Keep on the lookout for candlemaking equipment, especially when you visit garage sales! This way, you can build up your supplies bit by bit at minimum cost. For example, I once bought a terrific electric wok at a yard sale for $5.00—a can insert made a perfect double-boiler system.

Double-Boilers

As you can see, double-boilers are extremely easy to improvise. You need only an outer pot to hold water and an inner pot (insert) in which to melt the wax. The outer pot must be large enough to hold an amount of water sufficient to rise two thirds of the way up the inner pot.

Ideally, the inner pot will have a handle (a metal pitcher is excellent). A large can, such as the kind fruit juice is sold in, will work if you are willing to ladle out the wax. You can pour from such a can if you use mitts to protect your hands from the heat and are very careful.

If you improvise your double-boiler, you will need a support for the inner pot, such as a metal trivet (the kind used on the dinner table to protect it from a hot dish). A support can be improvised as well, for instance by using three short cans (tuna fish or cat food cans will do). Cut out both ends and wire them together to make a three-pointed support. Or, cut out one end only and fill them with water so they don't float.

You can buy ready-made double-boilers of many sizes. Some inexpensive, while others are quite pricey. Cast aluminum and stainless-steel double-boilers for cooking are readily available wherever cookware is sold. There is a marvelous utensil called a *bain marie* (literally, "Mary's bath") that you can get at specialty cookware shops. A *bain marie* has a copper bottom with a porcelain insert. The porcelain is heavy but has a long handle and makes for easy cleanup as wax won't stick to it, and the copper bottom retains heat. To my mind, this is a good investment.

Whichever kind of double-boiler you use, you will need to replenish the water in the bottom pot frequently in order to keep your boiling water at the correct level. Once again, experimentation will reveal just which type of setup works best for you.

Your working surface must be level and have ready access to a water supply. (I have a small stainless-steel sink in my art workroom.) You also need a heat source that is *not an open flame*. Your electric stove will work fine; a steady hot plate will suffice as well.

Concealed Element Approach

If you want to use the concealed element method, you will need a vessel that allows you to melt the wax directly in it, without the wax's coming into contact with the heat source. A slow cooker, an electric wok, or deep-fat frying kettle will all work fine. If you use one of these (remembering that it will be off-limits for cooking food), make sure that it has an accurate dial-type temperature control device marked in *degrees* (i.e., 0–450° is usual), not "Low–Medium–High."

You can use a concealed-element vessel as the bottom pot of your double-boiler. Set your wax-melting pot inside on a trivet or other support. Follow the instructions for the double-boiler method. It's necessary for you to know how much wax you have in your melting pot and to be able to judge how much solid wax to use to reach the level you need for the type of candle you are making (2 inches below the top of the can for dipping, for example).

To calibrate your can, first melt a pound of paraffin and score the can at the level one pound reaches. You can use any sharp instrument to make a mark—but be sure you don't puncture your can!

Continue the process with 2 pounds, 3 pounds, 4 pounds, and 5 pounds, marking each level separately. This will allow you to gauge the amount of wax in the can as you work.

As a precaution against water getting into your melted wax, always wipe dry the bottom of your melting pot when you lift it out of the water to pour off wax. Keep a roll of paper towels handy for this purpose.

Candle-Specific Suggestions

If you are making dipped candles, you will need a tall, cylindrical insert to hold your liquid wax. These are available at craft shops and from candlemaking suppliers. Your dipping can must be 2 inches deeper than your longest taper candles.

For making poured and molded candles, you can use a shallow round pot, big enough to melt as much wax as you will need. You can put one saucepan over another, or rest a fireproof bowl on a saucepan, but your wax may melt unevenly. Clean your melting vessel with paper towels after each use.

Miscellaneous Equipment

These ancillary but necessary items are listed more or less in the order of importance, but you will need most of them sooner or later, depending on the extent of your candlemaking efforts and the types of candles you make. If, for example, you start with dipped candles you won't need molds until you want to make molded candles, and vice versa—if you make only molded candles, you don't need a rack for hanging dipped candles. This list is not necessarily all-inclusive—you may think of other tools or implements that will be useful. Be innovative!

Molds. Molds come in an infinite variety of shapes and sizes. Anything that has a hollow center can be a mold—half an orange shell, a sea shell, even a rock with a convenient depression. You don't need to buy molds, though you can purchase fancy ones at craft stores. Supermarkets sell plastic food storage containers (usually in multiples) that are inexpensive. (Just be sure you get hard plastic ones that are impervious to heat. If in doubt, put your container in the sink and pour boiling water into it.)

Any glass jar or jelly glass will work as a mold. (I am addicted to saving jars of all types and even buy food in pretty or odd-shaped glass jars just to get the jar!) Jam and jelly jars come in interesting shapes—octagonal, square, round, short and fat, or tall and slim.

Wine bottles come in a variety of sizes, shapes, and interesting colors—from deepest forest green to pale aqua and from dark brown to honey, and other shades in between. They make wonderful holders for container candles and can also be used for molding.

To use a wine bottle as a container you have only to slice off the top with a glass cutter and smooth the rough edge down. If you are handy with tools, and either own or can borrow a glass cutter, you can do the job yourself. (As many craftspeople work in more than one medium, you may already have a glass cutter or know someone who does. Otherwise, an experienced glass cutter can do it for you. Check your yellow pages or ask your craft salesperson for a reference.)

Mold-Release Spray. You can use nonstick pan spray made of vegetable oil to prevent the wax from adhering to the mold. Or, you can put some vegetable oil in a spray designed for the purpose (for making salads and coating cooking pans with your own oil instead of the commercial spray can). These special spray cans are available through household outlets. Any vegetable oil will work; you can spray or wipe the mold with an oil-soaked paper towel. Just don't use a heavy hand—too much oil will mottle your finished candle.

You might also need a mold sealer or masking tape. They might be used to hold the wick in place.

Cake Pans and Cookie Sheets. Cake pans and cookie sheets are multipurpose. You can line them (as above) and pour unused melted wax to cool. You can use them for molds (see the instructions on how to make a wedding cake candle). They are also useful as pads for containers of hot wax.

Scale. A scale is an important piece of equipment as well, one you can't do without. Chances are you already have a kitchen scale that will do. It should have a range of 0–10 pounds, in ounces.

Or, and this is the most accurate, you can use a gram scale (as do all European cooks—in Europe, recipes are given by weight in grams). If you do, however, you will need to convert between grams and ounces and pounds. A scale is necessary for weighing not only wax but also additives such as stearic acid, colorants, and scent oils. For the latter, a gram scale can have the precision of ±1 gram.

ESSENTIALS

A scale with a knob that allows you to turn it back to zero after you have set your measuring container on it is handy. It will allow you to weigh only the wax without having to do the math to subtract the weight of the container each time.

Measuring Container. The ideal container for measuring in ounces and cups is an ordinary Pyrex measuring cup of the kind you no doubt already have. These come in 1-cup, 2-cup, 4-cup, and 6-cup sizes, and are heat resistant. Your measuring container has two uses: you can determine the *volume* of wax by displacement: for this you will need two measuring cups. Put wax in one cup in a block or chunks; then put water in the second cup and note the amount it takes to fully submerge the wax in the first cup. Subtract the volume of water added from the level of water needed to cover the wax. The result is the volume of wax you have just measured. Since Pyrex measuring cups can be heated, you can use such a measuring cup (or any heatproof calibrated vessel, such as a flask used in chemistry) as a wax melting insert when melting small amounts of wax.

Oven Mitts and Pot Holders. Oven mitts or pot holders are essential when it comes to protecting your hands when you handle a pot of hot wax. I hang an assortment of them on hooks hear the stove where they are easily accessible.

Metal Ruler or Straightedge. An artist's T-square is good, as are the heavy metal rulers they use. It's even a good idea to have both—

for cutting and for calibrating lengths of vessels, candles, and wicks. These tools are available at art supply shops, which often also sell craft materials. The straightedge is used to cut sheet wax, for rolled and stacked candles. T-squares and metal rulers come in various lengths: a 3-foot length is more useful than the ordinary l-foot length.

Cutting Surface and Tools. A cutting surface can be a laminated kitchen counter that can't be cut-marked or a wooden or plastic cutting board such as those used for chopping food. You can even use a piece of heavy cardboard such as the backing from an artist's sketchpad.

For cutting tools, I like Exacto knifes (as I am a graphics artist). The blades are extremely sharp and run cleanly along a straight edge. They come in different sizes, both handle and blades. You can use a single-edge razor blade as do artists, or a very sharp paring knife. Your cutting tool is for cutting sheets of wax for rolled and stacked candles, and for trimming the seams of finished molded candles. Scissors are also useful, especially for cutting wicks.

Ladle. You might also need a ladle—choose one impervious to heat, with a deep bowl and a comfortably angled handle to avoid spilling. A glass meat-baster is the perfect tool for sucking up melted wax and squirting it around loose wicks, or in other small spaces. Don't use a plastic one—it may melt!

Greaseproof Paper and Paper Towels. This includes waxed paper, parchment, brown craft paper (or brown paper bags flattened out), and foil. Keep a good supply on hand to cover work surfaces. And don't forget about paper towels—they are essential for cleanups, to use as oil wipes, to mop up water spills, and many other chores. I use up a lot!

Water Container. This can be almost anything—a plastic dishpan or a bucket—large enough to hold your finished molds for cooling. A cat litter pan works well for short molds, a dishpan for taller molds.

Dowels. Dowels are used to make a rack from which to hang dipped candles for drying. A short piece of narrow dowel can be used to hold the wicks of dipped candles apart while you dip them. A folded piece of cardboard will also work.

Wicking Tool. This can be a wicking needle made especially for candlemaking, an ice pick, a metal skewer, or a knitting needle. It is used to make a hole in hardened candles for the wick. A wicking needle looks like a darning needle: The hole at one end is elongated so that the wick can be threaded through it. You will need a long enough wicking needle to insert at the base and push through to the top.

Pliers. Pliers are used to grasp the wicking needle and pull it through the candle; to pull wicks through molds; to secure a candle that is being overdipped (by holding its wick in the jaws of the pliers); and to pinch the tabs on wick sustainers—it is a most useful implement! Regular pliers will work well, but needle-nose pliers will let you grasp and hold a wick more firmly.

Hammer. You might use a hammer to break blocks of wax into pieces. A sharp cleaver will also do this work well.

Use an old pillowcase to hold your block of wax while you hammer it into chunks. This will catch the crumbs and keep the pieces from flying about. But don't put the used pillowcase your washer/dryer—the wax may clog the pipes.

Paint Scraper. A paint scraper is excellent for easily scraping spilled wax off a hard surface, such as a counter. You might also use a putty knife.

Screwdriver. Some molds have screw-type wickholders. You will need a screwdriver to deal with these if you use them.

Weights. You'll need something heavy to keep a wax-filled mold submerged in its water bath. Depending on the size of your mold(s) you can use a brick, an iron boot scrapper (I have one that is a duck with a large flat bottom), unopened cans of food, an empty food can filled with quick-setting cement. Use your imagination!

Small weights with a center hole are required to weigh down wicks that are being dipped. Washers, curtain weights, and nuts will all do.

Plastic Bags. The zippered plastic bags work well for storing hard wax; open topped ones are best for measuring mold volume.

Safety First

Before you begin to work with wax, it must be heated to its particular melting point. Take care not to overheat your wax. The "burning point" of wax is that temperature at which the properties of the particular wax have been stretched beyond the safety mark. For example, paraffin should not usually be heated hotter than 200° Fahrenheit. Never leave melting wax on the heat source unattended—it is as volatile as cooking oil and can catch fire if overheated. *Always* keep a large pot lid handy to smother a fire, should one start. Also keep damp cloths handy for the same purpose.

Remember that waxes, including beeswax, are highly flammable (that's why candles burn!) and can catch fire. The temperature at which they will combust is the "flash point." This is approximately 440° Fahrenheit, depending on the type of wax you use. NEVER heat wax to the flash point. Watch your thermometer carefully.

Safety Considerations

Although candlemaking is rewarding, like any other craft it must be done with care. Remember that you are working with a flammable substance and a heat source. Don't use an open heat source if you can avoid it. For safety's sake, follow these precautions at all times:

- Always heat (melt) your wax in either a double-boiler or a concealed element heat device (both discussed above).
- *Never* put your wax-melting container directly on the heat source.
- Keep a careful watch on the water level in your outer pot. *Never* let it boil dry. Add water frequently while melting wax.

Rx for Safety

Make sure you have the following fire-extinguishing items and are familiar with how to use them:

1. A fire extinguisher of the ABC type (available at hardware stores).
2. A large metal pan lid to clap on your melting pot should it catch fire. The lid will smother the flame by depriving it of oxygen.
3. Several large cloths—old terry towels are best—to cover and smother a fire.
4. Lots and lots of baking soda (I buy it in 2-pound boxes at the supermarket) to dump onto a fire. It will smother flames immediately.

Rx for Burns

Baking soda's use is not only limited to smothering a fire; it can also soothe a burn on your skin, and works almost instantly. To use, make a smooth paste with water and baking soda and spread on your burn. Let it dry thoroughly before rinsing off. Repeat if necessary.

Hot paraffin, if not heated beyond its melting point, probably won't cause a severe burn, but caution is the rule. Keep a bucket of cold water handy in case you should splatter hot wax on your skin. If you spill a lot of hot wax on yourself, don't panic. Run cool—not cold or iced—water on your skin, or get in the bathtub or shower. If the burn is severe, call 911 and continue to keep the skin cool to avoid shock. If you get hot wax on your hand, plunge it immediately into the water until the wax cools.

Cooled paraffin will chip off, but sticky beeswax won't. If you get hot beeswax on your skin, cool it in the water thoroughly; then apply baking soda paste. If the burn is severe, consult your doctor.

Pour with Care

Always remember that the wax you are pouring is hot, and that it can burn you if spilled on your skin. Don't pour when you are feeling jittery or are distracted. Teach yourself to pour in a smooth steady stream by practicing with water, using the vessel in which you plan to melt the wax.

If the candle isn't taking proper shape, don't shift to an odd angle to correct the problem. It's best to start over. Never risk dropping the wax container or a spill for the sake of a perfect candle. And always keep plenty of pot holders and cloths accessible for grasping hot handles, and for cleaning up any spills.

A Clean Workplace Is a Safe Workplace

Craftspeople are by nature orderly—it is inherent in the work, and the very word "craft" implies professionalism and careful procedures. Originally, one learned a craft by apprenticing to a master craftsman. Today many of us are self-taught, but the same principles still apply.

The first of these is based on the old nostrum that "cleanliness is next to godliness." The less mess you have around you, the better—and more safely—you can work. The fewer items you have around to clutter counter space, to trip over, to move aside, or to spill, the better you will function and be able to focus on what you are doing.

ESSENTIALS

Line a shallow baking pan with greaseproof paper and pour your leftover melted wax into the pan after you have finished your candlemaking for the day. Leave the melted wax to harden, break it apart, and store for later use.

Clean Counters

Always cover your work surface with disposable non-newsprint paper. Don't use old newspapers to cover working surfaces as the newsprint may transfer to the undersurface if wax spills on it. Use brown wrapping paper or tin foil (use foil on stove) to facilitate cleanup. Or, if you can devote an entire countertop to your candlemaking, get a laminated one with a smooth surface from which you can easily scrape up cooled wax.

The Importance of Cleaning Up

After each candlemaking session, be sure to clean up your workspace—especially if it's in your kitchen. Then you won't have to clean up before you start another candlemaking session. It's like getting the dishes washed and out of the sink after lunch so you don't have to deal with a mess before you can cook dinner.

If you commit the following procedures to memory, you'll have an easy time of the tidying-up process:

1. Gather all your tools and materials—knives, scrapers, wicks, colorants, scent bottles, etc.—wipe or scrape any waxy residue, and store them in the place you regularly keep them.
2. Always keep rags and paper towels handy. Use them to wipe any waxy surfaces while they are still warm.
3. Think about how you want to reuse leftover wax. If you want to save different colors, pour each color into a muffin tin cup. If you want to mix everything, just pour it into a flat pan.
4. Pour the water from your double-boiler in the yard, or let it cool until you can skim off the congealed wax before pouring it down the drain. *Never pour water with wax in it down the drain!*
5. When your poured leftover wax has cooled, pop it out of its container, bag, and label with wax content and color mixes. You may want to match the color later and not remember exactly the proportions of colorant you used.

6. Peel any spilled wax off the paper you covered your work surface with and either save it or throw it away.

7. After you have cleaned up all waxy containers and surfaces, dispose of the paper/rags. Do not incinerate.

If you can't get all of the wax out of a container by wiping, you can fill the container with very hot water so that the wax melts. After it has cooled, the wax will float on top making it easy to remove.

SSENTIALS To clean your utensils, molds, etc., simply line a large cookie sheet with heavy-duty foil and place everything upside down on the sheet. Put inside a preheated warm oven (no hotter than 170° Fahrenheit) until the wax melts and runs onto the foil. While warm, wipe clean with paper towels; dispose of foil.

The Do's and Don'ts of Candlemaking

With any activity, there are some things that are "no-no's." Candlemaking is no exception. As you get underway creating candles of your own, there are some things to do and others to remember to *never, ever* do:

- *Don't* ever pour liquid wax down your drain. It will solidify and cause severe blockage—not to mention a huge plumbing bill. Don't learn this "no-no" the hard way!
- *Do* pour leftover melted wax into muffin tins or other small cups. Metal ice-trays are good for this purpose. You can then pop out the hardened wax and store it in plastic bags for future use.
- *Don't* throw away your leftovers, even the small scraps, including candle ends or the bottoms of container candles. Wax costs money. Recycling saves money and work.
- *Do* recycle all the wax you can save. You can ask non-candlemakers to give you their candle ends. Your church deacon may be happy to give you burned-down beeswax candles.

- *Don't* pour your hot double-boiler water down your drain. It may have wax in it unbeknownst to you, which could clog the drain.
- *Do* dispose of the water outside. Or, let it cool until the wax hardens and then remove the wax before pouring the water down the drain.
- *Don't* allow yourself to be distracted while making candles. Let the answering machine answer the phone if it rings while you are pouring or melting.
- *Do* make candles at a time when you can concentrate fully on the task at hand (maybe while the children are in school).
- *Don't* begin candlemaking without first assembling all of your materials and equipment in an orderly fashion, so that you can proceed step by step—safely.
- *Do* school yourself to know for certain exactly what you are doing at all times, where you are moving, which step you are taking when. *Practice* is the key to safety.

What to Wear

As there is always a risk of getting wax on your clothing, don't wear anything you aren't willing to throw away! Old T-shirts make good aprons—loose but not floppy enough to catch on pot handles. Smocks are available for cover-ups. Popovers—loose, shapeless dresses—are also good. Make sure your clothing is not flammable. Cotton is a good choice. Old jeans and denim shirts also work well.

How to Remove Wax from Clothes

Suppose you do get wax on a garment you don't want to discard. What to do? Here are some suggestions:

1. Remove the garment and let the wax cool. If you get a small spot of wax on a washable garment, use an ice cube to freeze it. If the spill is large, or on a "dry-clean only" garment, put the garment in

the freezer. Examine it—if the wax has not penetrated the fiber of the fabric, you can usually snap it off by bending the fabric around the wax.

2. Iron the fabric with a warm iron using several layers of paper toweling on both sides. The iron will melt the wax and the paper towels will absorb it. You may have to repeat this procedure, changing the paper towels each time.

3. Freeze the garment until the wax is brittle; then chip it off.

4. If all home remedies fail, take the garment to a good dry-cleaner. Advise the dry-cleaner that it is a wax stain.

CHAPTER 6

Handmade Rolled and Poured Candles

Rolled candles are made from sheets of wax, and as the name implies, the wax is rolled around a wick, much as you would roll a sheet of dough around a filling to make jelly rolls. This is the simplest method of making candles. It's easiest for the beginner— and a good way to introduce children to candlemaking.

Roll Your Own

What makes rolled candles so easy to produce is the availability of commercially produced sheets of wax made specifically for rolling. Although it is possible to make sheets of wax for rolling candles yourself, this is not advised. Wax sheets are available at craft shops and from candlemaking suppliers and they come in dozens of lovely colors. There are two types of commercially prepared wax sheets for making rolled candles: the majority are made of pure beeswax, which, although more expensive, are longer burning than paraffin or paraffin with stearic acid. The second type of sheet wax is a mixture of beeswax and paraffin, which is less expensive than pure beeswax. Also available, though less often, are sheets of paraffin without beeswax. These are the least expensive of all, but have the disadvantage of a much shorter burn time.

Be sure to check the label to determine what wax or blend you are getting, as the price will vary accordingly. Don't pay the pure beeswax prices if paraffin has been added to the mix!

Plain or Honeycomb?

Most wax sheets for rolled candles are formed in a honeycomb pattern. This type of sheet is embossed with a hexagonal (honeycomb) indentation—it looks like the wax from a honeycomb! The most common size is 8" × 16". You can cut the sheets to suit your specific purpose. The honeycomb-patterned sheets are rolled out under an embossing wheel. You can purchase these in the natural beeswax colors (pale honey to dark brown), or you can purchase them in various colors that have been dyed after the wax was bleached.

Another type of wax for making rolled candles is smooth and flat. These are useful when you don't want a textured candle. The pure-white smooth sheets make an elegant-looking candle that gives a stylish appearance.

Keeping Your Sheets Warm

Sheets of beeswax bought preformed in a honeycomb pattern are ready for use. However, they need to be warm enough to be pliable before you start to roll. A blow-dryer is a handy tool to keep on hand for warming sheets of wax. Beeswax is the easiest to work with because of its natural flexibility.

Paraffin or beeswax/paraffin blend wax sheets are used in the same manner, but paraffin tends to be brittle. Therefore a blend or straight paraffin will be a bit more difficult to handle, requiring extra attention in order to keep the sheets warm enough to be pliable. If your wax sheets have become cold and aren't pliable enough to roll, you can do several things:

- Using your blow-dryer, waft warm air over the sheets of wax
- Iron them with a warm iron between sheets of paper
- Quickly dip the sheets into hot water

ESSENTIALS

If you have a buffet warming tray that can be set on low heat, you can use that to keep your paraffin or beeswax/paraffin blend sheets warm and pliable. Just make sure that it is a concealed-element warming tray as you don't want the sheets near an open heat source.

Here are some tips for preparing to roll your own candles.

Making Your Own Wax Sheets

Although using purchased wax sheets is the easiest way to make rolled candles, if you are adventuresome—and if you have some leftover wax you want to make use of—you can try making your own wax sheets.

You'll need:

A piece of plywood the size of the sheet you want.
A large, deep pot for melting the wax. A deep steamer of the type used for asparagus or corn will work, as will a deep stock pot.

To prepare the plywood, soak it in water for 1 hour or more (to prevent it from absorbing the hot wax). Dip the plywood into the melted wax, using tongs or pliers to hold it firmly. Allow the wax-covered plywood to cool for about a minute. Dip the wax-covered board into the wax again, and again allow it to cool. Repeat this process five or more times depending on the thickness of the wax sheet you want. Scrape the wax at the edges of the board; then peel off the sheet.

Homemade wax sheets lend themselves to various uses. Although purchased sheets come in various colors, you can tint your own wax sheets any color you like, or make multicolored layers for an interesting effect.

Have Fun with Your Homemade Wax Sheets

What's nice about homemade sheet wax is that you don't have to warm it up before using it. It will be warm when you remove it from the board. While it is still warm, you can form it into different shapes as you roll it.

Should the wax cool too much, just drop it into hot water (100–110° Fahrenheit) for a minute or two to soften it again. Keep a pot of warm water at hand for this purpose.

Getting Creative with Wax Sheets

As you work with the wax, you'll think of many more ways to use it artistically. The more accustomed you get to shaping your homemade wax sheets, the more ideas you will get for using it. You'll find wax is wonderful for sculpting and hand-molding, like clay. If making mud pies was one of your favorite childhood pastimes, playing around with wax that's in between the liquid and solid states will give you a lot of satisfaction! Here are a few ideas for using your homemade wax sheets creatively:

• Make the sheets thicker and roll into votives or pillars.
• Roll three or more slender candles and twist them into a braid.
• Using a long wick, keep rolling until you have a long, thin candle.

Let the Kids Play with Wax Sheets

Give your children some warm—but not hot!—wax sheets and let them play to their heart's content. They can push the pliable wax around and make odd and curious shapes without making a mess. And you can always remelt the wax and use it later. Or, you can insert a wick (see p. 127) and burn their artwork.

Start Rolling!

You can make rolled candles any diameter you like. You can make tall slender rolled candles with two or three sheets. Medium and large size rolled candles can be made simply by adding more sheets until you reach the size you prefer. Rolled candles lend themselves to various shapes, the most common and easiest being a simple cylinder. To make this type of rolled candle, you lay out the sheet (preferably on a warm surface) and lay on it a wick cut to the proper size. Begin rolling at the short (8") end of the sheet and keep rolling until you reach the end. It's that simple!

 **SSENTIALS**
When making beeswax candles, be sure to keep your hands *clean*. If you don't, the beeswax will act as a cleaner for you! The result will be grubby, dirty-looking candles!

What You Will Need

- Purchased sheets of wax made for rolled candles
- Wick (or wicks if you plan to make several). Use a flat-braided wick for beeswax, a square-braided wick for paraffin.
- A blow-dryer or warming tray
- A sharp knife or razor blade
- A straightedge or ruler
- Scissors (for cutting wick)
- A hard cutting surface

Pick a Wick

There are no hard and fast rules for selecting wick size. This is especially true for wicks for candles that are thicker on the bottom (i.e., have a larger diameter) than they are at the top. The choice of wick size and type is largely a matter of judgement and experience. Follow the wick manufacturer's instructions when you start out, and then keep careful notes of your results. This will help you to determine wick size for different candles.

Generally speaking, the best solution is to use a wick size suitable for the largest diameter of your candle. However, be aware that the thicker wick will make the thinner top burn down more quickly. Candles that are the same diameter at the top and bottom, such as plain rolled candles, don't have this problem.

Another way to get the most burn time out of your wick is to keep it trimmed. Sometimes the wick on a candle gets long, making the candle smoke. If the candle flame flares out at the top, it needs trimming. There is no need to prime (pre-wax) a wick to make a rolled candle. However, the tip of the wick needs to be primed prior to being lighted. To do this, simply pull a small corner piece of wax from the edge of the sheet and press it around the end of the wick.

Remember that there is a relationship between the wax's melting point and the wick size (and type). The finished candle's diameter is a critical factor in determining how well the finished candle will burn. Always take notes so that you can repeat a success or adjust what went wrong.

Steps for Making Rolled Candles

1. Make sure your cutting surface is properly prepared. It should be covered with a piece of heavy cardboard or a mat.
2. Decide what size rolled candle you want to make. Cut a wick (or wicks) 2 inches longer than the size of the finished candle. Set aside.
3. Warm your wax sheets until they are pliable enough to roll easily. Use a blow-dryer (set on low) or put them on a heating pad or warming tray.

Be sure to watch your wax sheets carefully while they are warming. Depending on the warmth of your room, they can easily melt on a heat source. If you accidentally overheat and get a melt, just save the wax to make poured candles!

4. Lay the sheet of wax flat on a smooth surface, such as a countertop or a table. Then bend a ⅛" fold at the end of the short side to make a place for the wick. Press the wick gently into the edge of the wax before beginning to roll. Make sure the wick is firmly embedded in the wax.

5. Next, roll up the wax tightly, making sure that the wick is closely held in the wax at each turn. Keep rolling with a firm and even pressure. This is to avoid letting air bubbles form between the layers. Take care to roll in a straight line to keep the ends flat (for cylindrical candles).

Rolling a beeswax candle

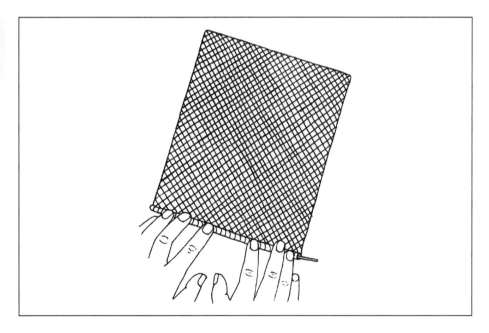

6. When you have rolled the entire sheet, press the final end into the candle so that it adheres to the last layer of wax.

7. Once you have finished rolling your candle, cut the wick to ½" in length and neatly trim the bottom end with your knife or razor to get a flat surface on which the candle can rest.

ESSENTIALS

If your candles seem uneven or the layers aren't quite close enough, roll the finished candle on your countertop back and forth (like fashioning a roll of cookie dough) until the candle has a round shape and the layers all hold together. Do this with a gentle but firm hand.

Making a Rolled Taper

You can carve a taper shape into your rolled candle. To do this, use a sharp knife to trim the wax into a cone shape, then smooth the edges with a heated butter knife. Trim the wick to ½".

How to Make a Diagonal Rolled Candle

To make a diagonal rolled candle, cut your sheet of wax in half to make two triangles, using your straightedge or ruler and a razor blade or other sharp implement such as an Exacto knife. Cut the wick to fit the longer edge (the 8" edge) and roll the wax sheet toward the pointed end. Take care to keep the long, straight edge even in order to end up with a flat bottom. This method will give you a spiral-shaped candle that is very attractive.

**E**SSENTIALS

To make sure the bottom of the candle is flat, melt it. Heat up an old metal pan—a pie pan, cake pan, or cookie sheet—over a low flame on the stove, gently press the bottom of the rolled candle onto the metal until it flattens out smoothly. This simple step also prevents unrolling.

Making a Square-Shaped Rolled Candle

Using seven sheets of beeswax (9" × 12" each) and a primed wick 10" long, plus 2 ounces of melted beeswax, you can make a square candle from the textured sheets of beeswax. These are quite easy to make, with little mess as you need melt only a small amount of wax.

1. Lay the primed wick across one beeswax sheet as described above. Roll up the entire sheet around the wick.
2. Place another sheet of beeswax next to the edge of the end of the first sheet and again roll tightly. Keep the edges even as you roll so that they remain the same length.
3. Using your metal ruler, press the sheets against a third sheet of beeswax at a 90° angle, pressing the roll into a square shape as you turn it over each time.
4. Continue adding the remaining sheets, using the ruler at each turn to make the sides square. After you have the edges shaped, lightly score each remaining sheet against the ruler to help you fold (not roll) the wax around the inner core of squared wax sheets.
5. Press the end of the final sheet firmly into place as you bend it around the candle. This step will insure that the finished candle does not unroll as it burns.
6. Holding the finished candle upside down over a cookie sheet lined with paper to catch the drips, use a small spoon to pour some of the melted beeswax into the cracks between the layer of wax sheets. Smooth some melted wax evenly over the bottom to seal the candle together and give a flat surface.

Homemade Birthday Candles

You can make your own birthday candles easily by using the rolling method. Just cut the sheets of wax (you won't need many) to the length you like and roll away. Since wax sheets come in various colors, you can make a set of birthday candles each of a different color.

You can also make multicolored rolled candles. This is a lot of fun, especially for kids. Buy wax sheets in various colors and roll your candles using a different color for each layer. You can mix and match for holidays—such as red and green for the Christmas season—or to go with your décor.

May I Pour You a Candle?

The pouring method is used to make many different types of candles. In fact, pouring is the most versatile way to make candles. Molded candles are poured candles; cast candles are poured candles; many novelty candles are made by pouring; and pouring is possibly the easiest method of making quantities of candles in different shapes and sizes. It's also an excellent method for making decorated and fancy candles. Poured candles lend themselves to many effects. Subsequent chapters will provide specific details on the various candles you can make with the pouring method.

Pouring oil and wax into containers to make rudimentary lamps is a technique as old as history. Most of these used some sort of liquid fuel, such as oil, or animal fat that would harden at room temperature, especially in cold climates. There are two types of poured candles: those made in molds, to be removed and used as freestanding candles, and those poured into containers in which they will be burned. The first type, poured in a mold and released, like a gelatin dessert or a fancy cake baked in a Bundt or other shaped pan, is a bit trickier to handle. The second type is the easiest poured candle you can make.

Molded candles are not a modern invention. They have been made ever since the fifteenth century. Originally made in wooden molds, often carved to give an embossed effect, these molds were tricky for the candlemaker to work with because, at that time, candles were made of beeswax, which is sticky and hard to remove from a mold without modern additives (such as stearic acid).

Today's candlemakers are fortunate in that additives make it possible to use just about anything that will hold hot wax as a mold.

Candle Hints

You can make a candle that is designed to burn itself into a shell, in which you can then place a votive or tealight. To burn a candle down the middle and use it as a holder, it is important that your burn it so that the well is created correctly. Light the candle and allow it to burn until the wax has melted to a diameter of about 1¾". When the wax collected in the pool around the wick reaches a depth of about ⅛", extinguish the candle and pour out the melted wax. (Save if you like.) Trim the wick and light the candle again. Repeat these steps until you have melted the center of the candle sufficiently to allow the insertion of a smaller candle.

Advantages of Additives for Paraffin Wax

Although it is possible to make candles from paraffin wax alone, and hand-dipped or molded candles do not absolutely require stearin added to the paraffin, there are definite advantages to adding stearin to paraffin no matter what kind of candle you are making. Here's why:

- Stearin makes candles easier to remove from their molds because they contract more during the cooling process when stearin has been added to the wax.
- Candles made with stearin have a longer burn time.
- Paraffin is translucent and can be dull-looking. Adding stearin makes the candle opaque and much whiter, giving a nicer appearance.

Remember, the paraffin wax you can buy in supermarkets to use for sealing jars of jams and jellies should not be used to make candles. It melts at low temperature and does not harden enough. Always use paraffin wax specially made for candlemaking to guarantee good results.

Special Additives for Paraffin Wax

In addition to stearin, there are other additives that are useful. One class of these is called "microcrystallines."

Micro Soft is a very soft wax. Adding it to paraffin keeps the wax mixture soft for a longer time, which is especially useful when making molded candles. Generally speaking, add 10 to 20 percent of Micro Soft to your paraffin when you want an especially pliable wax for shaping. It is also an excellent additive for floating candles.

Micro Hard wax, which has a higher melting point than paraffin, is used to make chip candles (see p. 178).

Supplier Information

Whatever additives you are using, check the label on the package. The supplier's information will make it clear exactly what use each is for and tell you how to use the micros and in what proportion.

Stirring the Pot

While you don't need to stir melting wax, you will need to stir in your additives—stearic acid, other waxes, colorants or dyes, and scents (if you use them).

Practically any old thing will do for stirring the melted wax—old long-handled wooden spoons are ideal. If you don't have any, chances are you can pick up some cheaply at a garage or yard sale, or at a flea market. I once bought a bunch of old wooden utensils—spoons, scrapers, mallets, and a couple whose purpose I didn't know—at a flea market for a few dollars. And I still use them.

There's a type of wooden utensil that's like a flat spoon with a hole in the middle. This is especially good for stirring wax that's beginning to thicken.

How to Get FREE Stirrers

Another handy stirrer can be had for free at your paint store. Paint stirrers are flat paddles given away with the purchase of paint, and paint store salespeople are usually happy to give you a few extra because they are imprinted with advertising for the brand of paint and/or the store. So when you have an occasion to buy paint, ask for extra stirrers and stash them away.

Making Container Candles

Container candles are a category of poured candles. This type of candle covers a broad spectrum of candles—molded and cast, as well as container. The definition of a container candle is that it is *not* removed from the mold (container) in which it is poured. It is produced simply by pouring hot wax into a container—and then it is burned in its container. Many containers can be reused indefinitely, especially those of heavy glass or metal (such as food tins). Since container candles are the simplest and easiest type of candle to make, we will begin our exploration of the art of pouring candles with them.

All about Containers

Container depth is important. Generally speaking, due to the need of the wick for adequate oxygen to burn the candle properly, it's a good idea to select containers no more than 5 or 6 inches tall. Shorter ones—even very small ones—are ideal as they burn well and can be made in quantity and set around different areas of your rooms to give a candlelit feeling to the entire space. For example, baby food jars or other votive-candle size containers can be utilized this way.

Not only jams and jellies, but all sorts of foods come in glass jars suitable for making container candles. These often come in interesting shapes. For example, I ordered by mail some sample all-fruit jam, made in France. The little jars in which the preserves came make adorable containers. Made of heavy glass, they are 1½" in diameter and 2" tall, and have a charming flared, fluted bottom. (Leave it to the French!) As you can see, the possibilities are almost endless. Once you become aware of them, you'll notice jars of food that will make excellent and attractive containers, so save them up and you'll have plenty of interesting-looking and original candle containers on hand! The following are some guidelines.

Selecting Containers

Always pick containers that are either the same diameter at the top and at the bottom, or are wide-mouthed at the top. Do not use anything with a narrow neck.

Glass and metal are the best materials for containers. Ceramic will also work, but it is opaque and will not give a glow as the candle burns down. Never use wood, milk cartons, or any other flammable materials for containers. Glass is a good choice, but make sure it is heavy enough not to crack under the burning candle's heat. All sorts of glass containers will work fine. For example, glasses made of heavy recycled glass (usually pale green: they are made from old Coke bottles) are perfect. Goblets or glasses of heavy glass, often hobnailed (that is, they have bumps on the surface), are very useful and can be refilled indefinitely. Another good choice is the square-shaped heavy glass containers that contain a jelled room deodorizer that evaporates as it is exposed to air. When empty and washed, these types of jars make perfect container candles.

ESSENTIALS

Before you remove the labels from food jars to use for making container candles, make a note of how many ounces the jar holds. You can put the lid on the empty jar with a label marked with the jar's volume. This saves measuring.

The list is virtually endless. Once you let your imagination run wild, you'll see containers for candles almost everywhere you look! If you select glass for your container candle, you have the choice of clear or colored glass. Colored glass will mask any color in the candle wax, so it's best to use untinted wax in a colored glass container and let its color glow with a jewel-like brilliance. On the other hand, if you want colored candles for a particular scheme of décor, or just because you like certain colors of candles or want to use them ritually for candle magic ceremonies, use clear glass containers instead.

 **SSENTIALS** Any clear jar or glass can serve as the foundation for an ornately constructed multicolored candle. Fancy glass—cut crystal, pressed glass, embossed glass ("depression glass" is wonderful, and comes in various colors)—will look beautiful as it burns when filled with plain wax. Medium to shallow glass bowls are also nice.

Preserving Jars As Containers

The possibilities for containers for container candles are practically limitless. Once you begin making container candles, your imagination will be ignited (as was mine). Here are some additional ideas I've developed that you can use. And you will undoubtedly discover many that I haven't thought of!

Jars for preserving (of the Mason type) are perfect for container candles. They come in a variety of sizes—the pint and half-pint sizes are recommended (the quart is too deep)—and shapes—some are cylindrical, higher than the diameter; others are short and squat with a larger diameter than depth (this shape is my personal favorite). The glass is heavy and made to withstand heat, as the preserving process involves a boiling water bath, so there's no need to worry about the candle flame cracking the glass. Also, these jars are always wide-mouthed, making them easy to fill when pouring, and their wide mouths make it a snap to balance a dowel or chopstick for a wickholder on the edges.

Most of these jars are beautifully embossed with fruit and/or flower patterns, which makes them ideal for gift-giving as well as decoration around the house. And, since they come with lids, you have a complete gift package—just tie a ribbon around the wide part of the lid's rim and make a nice bow. No muss, no fuss! Container candles in preserving jars are very popular and several upscale mail-order catalogs offer them—at high prices. You can make your own for very little cost—the jars are often offered for sale at big discounts during summer when most home-preserving is done.

You can even fool the recipients into thinking they are getting homemade jam or jelly by coloring your wax and scenting it to match different fruits, such as strawberries, cherries, blueberries, and so on. You can also use them to make chip candles (see p. 178) that will resemble pieces of fruit suspended in a jelly. Of course, the recipient of your gift will realize the "preserves" are a candle in disguise as soon as the jar is opened. I guarantee you they will be delighted at your subtle subterfuge.

A great characteristic of preserving jars is that they are hard to break. They can be used over and over again, and it's easy to refill them innumerable times, so if your friends aren't candlemakers, tell them to return your jars when the candles are used up. Just beware—they might ask for a refill!

Old preserving jars have hinged lids and are made of heavy glass. These make really nice container candles. You can often find them at flea markets—or look in your grandmother's basement! A few are still made today for use as canisters, often out of recycled green glass. I have one I bought ten years ago at a boutique in Vermont that is faceted like a cut jewel and makes a sumptuous container candle that glows with a wonderful mystery when it burns down a bit and the flame reflects off the many facets.

Another great container from my collection is an old piece of "depression glass," which was originally meant to be a canister. It's many-sided—like the facets of a crystal—and "gives a lovely light."

SSENTIALS   Keep your eyes open for old drinking glasses at flea markets or yard sales. They were made to last and are usually thick and heat resistant. Many are embossed (I have one with grape vines and bunches of grapes on it). These antique glasses make marvelous container candles.

Novel Ideas

Here are some more unique and interesting ideas:

- Metal ice cube trays—though new ones may be hard to find in this era when plastic rules—make splendid container candles. Using an ice cube tray has a double advantage. It's easy to pour and you get the effect of a multi-wick candle. When lighted, the tray of little cubes gives a brilliant light.

- You can also make neat miniature container candles in a mini-muffin tin. Line the cups with foil liners before pouring in the wax. When the wax has hardened, lift out each mini-candle. For a dinner party, you can set one of these little miniature candles at each person's place, perhaps placed on a saucer.

- Slice oranges in half and juice them. Then, carefully pull out the membrane and pulp until you are down to the shell of the orange peel. Fill with wax. When the wax is cool but not solid, insert a cored wick. These ingenious candles are wonderful for outdoor parties.

- I once found an old tin mold—what it's original purpose was I don't know, for it wasn't a cooking pan. However, this curiously shaped, age-tinged object, interesting in itself, made one of the best container candles you can imagine. If you look about you as you go, you'll find many such objects.

How to Make a Container Candle

What you will need:

- **Wax**—Usually plain paraffin with a melting point of 130° Fahrenheit
- **Stearic acid**—Optional but will give a longer burn time
- **Wick**—Medium-sized, one for each container; cored wicks are preferable, but not essential
- **Wick sustainers (tabs)**—One for each container
- **Colorant**—If you want a colored candle
- **Scent**—Optional but nice
- **Double-boiler or concealed-element heater**
- **Thermometer**
- **Ladle and/or vessel for pouring**—Preferably with a handle
- **Small sticks**—A dowel or chopsticks or even a slim garden stake will work for suspending the wick over the container

- **Weights**—You need to weight the wick in the container if you are using a noncored variety; small washers or nuts will work fine
- **Utensil for poking holes in the wax**—This can be a skewer, a chopstick, a pencil, or a small stick
- **Containers**—See above for various options

Though a thermometer is not absolutely necessary for melting plain paraffin (you can watch it carefully), if the wax is not the right temperature (the package will give the correct melting point), problems can result. Overheating the wax will change its chemical construction. Therefore, a thermometer is strongly advised.

Basic Steps to Making a Container Candle

Assemble *all* of your tools and materials in the order in which you will be using them *before* you begin your candlemaking operation. You don't want to have the wax melted and then start looking for a container or other needed tool!

Measure the wax. To ascertain how much wax is needed to fill your container (or containers, if you are making multiples), fill the container with water and pour the water into a measuring cup to determine the container's volume. Then dry the container thoroughly. To avoid this chore, you can first insert a plastic bag into the container and fill that with water to measure.

- 127 mp wax is sold specifically for use in container candles. It has a soft consistency and low melting point, and holds scent in until the candle is burned, without additives.
- 128 mp wax is also specially blended for use in containers (and votives), but it may require additives.
- 130 mp requires additives.

Once you have determined how much wax you need to fill your container (see how to weigh wax, p. 83), set up your pots for melting and begin melting the wax.

Attach a wick sustainer to the wick, which should be 1" longer than the height of the container you are using. Put the wick sustainer on one end, which will be the bottom. If you are using an uncored wick, you will need to tie a small weight to the wick.

In some large diameter candles, lead cored wicks are used because they burn at a higher temperature than fabric wicks. However, there is now concern about the health hazards of leaded wicks. No one knows just what the risk is but, to me, common sense dictates not to use lead.

Lay the dowel or chopstick across the top of your container. Tie the top end of the wick to it so that the wick hangs steadily in the container.

Warm the container before pouring wax into it. You can do this step one of several ways: place it in a warming oven (150°) for a few minutes; put it in the sink and run hot water into it; or set a pan of water on the stove on low heat and put the container (or containers) in the water to warm them before use. Be sure that the container is dried thoroughly before use.

If you are using glass containers, warm them slowly (the hot water method is safest). If metal, don't let them get so hot they burn your fingers. Always use a hot pad to handle a heated container.

After the wax has reached the proper melting point (usually 150–160° Fahrenheit; check your thermometer frequently), you are ready to pour. If you are not coloring the wax, go ahead and pour it into the warmed container. If you are using color or scent, add it to the wax and stir well before pouring.

For a multicolored candle, or several different colored candles, transfer the melted wax into other tin cans and add the colors and/or scents to each batch before pouring. Be sure to stir thoroughly to disperse additives.

The temperature needed to melt wax varies with the type of wax used. If your wax catches fire:

- Turn off heat immediately. Do not move the pan.
- Smother flames with a metal lid or damp towel.
- Never use water to put out a wax fire.

Begin pouring slowly, to one side of the dowel holding the wick. Be sure you keep the wick centered in the container, using the bottom tab or weight to do so. You may need to hold it in place for a few moments to allow it to set. This "tack pour," of about ½" of wax in the bottom of the container, is an important step, for a wick that is off-center will cause the candle to burn lopsidedly. Allow the ½" of wax at the bottom to cool sufficiently enough to stabilize the centered wick.

If you are making a single-color candle, continue pouring the wax until it is about ½" from the top. Wait a few minutes for the wax to begin to congeal. Then, with your skewer, poke a few holes into the cooling wax. Pour a bit more wax into these holes. This second pour (the "repour" or "cap pour") is to fill in spaces caused by air bubbles that formed in the first pour.

Repeat the repouring process until the wax cools.

Inexperienced candlemakers often underestimate the amount of wax needed for the finishing (filling of holes to eliminate air spaces and leveling) process. Keep a sufficient amount melted for this. You can always reuse any leftover wax for another candle.

Wax shrinks as it cools, and the candle will develop a depression in the center. Pour some more melted wax into this center when the candle is firm to the touch in order to make a flat surface.

When the candle has cooled completely (this takes from eight to twenty-four hours, depending on the candle's diameter), trim the wick to $\frac{1}{3}$" above the candle's surface.

Making a Candle of Many Colors

You can achieve a lovely and interesting effect in a clear glass container by pouring different colors on top of one another. First, divide your melted wax into batches, for however many colors you want—if you want only two colors, you need only two extra tins in which to mix them. If you want a many-colored striped candle—and there are no limits except the size of your container—you'll need a tin for each color.

If using only two colors, you can pour one layer of each color—or you can alternate the colors into more layers. Red and white would give a peppermint effect. If you are using several colors, pour one layer at a time, allowing each to harden before pouring the next to give a clean separation of colors.

ESSENTIALS   The National Candle Association offers a number of technical papers at *www.candles.org*. Especially interesting is "Dyes & Pigments." Also available: "Color Stabilization," "Dyes and Fragrances in Candles," "Color Fade Problems," and "Colorants for Candles."

For a vertical-against-horizontal effect, push the poker down into the wax layers while they are still congealing. Then pour one or more colors into the holes during the repour. Follow instructions above for finishing off the candle and preventing the center depression from forming.

CHAPTER 7
Molded Candles

Molded candles are made by pouring liquefied wax into a mold for a specific shape. For example, for an impressive square pillar candle, use a quart-size milk container as a mold. Or, for a nice squat shape, use a pint-size milk container. Tin food cans make good molds for cylindrical or round pillars. You can also create pillar molds yourself using cardboard, rubber, or metal.

Using Disposable Molds

Disposable molds are all around you. Just look about and you'll see them. (Check the trash bin!) Waxed milk, half-and-half, and heavy cream cartons, sour-cream and yogurt cartons, juice cans of various sizes—from individual servings, which make nice small pillars, to huge 48-ounce ones and several in between—can all be used. Tuna-fish cans and cat-food cans make nice candles that are larger in diameter than they are high. These are excellent for use on the dinner table for they don't get in the way of people seeing each other, as some tall candle centerpieces can do.

Some disposable molds—especially milk cartons and the like—may require reinforcement (that's what you'll need the masking tape for). Or, they may need wax that is somewhat cooler, so they don't collapse or melt. (Milk cartons are waxed inside.) Experiment with one first before making several.

Molds, Molds, Molds

Candlemaking has become such a popular craft/hobby that there are now literally hundreds of interesting molds available at craft shops and from candlemaking suppliers. These include reproductions of fancy antique European wood molds. Tin and pewter molds are also available from Colonial Williamsburg. You can even buy silicone molds of cartoon characters! Renaissance fairs, held all over the country, often feature candlemaking and sell various molds.

Commercially available molds are many and varied, from straight-sided to pyramid and other shapes. They may be made of acrylic, metal, or natural or silicone rubber material. All of these work well so long as you use the proper mold release agent. (Consult the package for information.)

For myself, I prefer using simple—usually disposable—molds, like milk cartons, tin food cans, and found objects such as sea shells (which we will cover later). Using a simple mold gives you lots of creative latitude, allowing you to create innumerable variations.

Molding Terminology

With this handy list under your belt, you'll have the all the scoop you need on molds.

Mold seal—This is similar to putty. It is used to hold the wick in place in order to keep the hot melted wax from leaking through the hole in the mold, which is there for the wick to be inserted. It is reusable.

Rigid plastic molds—These are available in a wide variety of unusual shapes—from hexagons and spheres to pyramids. For making unusual candles, these are the easiest and cheapest for the beginner. They may not be suitable for scent, however; check with your supplier.

A wide variety of molds is available commercially, from your local craft shop or through mail order. You can also order molds online. (Refer back to "Suppliers" section in Chapter 5 for more details.)

Metal molds—These are very sturdy, and can be used again and again. Metal molds sold specifically for candlemaking can be expensive, but tin cans are free. Check your tins for inside ridges (sometimes circular ones) and/or seams, which will leave imprints on your candles. These imprints can either be left as decorative elements or scraped and polished off.

Rubber/latex molds: These are made of a flexible material, which makes them quite versatile. You can achieve outstanding effects with much detail and relief. Their flexibility makes them good for making candles of odd shapes that could not have been removed from a rigid mold. The disadvantage is that they can be reused for only a limited number of times.

Glass molds—These give candles a nice gloss, after polishing. You can reuse them as long as you don't break them! A release agent is an absolute must. Also, glass makes great container candles that don't have to be removed from the molds.

Molded Candle Basics

To make molded candles you will need:

- **Wax**—Paraffin with a medium melting point of 135–145°F
- **Beeswax**—Up to 50 percent of the paraffin by weight (optional)
- **Stearic acid**—Approximately 10 percent of the paraffin by weight (a bit more won't hurt if you have to melt a second batch for filling holes)
- **Wick(s)**
- **Colorant(s)**—Your choice
- **Scent(s)**—Your choice

For a 2–3" diameter candle, use $^1/_{10}$" square braid. If adding beeswax at half or more, the wick should be increased by one or more sizes according to the size of the candle (diameter). Read the manufacturer's instructions carefully.

For equipment, gather together:

- A double-boiler or concealed-element heater
- A thermometer
- A pouring pot, pitcher, or ladle
- A thin rod-skewer, chopstick, or dowel
- Masking tape

- An ice pick (or knitting needle)
- Mold(s)
- Mold release agent (vegetable oil can be used)
- A pan for holding water to cool the filled molds
- A weight, such as a brick (full cans of food in large tins will work)
- A sharp-edged tool, like a razor blade, Exacto knife, or craft knife
- Nylon pantyhose (for polishing finished candle)

Candles made with rigid molds, that is, hard plastic, glass, or metal, need stearin added or they will stick to the mold and be extremely hard to release from it.

The Molding Process

After determining the volume of your mold, melt the amount of wax advised by the maker of the mold you are using. If you are using an improvised mold, such as a milk carton, you will know the volume (i.e., half-pint, pint, quart, etc.). As mentioned earlier, you can mark tin food cans and/or jars with the volume they hold by reading the labels before you soak them off.

Be sure your mold is clean and dry—water in a mold will spoil a candle. Wipe the mold with mold release or salad oil, but use it sparingly, for too much oil will give the finished candle a mottled effect (unless that is your aim).

Next, melt the amount of wax you need in the pot. After the wax has melted, put in additives, such as stearic acid, colorant, and scent. Watch your thermometer carefully and maintain the melted wax at a temperature of 160–180° Fahrenheit. Adjust heat accordingly.

Rubber Rules

Silicone rubber or "RTV" (room temperature vulcanizing) molds release the candles in them easily and so need extremely little mold release agent or none. You will note that the inner walls of these types of molds have an oily feel naturally. However, take note that natural rubber molds are allergic to stearic acid—it will make pockmarks inside the mold, making it unsuitable for reuse. To harden wax for use in rubber molds, use l to 3 percent of "Micro Hard," the hardening polymer discussed on p. 104. Vybar is an additive that increases the opacity of wax and helps it to burn more efficiently. Also, Vybar reduces the shrinkage of paraffin wax. It is ideal for candles made in rubber molds. Generally, allow l ounce of Vybar to 20 ounces of paraffin, or other wax. Proportions can vary with need. Disposable molds such as milk cartons don't need mold release agents. You simply cut the cardboard and peel it off.

Wick Preparation

Using a length of wick twice the height of the mold, prime it by dipping into hot wax. (See "Wick Priming," p. 73.) Thread a wicking needle with the wick and insert the wick through the hole at the top of the mold. Seal it with mold seal, pressing down firmly so that it is firmly attached. (Rubber molds do not need this sealing step.) Then, stick a toothpick through the wick at the base to hold it centered in the mold. Place the mold on top of an upside down cup or bowl, or whatever else will support the mold.

Prepare the Filling

Plan to make a wax blend of l0 percent stearin and 90 per cent paraffin. A rough guide for measuring how much wax you will need is weighing an already-made candle of the same size as the one you are going to make. Melt the stearin by heating it in a small double-boiler, improvised if necessary with two saucepans or a bowl over a saucepan. The stearin is melted when it becomes a clear liquid. If you want a colored candle, next add the colorant you have chosen to the stearin. Don't add too much at once. You can always add more if the color is too pale for your taste. If you do need to add more dye, simply melt a small amount of stearin and put the dye in it before adding to your wax mixture. (Ten percent is not an absolute proportion of stearin to paraffin.)

ESSENTIALS When using beeswax as an additive, a release agent should be used on the inside of rigid molds because beeswax is particularly sticky. This precaution applies if you are using more than 10 percent beeswax.

Transfer the stearin/dye mix to your major melting pot. Add the measured/weighed wax to the pot with the stearin and dye. Heat while stirring until everything is melted and the color is even and smooth. Add whatever scent you have chosen, being sure that it is made for use with candles. Some scents are not only unsuitable for candlemaking but can be dangerous.

Check the Temperature

Heat the wax to 180° Fahrenheit, being very careful not to overheat it. Keep the thermometer inserted into the melting wax until it reaches the correct temperature and stops rising. Remove the melting pot from heat at this point. (You can leave the melting pot in the hot water after removing the pot from the heat source to keep the wax warm enough to work with.)

Pouring into the mold

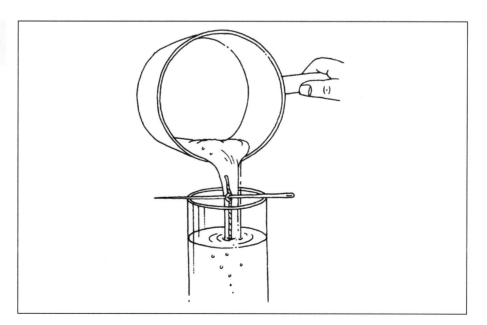

Make sure your mold has been warmed. When your mold is ready and your wax has reached the correct temperature required for the particular mold—*always follow the mold supplier's instructions*—you are ready to pour the wax into the mold. Pour slowly and evenly to avoid splashing hot wax on yourself and to avoid air bubbles forming in the wax. Pouring on a slant will help prevent air bubbles. Either pour directly from the melting pot (which should be a pitcher with a handle), or ladle out the wax (warm the ladle first) into the mold. Or, you can ladle wax into a separate pouring jug if you like. Pour smoothly and gently, avoiding any turbulence. Also, be sure to save some wax for the finishing process.

Add the Wick

After you have poured the wax into the candle, wick the mold. If you are using purchased molds, follow the manufacturer's instructions for wicking the mold carefully. (All commercially made candle molds come with detailed instructions on how to wick them.) One-piece molds—metal, acrylic, or rubber—have a hole in the base. You thread your wick through this hole to the top and pull it through the open end. You must then hold the wick taut by tying a rod to it. Two-piece molds—mostly for fancy shapes, like an egg-shape—require you to tape the wick to one half of the mold. You then must pull it tightly across the shape and tape it securely to the opposite end. Finally, you put together the two pieces and insert them into the purchased mold holder, which creates a seal between the two halves.

Wicking a Molded Candle by Suspension

This is a fairly easy method if your mold has a wide mouth, such as a milk carton or a medium to large tin food can. It works best with molds taller than they are wide. Lay a stick—a short dowel, a chopstick, a pencil, even a straight twig—across the top of the empty mold. Tie the wick to it and tie a small weight onto the bottom end. Keep it centered.

Wicking
the mold

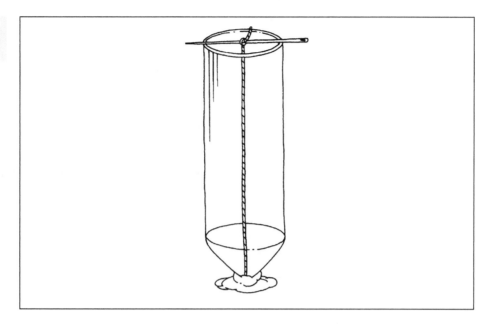

Give Your Candles a Bath

Wax shrinks away from the sides of the mold as it cools. To hasten this process, immerse the filled molds in a pan of cold water. Be sure the pan is large enough to hold them without crowding, or the hot molds will heat the water in the pan, defeating the cooling process. Water should not cover the tops of molds. Fill to within ½" of top of mold.

To determine the right size pan, put the empty molds in it and hold them down while filling the pan with water. Remove the molds—the pan is now ready to use. Don't try to fill the pan with water *after* you have put the filled molds in it: You may get water into the wax inside the molds, which would ruin the candles.

After you have filled your molds, transfer to the cool water bath that you have already prepared, handling the molds carefully (with mitts or pot holders) so as to not burn yourself—or suddenly drop one!

After the molds are placed in the water bath, place a weight on each one. This will prevent the filled mold from floating upward. The idea is to submerge the entire candle in the water just ½" from the top rim.

Finishing the Candle

Because wax contracts so much as it cools, there is a danger that the center of a candle might sink. The repouring process (described in greater detail in the preceding chapter, on p. 112) prevents this from happening.

After the wax has cooled enough to form a skin of about $\frac{1}{8}$" thick, begin repouring. To do this, poke holes in the wax, pushing down around the wick all the way to the bottom of the candle. Then add wax to refill the holes, but be careful to do it a little at a time so that it does not overflow.

During the repouring process, make sure that the additional wax you are pouring in is the same temperature as originally (180° Fahrenheit). If the wax is cooler, it will not adhere properly; if hotter, the candle may crack. You may need to refill the center to get a level surface. Molded candles are usually finished from the bottom end, unlike container candles, which are finished at the top. Therefore, if you need more wax to make the candle flat, it won't matter if it is a different color than the original candle as it won't show—unless you set it on a plate. An easy way to level the base of a candle is to stand the candle upright in a warm pan. This will melt the base just enough to create a nice flat surface.

Leveling the base

After repouring, leave the mold in the water for 1 hour or more to cool thoroughly. If the water in the pan is getting warm, just add a few ice cubes.

Before attempting to remove the candle from the mold, make sure it is completely hardened and cold throughout. This can take from several hours to twenty-four hours, depending on the size of the candle and the type of wax mixture you used. A properly set candle will release from the mold easily. The general rule of candlemaking is to wait for eight hours before removing the candle from its mold. The point here is that if the candle is not completely cold through and through, into its center, removing it from the mold may cause it to have a distorted shape.

Never hit or pry at a mold to get the candle out. Be patient and wait until it's completely cold. If you bang your mold you may make marks in it that will be permanent. These will mar any future candles you make in that mold.

A Candle Is Born

When you see that the wax has shrunk away from the sides of the mold (just like a cake, when done, shrinks from the sides of the baking pan), it is ready to be released. At this point, turn the mold upside down very carefully and remove the wick sealer. Then remove the candle.

If you have reused old wax to mold a candle and the color turns out to be less than pretty, the remedy is "overdipping." Just melt some new wax in a container deep enough to immerse the molded candle and give it a quick dip to coat it.

Occasionally it will happen that there are seam lines at the sides of molded candles. These can come from use of two-part molds, or from tin-can molds. If you get a seam line, simply give your candle a shave along the seams. Any sharp blade will work, but there is a special tool used for scraping dry paint off glass that is superb. This item holds a single-sided razor blade and is easy to manipulate. You can buy such a tool in a paint store or hardware store.

To get a candle out of a mold made from an empty tin food can (washed and dried well), simply use your can opener to cut out the bottom end and push the candle out through it using the cut-out bottom end as a pusher.

Help, It's Stuck!

Into every life, some rain must fall. Sometimes, despite your most careful preparation, a candle will refuse to come out of its mold. If, having tried all of the standard methods already described, you still can't get the candle out of the mold, don't despair. There are some alternative means you can try to get that stubborn wax free of its mold.

1. Put the candle in its mold in the refrigerator for half an hour. Remove it and again try to release it. This usually works.
2. If the fridge fails, run the mold under hot water. This will warm the wax enough to get it to release, but it will also mess up the smooth, shiny surface that was effected by the water bath. Again, don't despair. You can polish the candle (use the tried-and-true nylon pantyhose method) back to a sheen.

If polishing the candle doesn't give the shiny result you want, overdip the candle into a new batch of melted wax for a fresh outer coat. Dip it into a batch of colored wax, which will cover a bad surface more completely than translucent plain paraffin.

Save Your Pantyhose!

Nylon pantyhose make excellent polishing cloths for finished candles, so if you get a run, don't fret—just put it in a plastic bag in your work area to store them. After you have removed the seam lines, if you need to do so, rub your finished candle with old nylon pantyhose to give it a nice polish. This will also smooth away any shaved-off seam lines.

Voilà! You now have a finished molded candle. Stand back and take pride in your accomplishment. And there are now lots of creative things you can do with your molded candle. We'll be discussing those throughout the book.

Automatic Wicking

It's possible to insert a wick into a candle that has already hardened. This is an easy way to make candles. Just pour your wax into the mold, let it harden, release it, and insert a wick. To do this, you will need an ice pick, a heavy knitting needle, or a wicking needle. Heat the implement over a burning candle or other heat source and, holding the hard candle firmly in one hand, slowly and carefully push the hot needle through the candle from one end to the other until you have a hole clear through. Now, using a stiff wick (primed or cored), push the wick through the hole. If the hole is bigger than the wick and there is air space, pour in a little melted wax to fill in the gap.

Wicking Disposable Molds

The easiest way to wick a candle made in a disposable mold is to use the method for wicking an already hardened candle. There are, however, other choices.

If you don't want to make a hole in a disposable mold in order to use it again, use the method for wicking a hardened candle. A hot ice pick works best, but any heated pointed instrument will work fine.

You can punch a hole in the bottom of the mold, using an ice pick or screwdriver (or hammer, if the mold is metal). Then, seal the hole with mold sealer—or use putty, chewing gum, modeling clay, or masking tape. Since the bottom of the mold becomes the top of the candle, this method seems to work best since the end into which the wax was poured will always have an irregular surface.

Technical Assistance Online

The National Candle Association offers a number of technical papers for sale at *www.candles.org*. Here are some you might find useful for making molded candles:

Topic: Wicks
- "Wicking, Function and Structure"
- "Baseline Wick Developmental Data"

Topic: Paraffin Waxes
- "Vybar Polymers—Synthetic Additives for Paraffin Modification"
- "Additives for Candles: Epolene Polyethylene Waxes"
- "A-C Polyethylene Waxes for Candles"
- "Elvax Ploymers: Its Use and Properties"
- "The Crystal Structure of Paraffin Waxes and the Effect of Polymeric Additives"

Topic: Non-Paraffin Waxes
- "Beeswax and Other Non-Paraffin Waxes"

The Craft of Moldmaking

The easiest molds to use are the simple shapes we have already described—squares or rectangles (such as milk cartons) and cylinders (such as food tins). However, if you are the adventurous type—or artistically inclined—you may not be satisfied with these basic shapes (although they can be used to make some extremely interesting-looking candles).

Once you progress beyond these block or cylinder shapes and want to extend your repertoire of candlemaking, you will need two-piece molds (extensively described below). Many of these can be purchased, and you can make your own.

Moldmaking is not easy. It is exacting and complex work. As with any other technical art, people spend years mastering the moldmaking process. But it's fun to try. There are many books that cover this topic. Check out your library or the Internet for books dealing specifically with moldmaking.

You can also learn from professional candlecrafters. Your local craft store may give classes in moldmaking. Also, adult education programs given at local colleges and universities may have such courses available. If you are interested in gaining expertise in this challenging but rewarding art form, investigate these options.

Moldmaking Step by Step

Molds can be made from many materials. You can choose plaster, clay, natural rubber, or silicone rubber. Whichever material you use, the basic technique is the same. Follow these steps carefully to insure success.

Carefully choose the shape you wish to duplicate. Obviously, simple shapes are easier than complex shapes. Take some time to examine the piece and determine if it is truly suitable to use as a model. That wonderfully interesting widget with all sorts of protrusions might look great as a knick-knack—but how hard will it be to get wax out of a mold made from it? If the model you want to duplicate has "undercuts," a one-piece mold is not advisable. Determine which direction the mold will come off of the model. Will it have to be pulled off in such a way as to risk damaging the hardened wax inside? Ask yourself if the model lends itself to being made as a one-piece mold. If not, you'll have to devise a two-piece mold.

Problems: Draft and Undercut

The biggest problems for the moldmaker are draft and undercut. Draft is the taper form intentionally given to molds in order to make removal of the candle easier. An undercut is any flaw—such as an indentation or protrusion—in the model. Undercuts make candle removal (from a one-piece mold) difficult, if not impossible.

The shape you choose from which to model your mold is the clue to easy or hard removal. Latex molds can be peeled off like an adhesive bandage. However, remember that hardened wax is frangible. Trying to peel off a mold from the outstretched wings of an angel might break them off. So when choosing models, take their basic shape into consideration: the simpler the better (and easier).

ESSENTIALS

If you want to make really fancy shapes, there are many good books available on candle moldmaking. Your craft store may carry a line of candlemaking books. Or, search the Internet's many candle Web sites. Your library is also a good source.

Materials for Home Moldmaking

There is no one best material to use for making your own molds. As you experiment and gain experience, you may well develop preferences. You may find one or another material easier or more difficult to work with. Once again, there's always a lot of trial-and-error to home candlemaking. That said, here are some general guidelines for moldmaking substances.

- **Clay**—Clay is an excellent substance for replicating a shape (model) you have made yourself. It's hard to reuse and best for making one-of-a-kind shapes. Don't attempt to use clay for quantity candlemaking.
- **Latex**—Latex is fairly easy to use as a brush-on liquid. (See "Making a Latex Mold: A Step by Step Guide.") However, latex is somewhat time-intensive as you have to apply ten to twenty coats and wait for each one to dry before applying the next. The good news is that a latex mold can be reused several times,

sometimes—depending on the shape—as many as twenty. The downside of latex molds is that they shrink as they dry. This can distort the shape. To avoid this problem, simply support the mold as it is drying. Although latex can be reused, it's also great for a single use, especially if you are using an odd-shaped model. Be prepared, however, for your candle to emerge from the latex mold a bit smaller than the mold itself.

Natural Rubber—Natural rubber has many advantages. It is flexible and easy to handle. However, it has one big disadvantage: you can't use stearin with a rubber mold. A chemical reaction between the two will ruin the rubber due to the corrosive quality of stearin (stearic acid). The good news is that natural rubber can be reused with candles made from wax that doesn't need stearin as an additive. If you want to use a natural rubber mold just a few times, you can use stearin as part of your wax mixture because the chemical corrosion is a slow process. But, eventually, the stearin will make pits in natural rubber.

Plaster—Plaster of Paris makes excellent molds but it is entirely without flexibility. From a practical standpoint, plaster is best used to make a master mold from which you can then make molds of flexible material. Plaster can be used to create a two-part mold.

Polysulfide—This material is reasonably priced and fairly easy to use because of its flexibility. It can be poured over almost any object. Just remember to coat the model with a releasing agent. Petroleum jelly and liquid soap are good.

Polyurethane—This substance is inexpensive and mixes up easily. It is not advised for quantity production, especially if you are using stearin as an additive. Like natural rubber, there is a chemical reaction between the two, though less severe. The downside to polyurethane is that is doesn't keep well. You have to plan to use it as soon as you open the can. It's probably best used for molds with which you are going to do a short-run production of no more than a dozen candles, and make them at the same session of candlemaking.

Every mold material (except plaster bandages!) comes with a sheet of instructions and information about the material's attributes and recommended uses. Be sure to read it and follow all instructions carefully. You may need to wear rubber gloves or take other precautions.

If so advised, be sure there is sufficient ventilation when using the moldmaking material. This caution cannot be emphasized enough, especially when using the chemically based materials.

Two-Piece Moldmaking

Once you have determined a suitable location for the break-line of a two-part mold, you will need a cardboard box out of which you can cut the bottom. This will be the container for your clay bottom layer, the mold model, and the moldmaking material. Its purpose is to hold the model in place while you cast the two separate parts, one after the other. The box needs to be the same size as your mold model, with an additional 2" in all directions—width, height, and depth. This extra space will be filled with clay to hold the model in place while you pour the moldmaking material over it.

What you will have is a four-sided box with no top and no bottom. Place the open-ended box on a flat, hard surface. A piece of plywood is good. Or, depending on the size, a cutting board. Layer some clay on the bottom—about 2"—to form a surface on which the mold model will rest. Prior to inserting the model, coat it lightly with mold release agent or vegetable oil (nonstick pan spray is good) to prevent its sticking to the clay.

Remember that poured candles are normally made upside down. Therefore, place your model in the box with its base flat up against one side of the cardboard box. Secure it with tape or mold seal so that no moldmaking material will get between the model base and the box wall. This end of the mold will hold the pouring hole for your mold.

After you have placed your model in the clay bed and secured its base tightly against one cardboard wall of the box, add more clay up to the location of the line of separation between the two parts of the mold you have chosen. Carefully embed the entire part of the model that will be the other half of the mold. The upper part, the exposed portion of the model, will be the half of the mold you make first. It should be clear of all clay to the line you have decided upon.

At this point, you want to smooth down the surface of the clay very carefully so that the level of the clay is in the exact place where you have decided the seam of the mold will be located. When selecting the parting line, remember that the more strategically you place the seam line the less it will be obvious in the finished candle (even though you can scrape and polish the seam line to some extent). Check your model before starting to see if there is a natural place for a break in the mold. If you can find such a place, and align the parting line with some decorative area of the model, the seam line will be almost invisible.

Having leveled off the clay to the parting line, you must now insert several small pegs or other objects (such as little beads) in a line around the model. These will serve as the registration points on the seam line so that when you put the two pieces together they will fit exactly.

At this point, you are ready to spray or coat the model embedded in the clay with mold release. For plaster or silicone, use petroleum jelly. For rubber and Latex, use mold release of the commercial variety.

Part One

To make the first piece of your two-piece mold, pour your moldmaking material over the model. Fill the space with sufficient material to create a mold wall thick and sturdy enough to hold the hot wax without distorting its shape by bending or buckling.

After filling the box with the moldmaking material, allow it to dry thoroughly. The time needed will vary with the moldmaking material you have chosen.

Part Two

To make the second part of the mold, turn the box upside down to remove the clay bottom. Do not remove either the model or the top half of the mold. Take out the mold registration pegs or beads.

Repeat the process for making the first half of the mold. Coat the exposed model with the appropriate mold release substance. Pour in the moldmaking material. Allow to dry. You now have the second half of your two-part mold.

All Together Now

Lift the cardbox off the mold, after it has dried thoroughly. The finished mold should split neatly apart along the separation line. Take out the original model. The space left behind is the mold into which you will pour the wax. The end of the mold that was pressed flat against the cardboard wall is the opening through which you pour wax.

When making candles from handmade molds such as we have been describing, you will need some sort of clamp system to hold the two pieces together while the wax hardens. This can be heavy rubber bands, duct tape, or whatever else you can improvise. (Store-bought two-piece molds come with their own clamp system provided.)

Making a Latex Mold: A Step-by-Step Guide

Liquid Latex can be purchased from most craft shops. It comes in jars or tubs, and approximately $15.00 worth of Latex will be enough for four or five molds, depending on size, shape, complexity, etc. Alongside the Latex in the craft shop you will usually find the Latex-thickening agent. It's a good idea to have this as well, or your Latex may be too thin.

Be sure to cover your work surfaces with heavy brown paper (old grocery bags are great—you can cut them flat) and wear disposable clothes. If spilled, Latex is nearly impossible to get off of clothes, fabric (such as rugs), and most other surfaces.

Before beginning to make a Latex mold, carefully choose the object from which you are going to create the mold. You can use ornaments, plastic children's toys, and any number of shapes. A stone ornament of a cat or a turtle makes a wonderful mold shape. Use your imagination—look around and see what you have that will serve the purpose.

The Next Step

Secure the base of the object you have chosen on a smooth surface, such as your kitchen counter, with blue tack (a type of mold seal available at craft stores) or double-sided masking tape.

Next, with a large brush—it can be the type artists use, or a small, disposable paintbrush—begin to paint your object with the liquid Latex. As you work, be sure to get the Latex into the crooks and crannies of the mold. Fill in any crevices carefully. Keep painting until you have completely covered the object with latex. Then paint another two inches around the base to form a lip for the mold. If you want to reuse your brush, immediately wash it in hot soapy water. Disposable (cheap!) brushes can simply be discarded.

Allow the mold to air-dry (liquid Latex dries fairly quickly). The thinner the coat, the faster it will dry, and vice versa. Continue this painting/drying process until the Latex covering your object is approximately 2 mm thick.

Once you are satisfied with the thickness of the mold, allow it to dry completely. Using liquid dish detergent as a release agent, carefully peel the mold off the object. Clean it and allow it to cure (dry) at room temperature for seventy-two hours before attempting to fill with wax.

Use the mold to make your molded candles, following the basic instructions given in this chapter. However, *do not use stearin in rubber molds*. It has a corrosive effect, which will rot the rubber.

Tips for Successful Latex Molds

- Watch out for deep undercuts in your model. If it has these, the mold will be extremely difficult to remove.
- Use untreated/unpainted plaster cast models to make interesting molds. These can be found at shops that carry ceramic craft materials.

- Remember that handmade molds cast from objects have a limited lifespan. You cannot use them indefinitely.
- Don't make the mold too big. A too-large mold can distort the wax poured into it.
- Don't touch the rubber in between coats—this will interfere with the adhesion of subsequent coatings.
- Don't use metal objects for making Latex molds. Certain chemical reactions may occur that are inadvisable.

A two-piece mold makes removal a snap. But you have to carefully determine the parting line, where the mold separates into two pieces. It must be so located that you can pull the two pieces apart, free from any protruding areas of the shape (such as the angel's wings).

Complex Molded Shapes

With patience and a little practice, it can be fairly easy to make molds at home, as long as you stick to shapes that lend themselves to a natural part line. But if you want to get really fancy, it's possible to make three-part molds. Just remember that the more parts, the more possibility of wax leakage. Wax may leak from a mold that has more than one part line, and this can ruin the candle. Experienced candlemakers don't advise beginners to attempt to construct molds of more than two parts. Once you have mastered the two-part mold construction, you may want to move on to more complex shapes.

Objects for Moldmaking

Here you are limited only by your imagination and your skills at moldmaking. Naturally, you will want to choose objects whose shape appeals to you aesthetically—or even to your sense of humor! Almost any object can be used for a mold. However, *it must be made of nonporous material.* Anything that can absorb water or any other liquid will be able to absorb wax as well. Follow this basic rule and then let your imagination run wild!

Models, Models Everywhere!

The object you use as the model for your mold can be just about anything (again remembering the caution about overly complex shapes). It might be an object you particularly care about—such as a pressed-glass jar (I have one of those, a tall cylinder that is "just right," and makes a lovely and intricately patterned candle).

Your model could be a unique (one-of-a-kind) object that has surface texture that you'd like to reproduce in wax form. If you sculpt, it might be something of your own design that you would find appealing as a candle. Or, you might make a specific shape just to be a model for a mold.

Your child might be playing with modeling clay and come up with something that could be used as a model. Think what a thrill for him or her to see his or her artwork reproduced as a candle! Such an item would make an outstanding gift for a grandparent or other relative. Or, your child could take the candle made from his or her artwork to school for "show and tell."

Garage and yard sales are prime sources for objects to be used as models. At them, you are likely to find oddly shaped—often old-fashioned or antique—objects perfect for moldmaking. For example, I once found an antique butter mold that was beautifully shaped. All sorts of glass containers, particularly cut glass or pressed glass, make good models. You could even use a piece of fruit such as an apple or a mango. One candlemaker I know looks for old carved wooden moldings—their intricacies make very unusual candles. You are limited only by your tastes and imagination in choosing models for your moldmaking.

Plaster Bandage Molds

Some molds you make you might want to reuse. On the other hand, you might want to make a temporary model out of clay, which you just peel off the finished candle and discard. Gauze, a type of plaster that doctors use to make casts for broken bones, is also good for making your own models. (I learned about this from doing mask workshops where we used the material to form masks right on the faces of the participants.) You wet the plaster bandage material and then use it to form a shape. You can either wrap it around an existing object, leaving a hole through which to pour the melted wax, or create a freeform shape (also leaving a hole). To use a plaster bandage for a two-part mold, wait until your form is thoroughly dry and then, using a sharp knife, slice it down the center, either vertically or horizontally. Proceed with the candlemaking process as described for two-part molds.

CHAPTER 8
Dipped Candles

Dipping is probably the oldest method of candlemaking in the world. There is some evidence that the ancient Romans made dipped candles. And, aside from the newer method of container candles already described, dipping is perhaps the simplest and easiest method by which to make candles.

Dip Your Wick

Actually, a dipped candle is nothing more than a wick that has been primed—that is, a wick that has been first dipped into hot wax to eliminate air bubbles—and then re-dipped into the wax several times so that the wax forms a thick coating around the wick. As the wax drips off the dipped candlewick, it naturally forms a tapered shape. Dipped candles can be made any diameter the candlemaker chooses, although commercial dipped-type candles are made in standard sizes (with which we are familiar) to fit into standardized candleholders. Tapers are generally made ½" or ⅞" in diameter at the base because most purchased candleholders come in these sizes. Exceptions are birthday candles (to be stuck in the cake icing or fitted on special holders with points), and Danish tapers, which are only ¼" in diameter.

QUESTIONS?

What is a dipped candle?
Dipped candles are made a pair at a time by repeatedly dipping a double loop of wick into molten wax. Dipped candles have a pleasing tapered shape. When done by hand they are uniquely beautiful. No factory-made taper can match them.

The simple process of building up wax in layers on a wick creates the lovely tapered shape—without any effort on the part of the candlemaker! However, you can manually effect the dipped candle's shape while the candle is still warm. (We'll discuss that in detail later.)

From Labor to Love

At today's popular Renaissance Fairs, candle dipping is a big attraction, as it is at the town of Colonial Williamsburg. There, you can watch—and it's fascinating to see—the women methodically dipping racks of wicks that will become tapered candles. If you visit Williamsburg, you'll learn that Colonial women dipped candles as part of their domestic work. Every Colonial home was the producer of all things needful to life, including candles. Candlemaking was not a *hobby* then—it was a labor assigned to the housewife. And a backbreaking, smelly, greasy task it was. Yes, today candlemaking can be fun—and a rewarding hobby. But back then it was pure *work*, and lots of it.

For a long time, candles were made only of animal fat, and housewives collected every scrap after butchering and cooking of meats was completed. These precious fats were hoarded carefully, protected in covered crocks. At candlemaking time, the fat was melted down and the dipping process began.

Fortunately for early American women with the wherewithal to get them, there were other candlemaking materials available to them, besides ones available in Europe. New England gave them bayberries, which have a heavenly scent—quite a change from the stinky animal-fat candles. Bayberries were introduced to the Colonial women by their Native American neighbors, who also showed them how to get the wax out of the berries.

As you realize by now, another source of candle wax was beeswax, and many farm families raised bees, primarily for their honey and their pollination work, but also to get the sweet-smelling beeswax. Lucky was the Colonial farmer with a hive or two of bees! (Always think twice before you swat a bee—they are beneficial insects!)

FACTS

In all probability, the technique of dipping was developed from the earliest form of candlelight we know, the "rush dip." This was made by dipping long stalks of dried grass repeatedly in melted tallow (animal fat). These were then lit and used for light both outdoors and indoors.

Today, most dipped candles are made of paraffin, which is sometimes mixed with various additives, like stearic acid. The more expensive tapers available commercially may be a blend of paraffin and beeswax. Pure beeswax tapers are rarely available, but recently I have noticed some upscale mail-order catalogs are offering pure beeswax pillar candles. Beeswax needs no scent. It gives off a delightful fragrance of honey; depending on what diet the bees have had, the honeyed scent will vary slightly, from clover to wildflower.

The Skinny on Dipping

The basic dipping technique is simplicity itself. Find a can that is 2" taller than the desired length of the candles, and use it to melt wax in a pot of hot water. Ordinarily, candles are dipped in pairs, which means that one wick supports two candles. The wick is therefore cut long enough to accommodate the length of two candles. You will actually dip one wick, but hold the middle part above the wax, which is what makes the pair.

Each end of the wick is weighted, so that it will drop to the bottom of the wax receptacle. The weights also serve to keep the wicks straight in the wax bath until enough layers have been built up so that the candle itself is heavy enough to hang straight. The pair of candles is held apart with a rod, which prevents them from making contact in the hot wax and adhering to each other.

Sound easy? Let's look at this technique more closely.

Gather Together

Before you begin, assemble all of your materials and equipment. If you are going to make a quantity of dipped candles, cut all of your wicks in advance and lay them out. Prime them and allow to harden before beginning the dipping process. You will need to have the following materials on hand:

- Wax
- Beeswax
- Stearic Acid
- Wick(s)
- Colorant(s)
- Scent(s)
- Double-boiler setup or concealed-element heater
- Thermometer
- Can for dipping, at least 2" taller than the length of the candles you plan to make
- Rod or dowel
- Bucket
- Small weights
- Sharp knife
- Nylon pantyhose (for polishing finished candles)

The recommended length of primed wick is 24" for each pair of candles you plan to make. A medium sized wick is recommended, such as $\frac{1}{10}$ square braid, or 30-, 36-, or 42-ply flat braid. Again, experiment and *keep notes*. If you are using 50 percent or more beeswax, the wick should be increased by one or more sizes according to the diameter of the candle. Read the manufacturer's instructions carefully.

Use the knife for slicing off the bottoms of the candles when finished. (When doing this, take care not to mark your newly made candles with fingerprints!)

The dowel is used to hold candles for dipping (although you can do this with your fingers, a "spacer" is a good idea.) A coat hanger works fine. You'll also need something to hang drying candles on, such as hooks, nails, or pegs. For quantity candlemaking, you can use a frame.

The bucket will be useful for holding sufficient water in which to submerge the finished dipped candles. Washers, nuts, or nails are suggested to use as weights to tie at the ends of the wicks to hold them straight while dipping.

Wax Formulas for Dipped Candles

As with most candlemaking, there are no hard-and-fast rules about wax mixtures. The important factor in whether a candle will burn well is the relationship among the wax mixture's melting point, the finished candle's diameter, and the wick type and size. Ask yourself what you want to achieve with your dipped candles. Do you want long burning time? Do you want a slim, elegant shape? How are you going to use the candles—for a special occasion party or everyday home dining?

Here are some options for waxes used in dipping:

- *Pure beeswax.* See "Create a Pure Beeswax Dipped Candle" later in this chapter.
- *Beeswax mixed with paraffin.* Proportions are optional.
- *Paraffin, stearic acid, and beeswax.* Proportions can vary. Try twice as much paraffin as stearic acid, with $\frac{1}{3}$ as much beeswax, i.e., 6 pounds paraffin/3 pounds Stearin/1 pound beeswax.
- *Paraffin, with stearic acid (usually 10 percent).* Pure paraffin is not advisable as it generally needs stearin to hold a shape.

Keep notes to see what works best for you. Make a test pair before going on to make quantities using the same formula. Add color and scent as you wish to any of the suggested wax mixtures. Again, experimentation is the key to success. Always make a test candle, and always keep notes of the amounts and kinds of colorants and scents you use in your wax formula.

SSENTIALS

Three sets of two pairs of l0" × ⅞" tapers require approximately 6 pounds of wax. With a large dipping can, you will need more in order to submerge the wicks entirely. If wax is left over, pour it into lined, shallow baking pans to cool and reuse.

Take the Plunge

Begin by measuring the wicks. Each wick should be twice the length of the candle you are planning to make (in pairs) plus an additional 4", to allow the candles to be held apart when being dipped. You'll find that while being dipped, the candles have a natural attraction to each other—they seem to want to be just one candle! To prevent them from sticking together, you have to take extra care as you lift them in and out of the melted wax. This can take a bit of practice if you use your fingers, but you can also use a small piece of cardboard or a rod as a spacer/holder to keep the forming candles separated. If you are new to candle dipping, experiment with various methods of holding the pairs of candles apart before attempting to dip a quantity of pairs.

Tie a small weight—for example, a washer, a nut, a nail, or a curtain weight—to the end of each wick you are going to dip.

Although you can dip each pair just by holding it with your fingers, that can be cumbersome, especially if you want to make more than one pair at a time. If you are making a single pair of dipped candles, you can take a small piece of cardboard, about 2" square, and cut ½" slits on either side of it to make a channel to hold the wick. You then hold the cardboard "spacer" with your fingers to do the dipping.

Luckily, there are several simple dipping frames you can improvise for dipping multiple candles. One is a slender rod or dowel. Loop the upper ends of the wick around it and tie them securely. You can use a heavy coathanger (one that won't bend with the growing weight of the candles as they are being dipped). A metal rod, such as those used to hang curtains, will work well. There's a type of curtain rod called a "tension rod," which has two pieces that fit together with a spring in between. You can use just one piece. These rods are very sturdy.

Next, prepare your double-boiler setup for heating the wax—and remember that your wax receptacle must be 2" taller than the length of the candles you are going to make. Fill the bottom pan with water. Put the dipping can in the water receptacle (it can be a large saucepan). Cut up or break your wax into chunks and place them into the dipping can. Heat the water slowly to begin the melting process. Stir occasionally. Put in any additives you are using in addition to stearin, such as colorants and scents. Mix well to distribute these elements throughout the wax.

The Importance of Temperature Control

Keep a constant check on the temperature of the wax with your thermometer, and leave the thermometer in the wax while you are working. This will tell you how long the wax maintains the correct temperature before it needs reheating. At 160° Fahrenheit (or whatever other melting point your wax has, whether it is above or below this temperature), lower the heat under the pot of water.

Wax shrinks as it cools, so each dip should be in the same temperature of wax. Use your thermometer to check temperature. The candle should cool before re-dipping, but it should not be *cold*. Your work area should be normal room temperature. You may want to use a water bath to cool the candles between each dipping.

Using Colorants

There are two ways to make a colored dipped candle. You can add color to the wax and have the candle colored throughout. Or, you can "overdip," a process we will describe in full later, by dipping white candles into colored wax for the last few dips, just enough to coat the white wax with color.

If you want to dip in colored wax, do not add too much coloring agent at first. If after you have made a pair of candles you want to intensify the color, you can always add more colorant to the remaining wax. Again, keep notes of how much colorant you use to which proportion of waxes.

Candle Colorant Technical Papers

You can order several fairly inexpensive technical papers on dyes and pigments from the National Candle Association. Available are the following:

- "Color Stabilization"
- "Dyes and Fragrances in Candles"
- "Color Fade Problems"
- "Dyestuff—Dyes and Pigments"
- "Colorants for Candles"

If you want to get into candlemaking at the advanced level, or if you simply want to color and scent your basic candles, these are worth your consideration and could, in the end, save you money and a lot of trial-and-error candlemaking.

Be careful what you put in your wax mixture. Don't ever use lipsticks or house paint for a coloring agent. Stay away from crayons, unless they are made of wax. To stay on the safe side of this nasty problem, always use color material that is made especially for candlemaking.

Ready to begin?

Hold a length of wick in the center (looped over your fingers) and dip both ends into the melted wax, keeping your fingers 2" above the melted wax. Leave the wick in the wax for about three seconds. Remove and allow to cool on a holding peg for about three minutes. Don't touch the candles while they cool down. If the first layer of wax is smooth when cool, continue the dipping and cooling process until you have produced candles of the thickness you desire.

You can speed up the cooling process in between dips by submerging the growing candle into a water bath. However, if you use this cooling method, *make absolutely sure that all the water residue has evaporated from the surface of the candles.* If you dip candles that have water on

Dipping candles

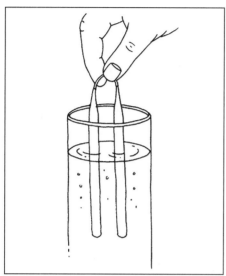

their surface, you will get wax-covered water bubbles in the finished candles. These cause candles to sputter when burned, and they mar the finished appearance of the candles.

Before re-dipping, make sure the previous layer is cool. Dip the candles in the melted wax quickly, to the same level as the first dip. Pull them out slowly and steadily. You should begin to see a waxy buildup on the wick by the third dip. If the wax isn't adhering properly to the wick, let the wax

cool a bit (about 5° Fahrenheit) and re-dip the wick until you see the wax beginning to grow.

Your dipping can will initially contain much more wax than you will actually use for making the many layers of the final candles. However, because you are *taking wax out of the dipping can*, you will need to replenish your supply of wax frequently. The best way to do this handily is to keep a second double-boiler setup going with a supply of extra wax for refilling the dipping can. In order to be consistent, remember to first determine the exact wax formula, including color and/or scent, that you want to use for all of the candles you are dipping in one session.

Growing Your Dipped Candles

The dipping-and-drying process can take fifteen to thirty dips, depending on the thickness you want the candles to be. This requires a certain amount of patience, but it is quite fascinating to watch the candles grow into their lovely tapered shapes as you work with them. As your candles begin to accumulate layers of wax, the cooling time in between dips will increase. Make sure the candle is cooled each time before you re-dip. Also, it's best to rotate the dipping frame so that you can see the opposite sides of the growing candles as you dip to make sure you are getting a smooth effect all around.

Progression
of dipped
candles

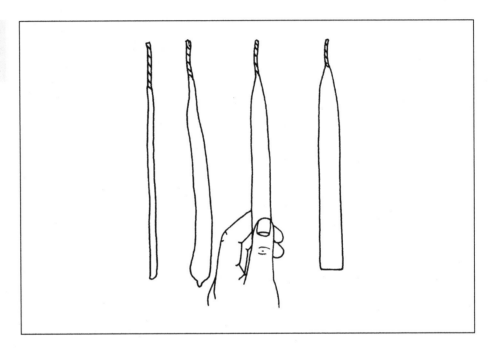

After several dips, the candles will have thickened enough to serve as their own weights. At this point, before doing your final dips, take the sharp knife and slice off the bottoms of the candles where the weights are embedded in the wax. When cutting off the bottoms, make sure the candles are cool and hard enough not to be imprinted with your fingertips. Do this as cleanly as possible so that the candle base will be finished nicely. If you don't get it quite right, you can always repeat the process later. Save the candle ends with the weights in them to remelt and use later on. You can achieve a shiny surface on your dipped candles by submerging them into cool water after the final dip. After doing this, hang them up to dry for one hour or more. Store newly made candles laid flat and away from direct sunlight.

Marbled Chipped Pillar

Molded and Dripped

Chipped

Carved

Twisted Taper

Pyramid

Specialty

Chip

Marbled

Molded Floating

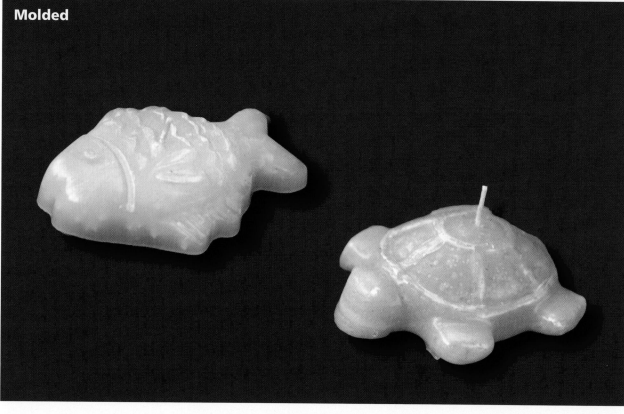

Molded

Molded

Multiwick

Molded

Rolled Beeswax

Carved

Specialty

Danish Tapers

Carved

Molded

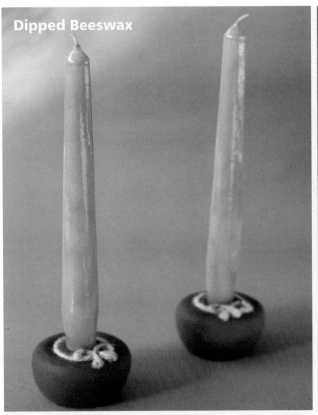

Dipped Beeswax

Dripped

Chipped

Molded

And don't forget to take notes. This is an all-important step for the candlemaker to be able to repeat successes and avoid future failures.

SSENTIALS

For an ultra-smooth surface, on the final dip increase the heat of the wax to 180° Fahrenheit. After the last dip, lower the heat immediately so as not to overheat the wax. And always watch your thermometer carefully as you work.

Reverse Dipping

Although this reverse process of bringing the wax to the taper strikes me personally as a bit cumbersome, it is the preferred method for some experienced candlemakers. Instead of dipping the wick into the wax, reverse the procedure by raising the container to the wick. This allows you to coat each wick, one after the other, pausing only to reheat the wax when it cools off.

If you are going to use the reverse method you will need a dipping can or pot with a sturdy handle, like a metal pitcher. Also, you will have to hang your wicks far enough apart to accommodate the size of the pot. Still, some people find this easier than the traditional dip-the-wick method.

Reverse dipping

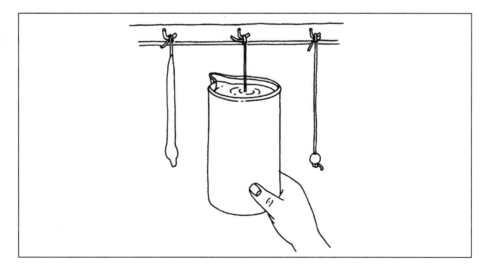

Drying Dipped Candles

As dipped candles are usually made in pairs, the wax is still warm when they are finished. Therefore, when hanging dipped candles to cool, make certain they do not touch each other, or they may stick together. You can hang them over two nails or a dowel rod. A coathanger makes a great frame.

SSENTIALS You can use hooks or pegs for hanging just-dipped candles to cool. An old-fashioned peg-board—a long board with several pegs inserted—is a good choice for several sets of tapers. You can make such a board easily with screw-in hooks.

Troubleshooting

Dipping candles requires technical mastery. Understanding wax temperatures is crucial, as is how long the wick being dipped stays in the hot wax. Shaping the final candles can be a problem; beware of leaving surface blemishes. Here are some troubleshooting tips:

1. If during successive dips your candle is not growing, it may be because the wax is too hot. Or, you may be keeping the candles in the wax too long.
2. If the wax buildup is melting off the candle in the successive dips, the wax is too hot or you are keeping the candles in the wax too long.
3. If the surface of the candle is forming bumps or blisters, it is because you are keeping the candles in the hot wax too long.
4. If the candles have lumps and bumps, the wax is too cool.

That's Wicked

The correct burning of a wick is directly related to the melting point of the wax mixture during the dipping process and the diameter of the finished candle. If your wick doesn't burn correctly, you can analyze the problem and learn to avoid it in the future. Here are some common wick problems and how to recognize them:

Guttering

You will know when you see a guttering candle that the amount of wax being consumed by the flame is more than the wick can effectively absorb. The melted wax will overflow the candle and drip down its side. This dripping is called *guttering*.

What causes guttering?
The wick is too small for the wax mixture you are using and the diameter of the candle you have made.

In severe cases of guttering, all of the melted wax will run down the side of the candle, emptying out the pool of liquid fuel. Since the wick will then have no fuel, it will begin to smoke until it burns enough of itself to melt enough candle wax for fuel. At this point, it's best just to put the candle out, as you will have a drippy mess on the candleholder and whatever is underneath it.

SOLUTION: remelt the candle and try again with a different wick.

Guttering

Cratering

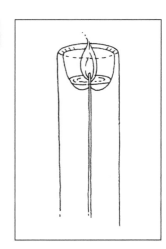

Cratering

This condition occurs in pillar candles when the wick is too small for the type of wax mixture and the diameter of the candle. With cratering, the wick will burn a deep hole in the center of the pillar, creating a "crater" that will fill with the melting wax. As the wick surrounds itself with melted wax, it will extinguish itself in the pool it has made.

SOLUTION: You can take a sharp knife and cut off the top of the candle until the wick is above its surface, then try again to burn it.

Another cause of cratering is when the wick is too large for the candle and absorbs more liquid wax than it can burn for fuel. When this occurs, you will have a smoking wick and a small bead of carbon will form on the tip of the wick.

SOLUTION: You can trim the wick and pour off the excess melted wax. Or, you can simply remelt the candle and use the melted wax to make another candle.

Sputtering

This condition occurs when the candle is not properly made. It may have air or water pockets inside it.

SOLUTION: Depending on the extent of the problem, it is possible that, as the wick seeks its fuel, it will burn past the problem area and be fine. However, if the air/water bubbles are throughout the candle, consider it a total loss and put in the "save for remelting" bag.

Wick Won't Burn

Occasionally, a wick just won't let itself be lit, or you light it and it instantly goes out. This problem is usually caused by additives, mostly color pigments of various types, clogging the wick's wicking system.

SOLUTION: Chances are, this is an unsolvable problem, for if you remelt you'll still have the clogging additives in the wax mixture. Make a note in your journal to avoid that formula and write it off to experience.

Surface Defects

If you don't get a smooth surface on your candles (like all the pretty pictures in candlemaking book displays!), it's because your wax is either too hot or too cool. Wax that is too hot can cause air-filled blisters. Wax that is too cool will thicken and produce a lumpy surface.

SOLUTION: Watch the temperature!

Make It Stick

Adhesion of the layers of wax being built up as you dip is important. If the layers do not meld properly during the successive dips, the candle may separate into concentric circles, like slices of an onion. To achieve good layer adhesion is the aim of the candledipper. Only thus can you produce a candle that is solid wax from core to outer layer. Such a candle won't come apart unless broken intentionally.

If you are having problems with layer adhesion, there are four things you can try:

1. Increase the submersion time
2. Decrease the time between dips
3. Increase the temperature of the wax
4. Raise the temperature of your work area and eliminate any drafts, especially cold ones

Use Your Notebook for Troubleshooting

We've said it before, and we are saying it again: Keep a notebook—especially when dipping candles. Because submersion time, time between dips, and wax and room temperature are all crucial elements, these should be meticulously recorded in your notebook. Then you can refer to these notes whenever you encounter trouble with dipping candles.

Note any adjustments you make to the temperature of the wax, and record the wax formula used. By doing this, you will know what wax mixture needs which temperature in order to work best. Since each wax mixture will have a different ideal temperature for dipping, notes are invaluable—if any time elapses, you may forget what you did that worked best.

Dipping in Quantity

On occasion you may want to make a large number of pairs of dipped candles—for instance, to decorate the tables at a large party such as a wedding or birthday fete, or to give as gifts during the holiday season. Candles can be dipped in quantity by tying pairs of wicks to a frame, such as has been described above. However, to dip candles in large quantities, you must be certain that your frame is very sturdy. The frame can be a rod, a hoop, or a square. Metal racks such as are used for cooling cookies, or metal broiling pans that are made of parallel rods, can be especially useful to the home candlemaker who wants to do a large production run.

ESSENTIALS

Another way to make dipped candles in quantity is with the coathanger method. Simply use ten hangers (holding two pairs of candles each). Because you have to wait two or three minutes in between dips, you can increase efficiency if you work with several hangers, dipping one after the other.

Helpful Hints for Dipping in Quantity

There are two important points to remember when choosing a frame for making dipped candles in quantity: one, when tying the wicks onto the frame, be careful to leave sufficient space between them to accommodate the finished candles. You will have to decide their thickness in advance in order to do this. About three candle diameters between wicks is suggested for adequate spacing. The second point, and a vital one, is to remember that a frame of many candles is going to be heavy, and will get heavier as you dip and add the layers to make the final candles the thickness you desire.

Dipping for Kids 101

For a children's project, it's best to dip a single candle at a time, which avoids the problem of the pair making contact. This also gives the child a long length of wick to hold, thereby avoiding danger of burns or the child's accidentally getting a hand or fingers into the hot wax.

Keep safety at the top of your priorities. Be sure children are properly protected—an old T-shirt over regular clothes is a good apron. And of course, adult supervision is a must.

What you will need for this is plain paraffin, an empty can for melting the wax and dipping the wicks, a saucepan to use as the bottom half of the double-boiler setup, and wick lengths of 24", one for each candle to be made.

Fill the saucepan with about 2" of water and heat it over low heat on the stove. Add the paraffin block (or cut it into pieces for faster melting) and let it slowly melt while keeping a close watch. Give each child a prepared wick with the weight already attached to the bottom end. Also provide each child with a small piece of cardboard to hold under the just-dipped candle, to prevent drips on the floor.

When the wax is melted, allow the child (or each child involved in the project) to dip a wick slowly down into the melted wax and then slowly pull it out again. Have the children stand in a line and approach the dipping can of melted wax, under supervision. Have some hooks or a rod available on which to tie the tapers to dry. Allow the children to repeat the dipping process eight or ten times until enough wax has accumulated on the wick to make a nice size candle. The candles will be thinner and smaller than usual, but that's not important. It's the experience and the fun of it that count!

When each child has made his or her candle, hang all the candles on the drying rack (with nametags for identification later). When the candles are dry, trim off the extra length of wick used for tying the candles onto the rack, to about ½". An adult should be in charge of trimming off the candle bottoms. If this is a school project, send the candle home with the child. If this is a home project, allow the child to light the candle—be sure to give appropriate warnings about candle-burning safety.

Be aware that these simple, paraffin-only candles will not burn as long or as well as those made with additives. But pure paraffin is lovely to watch burn as it gives a translucent glow—and what could be lovelier than helping kids to get creative?

Teacher's Tip

Candlemaking at school by a group of children can become a festive activity during the holiday season. A field trip to a candlemaking facility, the telling of a story about how the candle represents the light of life, the singing of a holiday song—all could be adjuncts to the candlemaking project.

If you make special candles for holidays such as Christmas, it's especially important to keep careful notes. You may know your everyday procedures by heart, but after a year has passed, you are likely to have forgotten exactly how you made those lovely beeswax candles that everyone so admired!

Candle-Burning Safety

Fire can be a friend—or a foe. The following precautions will ensure that the pleasure of using the candles you've made doesn't become a disastrous experience.

- Never leave a burning candle unattended
- Always put tapers in candleholders that fit properly
- Place candles in a secure area away from drafts or pets
- Make sure the candleholder is nonflammable
- When lighting candles with kitchen matches, dip the match in water before discarding—many a hot match has ignited paper in a trash basket!
- Keep the candlewick trimmed to ½–¼" for better burn
- Avoid splattering melted wax when blowing out a candle by cupping your hand around the flame first
- Trim candle after extinguishing it, while the wick is still warm—trimming a cold, burnt wick can damage it and make it difficult to relight

Good News about Wax Removal

Throughout this book, we have cautioned you to carefully cover all work and surrounding surfaces to avoid the problem of spilled wax. We've suggested you wear old, disposable clothes. Now—as an avid reader of mail-order catalogs—I am able to bring you some *good* news. I have recently discovered some wax-removal products that actually work!

The Vermont Country Store sells a product called "Wax Away," which they claim removes spilled candle wax even from delicate linens, works fast with no scraping, and will not stain. An 8-ounce bottle is $8.95. Call (802) 362-0285 or reach them on the Web at *www.vermontcountrystore.com.*

Called simply "Wax Remover" by its purveyor, this product loosens wax so you can simply lift it off. A liquid, it can be used on wood, plastic, or painted surfaces, carpets, tablecloths, and clothing. An 8-ounce bottle costs $9.95. Contact Illuminations at (800) 226-3537 or visit their Web site at *www.illuminations.com.*

Candle Care Kit is an excellent collection that contains a silver-plated candle shaver, stainless steel wick trimmer (angled to reach deep-set wicks in pillars), steel tweezers to remove wick debris, Wax Remover, and Candle Stickers. The Candle Care Kit is also available from Illuminations (see their contact information in the preceding paragraph).

Create a Pure Beeswax Dipped Candle

In the Middle Ages, only churches and the royal families had access to beeswax. (Incidentally, the bee has long been a symbol for royalty!) Although it is possible to purchase pure beeswax candles today, they are extremely expensive. Making your own is gratifying—and a lot cheaper! And hand-dipped candles have an appearance that can't be beat by factory-made ones. They burn beautifully, and no wax is better suited to this method of candlemaking than the beautifully colored and scented wax made by those industrious and useful creatures we call bees.

FACTS

To produce two pounds of wax, bees have to consume about fourteen times this weight in nectar. The wax is secreted in small flakes from glands on the underside of the bee's abdomen. The bee strips off secreted wax to use for the construction of the honeycombs. Fresh wax—known as "pure" wax—is white. Its fragrance depends on the bees' sources of nectar, which could be a single source like clover, or wild flowers, or other types of plants that produce nectar the bees can consume.

Getting Started

To make one pair of pure beeswax candles, you will need these materials:

- A 1½"-primed wick, about 20" in length (beeswax requires a heavier wick than paraffin mixtures)
- A dipping can 2" taller than the length of the candles you plan to make, filled with pure beeswax
- A saucepan or Dutch oven deep enough to hold water two thirds of the way up the dipping can
- Wax thermometer
- Soft cloth for polishing, such as those used to polish silver

Steps to Making Pure Beeswax Dipped Candles

1. Heat the wax until melted. Hold the measured piece of wick in its center and dip both ends into the wax. Remove. Repeat three times.
2. Continue dipping the wax-coated ends of the wick into the melted wax until the wax builds up. By hand-dipping you can achieve candles much thicker than those commercially produced, and with a nicer shape.
3. Beeswax melts at 140–145° Fahrenheit. Use the thermometer to maintain a constant melt; otherwise you may find a skin forming over the wax as you work and the wax cools. Either maintain a low heat under the saucepan, or return the dipping can to the hot water for reheating when necessary.
4. After about thirty dips, your beeswax candles will be approximately the diameter of standard-sized tapers you buy in shops.
5. Continue the dipping process, allowing the candles to dry a bit in between dips, until they have reached a diameter of approximately 1½" at their base.
6. Immediately dip the candles into a bucket of cold water, which will give them a beautiful sheen, then hang them up to dry. When they are completely dry, buff the candles with a cloth.

Once formed into a beehive, the white honeycomb wax begins to turn yellow. As the combs age, the color darkens to the familiar honey-color we know. This aging process explains why there are differently hued beeswax sheets and candles.

Beeswax is used not only for candles but also to make artificial fruit and flowers. It's also a good modeling wax. Further, it is an ingredient in the manufacture of furniture and floor waxes, leather dressings, inks, ointments, cosmetics—even waxed paper!

Overdipping: Another Kind of Dip

Dipped candles by definition (see above) are pairs of candles on which wax has been built to a certain thickness by repeatedly dipping a single wick into the melted wax.

There is, however, another kind of dipping—called "overdipping." Overdipping, put simply, is submerging a finished candle in a final wax bath either to layer a candle with color or to put a layer of super-hard wax on the candle, with a higher melting point than the wax in the center of the candle, to prevent dripping. This process makes the wax on the outer layer burn more slowly than the wax at the center of the candle. The wax closest to the wick is consumed by the wick's flame before it can pool and drip over the side of the candle, or, in the case of pillars, make a crater or deep pool of melted wax that will extinguish the wick.

Overdipping in a higher melting point wax creates a hard shell on the candle, which protects its surface. It can also serve to cover up any surface blemishes on finished candles. Or, it can be used to change the color of a tinted candle. You can even make a half-and-half (say, blue and white) effect by overdipping only the bottom half (or other portion) into the colored wax. Quite dramatic color effects can be obtained by overdipping, such as adding strongly contrasting colors over white. As the candle burns, the contrast is revealed. Or, you can overdip a second color over a first color—for example, a red over a pink—for an unusual effect in the burning candle.

Overdipping rolled candles will seal them together and prevent them from coming unrolled (which can happen in hot weather or an overheated room). Simply overdip your rolled candles in clear wax. This process gives a nice, finished look to the rolled candle; it is especially recommended if you have rolled the candle into a spiral shape.

Overdipping is also useful for creating decorated candles. By overdipping the finished candle in plain paraffin, which is translucent and won't affect color, you can adhere small decorations, such as beads or sequins, to the candle's surface.

Additionally, candles can be overdipped with the same wax you used to make them if you add l0 percent of the hardening agent microcrystalline.

SSENTIALS   When overdipping in beeswax, no additives are needed. As an overdip, beeswax is more economical than making a pure beeswax candle—it gives the *appearance* of pure beeswax, its color, and signature honey fragrance, without using up a lot of beeswax. Plus, overdipping in beeswax will give a longer burn time.

Method for Overdipping Candles

Don't confuse *overdipping* with *dipping*. You can overdip tapers, but you can also overdip almost any kind of candle you make. Pillars especially lend themselves to overdipping and special effects from overdipping.

Here's what you'll need for overdipping:

1. A wax or wax mixture with a high melting point (check the temperature with your thermometer)
2. Stearic acid—5 to 30 percent relative to the wax, depending on the effect you want to achieve (remember that stearic acid makes paraffin opaque)

3. A container of cool water deep enough to submerge the candle, to add shine to the finished candle and to cool it
4. Your double-boiler setup
5. Pliers (needle-nose pliers work well)
6. Colorant or dye, if you are going to overdip in color (usually over a white candle, but not always: you could overdip a lighter colored candle in a darker color)

Overdip with Clear Wax

Melt the wax about 20° above its melting point. For proper adhesion of the overdip layer, the candle should be still warm, not cold. If you have a cold candle (for example, if you purchased white candles and are going to overdip them in color or beeswax) you must warm the candles a bit before dipping. Small candles and tapers can be held between the hands; larger ones, like pillars, can be put in a warm spot—but not too warm and not for too long, or they will begin to melt!

Holding the candle by its wick, using the pliers (recommended for bought candles or those with already trimmed wicks), or your fingers if the wick is sufficiently long (as it would be with handmade dipped pairs), completely submerge the candle in the clear wax. Pull it (or them, if a pair) out steadily. The overdipping must be done quickly because the wax is hotter than usual and you want to avoid beginning to melt your candle.

The overdipped candle will be quite warm, a bit soft, and slightly pliable for a few minutes. Continue to hold it aloft by its wick until it begins to set. Although some candlemakers consider a single dip sufficient for an overdip, others recommend dipping two or three times, allowing about thirty seconds between dips. This is your choice. Again, experimentation is the answer. And, yes, keep notes!

After the final dip (if you use more than one) plunge the whole candle into a bucket of cool water for a glossy sheen on its surface. Then polish lightly.

Overdip with Colored Wax

If you want to overdip a white candle with color, or a colored candle with another color (or several colors) to achieve different and exciting effects, you will need a container for each color you plan to use. For example, if you wanted to dip a candle half in green and half in red for Christmas use, you would need two containers, plus the candle(s).

Overdipping in colored wax requires a large amount of wax, because you have to either submerge the candle entirely or do it by halves or sections. However, any leftover wax can always be reused another day and another dip.

ALERT

If your candles are not picking up sufficient color in two or three dips, your wax is too hot. If, on the other hand, the coating of colored wax is blemished, or scaly, the wax is too cool. Solution: Always use your thermometer and keep a close watch on it. And—always take notes.

Follow the instructions above for preparing to dip in clear wax and add the color or colors you want to use to each container. You will need to melt the wax in each container, so either do all of one color at once and then switch to the second, third, etc. colors in sequence; or, if you have the space and the equipment, you can set up more than one double-boiler for melting the wax for overdipping.

There are many interesting, dramatic, curious, fun effects to be made with overdipping. We'll explore these unusual types of candles in the following chapter.

CHAPTER 9

Introducing Unusual Candles

Now we arrive squarely in the territory of contemporary candle-making. In times past, *all* candles were unusual, so much superior to rush-lights, which had been used for centuries for lack of better options. And, once the wicked candle was invented, the most "unusual" candle was beeswax—ordinarily reserved for the Catholic Church's ceremonies, and available only to nobility and later the very wealthy.

A Most Unusual Candle!

Although candles as timekeepers were known and used until quite recently, the "candle clock" of the Islamic world stands out for its qualities of unusualness. As described by Al-Jazari, Islamic candle clocks worked on the following principle. Each design specified a large candle of a uniform cross section and known weight. So precise were these Islamic candlemakers that they even calculated the weight of the wick! The candle to be used as a clock was installed inside a metal sheath, to which a cap was fitted. The cap was fashioned to be absolutely level (flat) by turning it on a lathe. It was provided with a hole in the center, which on the upper side had an indentation around it.

The burning time of the candle was also known. As it burned, it bore against the underside of the metal cap and the wick passed through the hole. Wax collected in the indentation around the hold. Periodically, it was removed so that it did not interfere with the steady burning of the flame. The bottom of the candle was set in a shallow dish which had a ring on its side connected through pulleys to a counterweight. As the candle burned away, the weight pushed it upward at a constant rate. The automata were operated from the dish at the bottom of the candle. No other candle clocks of this sophistication are known. (*Source:* History of Sciences in the Islamic World: *http://home.swipnet.se/islam/articles/ HistoryofSciences.htm.*)

Progressive Candles

Next in Western candlemaking history, along came the whaling industry, and spermaceti was discovered and put to use for the next extraordinary candle—one that burned whiter, brighter, and odor-free. Now, *that* was unusual in a time when candles were generally made of tallow, which was difficult to render and nasty to work with. Lastly, after petroleum was discovered and taken out of its snug hiding place in the earth's depths, paraffin, a petroleum derivative, became the most unusual candle available. After that, with stearin, which hardened paraffin and made it opaque, most people thought candles had reached their pinnacle.

Creative Contemporary Candlemaking

But today with new additives and leisure time for hobbies (no Colonial woman would have thought of candlemaking as a hobby!), we are free to investigate the subject of unusual candles and how to create them. And we have the great good fortune to be nearly unlimited in our abilities to make these unusual candles. The materials are readily available at reasonable cost, and many of us have the free time to indulge ourselves in crafts and hobbies.

As there is such a wide range of unusual types of candles, and as we are going to cover some of the more specific, detailed ways of making all sorts of candles in the remaining portion of this book, you can consider this chapter to be an introduction to the making of unusual types of candles, as a basic step to the making of more complex, artistic, creative candles to be described in later chapters. For now, we are going to stick with the basics. Once you learn some of the simpler ways of making unusual candles, you will have a base of experience from which to move out into your own creative exploration of candlemaking.

You can purchase candlemaking kits that have preformulated wax for different purposes from some suppliers. Your local craft store probably also carries kits—mine does. (See list of suppliers, p. 69.) Be sure to tell your salesperson what kind of candle(s) you want to make.

We have discussed all of the basic candlemaking techniques in Chapters 5, 6, and 7. Any and all of these primary techniques lend themselves to making unusual types of candles. For example, the basic—and oldest we know—dipping method can be used to make the following types of tapers.

Danish Tapers

Danish tapers are simply smaller, thinner, dipped candles. There is a special wax available for making them, but if you can't find it, you can substitute one part stearic acid and one part plastic additive to every twenty parts of wax (usually paraffin). The addition of the stearic acid and the plastic additive makes a stronger Danish taper, which compensates for their smaller size and slenderness and prevents them from drooping in hot weather. It also increases their burn time.

Following the directions for making dipped candles (see Chapter 8), make the Danish taper in the same way as you made the regular taper. You can also overdip your Danish tapers in a colored wax. If you choose to overdip your Danish tapers in a coating of colored wax, curve the taper slightly before dipping it into the water bath.

Making Taper Trees from Danish Tapers

You can fashion charming taper trees from newly made Danish tapers. Simply dip four or more of these miniature taper candles and lay them on a clean surface (wax paper is good). Then, taking two tapers at a time, firmly squeeze them together about a third of the way from the bottom until they adhere to one another. Now, dip the bottom parts in hot wax a few times until they hold firmly together. Next, holding the two joined tapers at the bottom, dip them into cold water to cool. This will allow the new wax to set and prevent the tapers from drooping.

Repeat this procedure with the second set of two Danish tapers. Then, after you have dipped the bottoms of the second pair in hot wax and set the shape in a cold water dunk, hold the two sets together firmly and dip them into the hot wax until they adhere securely, repeating the cold water bath. If you wish, you can add a third or fourth pair of Danish tapers to your taper tree, although that's a bit trickier to manage.

Cutout Tapers

You can make cutout tapers from regular taper candles fairly easily. Do this by dipping your taper in one color of wax until it is approximately ½" in diameter (or, depending on the size of the finished candle, thicker). Next, dip the taper into a second color until you have built up the wax to another ½" thickness (or more).

You can make a simple two-color cutout taper by cutting through the outer layer of colored wax with a sharp knife, incising any design that suits your fancy—such as squares, triangles, circles, or flower shapes. Or, you can make a multicolored cutout taper by continuing to dip the taper into different colors of wax (you will need a separate container for each color) until you have built up several layers of different colors. This will make a thicker taper than the usual. Then, using the same procedure, cut through the colored layers so that all of the different colors show through.

Don't make the cuts in your cutout candle too deep—if you cut too far into the core, the candle will tend to droop when the flame reaches the incised parts. Starting with a thick taper and using fairly thin outer coatings will help prevent this problem.

Birthday Candles

There's nothing more charming than handmade birthday candles. Birthday candles can be made in several different ways. The simplest is to merely dip an extra-small wick (15-ply or smaller) in the same way you dip a regular taper. However, their short length makes dipping them in pairs an ineffective way of producing them.

A second method of making birthday candles by dipping is to dip the wick in the same manner as if you were making a long taper. Once the candles have accumulated enough wax to reach the required diameter (usually $^3/_{16}$"), you can carefully cut the long candle into short sections, while it is still warm. Trim away the wax from the top ½" of each section to expose the wick.

Birthday Drawing

A third method of making birthday candles involves melting the wax in a container with a large surface, such as a baking pan (9" × 9" or larger). Using a yard (36") of wick, pull it through the melted wax, from one end to the other, repeatedly until you have accumulated the desired amount of wax on the wick. Though a form of dipping, this process is known as "drawing," as you literally draw the wick through the wax.

As you draw the wick through the wax bath, wait a few minutes in between each dipping to allow the newly added wax to cool a bit—but make certain you re-dip while the wax-coated wick is still warm enough to be pliable (or it won't "draw" through the melted wax). When you have reached the desired diameter, snip the long wick/candle into short lengths, trimming the top of each about ¼" to expose the wick so the candles can be easily lit.

Long in the Candle

The usual length of a birthday candle is 3", but if you like, you can make taller birthday candles, which will burn a bit longer. Depending on the age of the person for whom the birthday candles are being made, this is sometimes a good idea. You don't want the candles on the cake to go out on their own before the birthday person gets to blow them out! Also, if you want to carry in a cake with its candles already lit—a spectacular presentation!—having taller, longer-burning candles can prevent them from going out during the trip from the kitchen to the dining room.

Making Wax Matches

Called "vestas," in honor of the Roman goddess of the hearth and fire, Vesta, wax matches are a real boon to the person who lights many candles at one time. They are also great for lighting pillars which have already been used and therefore have a deep well in them. If you've already tried to light a used pillar with an ordinary kitchen match and either had it go out or burned your fingers holding it inside the well to ignite the wick, you will appreciate wax matches.

Vestas are not difficult to make. Follow the basic dipping method (given in Chapter 8). Note, however, that you will need only enough wax for two to four dips. Use a medium size wick.

QUESTIONS?

What's a vesta?
A vesta is simply a wick coated with fewer layers of wax than a birthday candle. Usually two to four coatings will suffice, depending on the wax formula you are using. Beeswax, for example, being thicker, will take fewer coatings to produce a satisfactory vesta.

You can make your vestas at regular taper length for long wax matches, or if you want shorter ones you can snip the finished wick/candle and trim the tops to expose the wick for lighting. Vestas make unusual gifts (many people have never even seen one) and can be made in colors as well as in white. You can even take two warm vestas and twist them together into a candy shape if you want to get more unusual. These can be of either a single color or of two colors. Try tying a bundle of vestas together with a raffia ribbon and bow for a charmingly rustic gift package. Vestas are a wonderful reminder of the past, when they were in regular use before matches were invented.

To use a vesta, simply light it with a match and then carry it to the candles you wish to light. Keep a supply of vestas in your candle drawer. They come in extremely handy if the power fails as you don't have to go about the house lighting candles with a box of matches in your hand. A vesta not only lights your candles, it lights your way in the dark!

Making Glow-Through Candles

Another unusual candle you can make easily is the "glow-through" candle. This is basically just a block candle (see the section on milk cartons in Chapter 7), made from pure paraffin with no additives, overdipped in colored wax. As the candle burns and makes a well in the center, the flame glows through the outer shell of color, giving a lovely effect that is interesting and beautifully warm-looking, like a light shining through a window seen from outside.

Make It So

To make a glow-through candle, first make a regular block candle—any size in any type of mold (milk cartons are the easiest and simplest molds for block candles of many sizes). After the block candle has cooled thoroughly, remove it from the mold. (If you are using a milk carton, you can simply peel it off.)

Next, holding the candle by the wick either with your fingers or with a pair of pliers, dip it into colored wax heated to about 190° Fahrenheit. Remember to always use your wax thermometer when heating/melting wax. (For a more detailed review, also see "Overdipping," p. 160.)

Dip the entire candle into the colored wax, swirling it around to melt off any rough edges and give it an even shape. Allow the overdipped candle to cool for a minute and then dip again. Always use a smooth in-and-out motion when dipping. Take care not to leave the candle in the hot wax too long. The first dip should be the longest. After that, you are building up layers of color and the subsequent dips should be shorter. Continue to dip and cool until you have a nice coating of the colored wax on the outside of the candle.

Rainbow Glow

Once you have mastered this process, you can move on to multicolored glow-through candles. If you want to try this, dip the entire candle first into a yellow wax four times. Then, dip two-thirds of the bottom into pink three times. Lastly, dip the lower third of the candle into blue three times. What happens is that the pink-over-yellow dip turns orange; the blue over pink turns purple. Then, when burned, these multicolored glow-through candles give off a soft and glowing light that is most pleasing to the senses.

Hand-Molded Candles

This is one of the most exciting—and simple—methods for making candles. The creative possibilities of making unusual candles with hand-molded wax are practically limitless. With a little wax and a lot of imagination, you can create most unusual candles by hand-molding. It's just like working with modeling clay. Hand-molding is particularly good for children's projects, because it requires a minimum of coordination while at the same time stimulates kids' creative juices.

For hand-molded wax, you will need a soft, interior wax—such as paraffin alone—and a harder exterior wax, such as paraffin with stearin or micro-hard (see p. 104). To prepare wax for hand-molding, melt the *interior* wax in your double-boiler system over low heat, stirring frequently. When wax reaches its melting point, pour it into a mixing bowl and stir gently until it is cool to the touch.

While you are doing this, have your *exterior* wax melting in the double-boiler system. When the wax in the mixing bowl is cool enough to handle, begin to press it into any shape you like—a ball, a figurine, a freeform shape. (Pay no attention to imperfections in your hand-molded form.) Poke a hole through the middle of the candle while it is still warm, using a skewer or wicking needle. Now, leave it to get completely cold and hard.

SSENTIALS

If you live in the United States, a good source for beeswax is through your local Agricultural Extension Office. The Agricultural offices keep a listing of local beekeepers, because bees are in demand by farmers. Through them, you should find many beekeepers to contact.

After the candle has cooled completely, thread it with a wick that has been primed (see p. 73), tying a knot in the bottom end, or base, of the candle. Make sure your knot is large and secure so that when you overdip into the exterior wax it won't slip off the wick. Trim excess wick from the knot. Leave the wick at the top end of the candle about 2" long.

If you are going to use colored wax for your overdipping, add the colorant and stir thoroughly until it is dissolved and evenly distributed throughout the wax. Dip the hand-molded candle into the overdipping wax smoothly and quickly. Have a drip-tray ready to hold the dipped candle over while it cools for two minutes. Repeat the dipping process three times. Then allow the candle to cool completely. If you wish to decorate your candle, see Chapter 14, "Surface Techniques for Decorating Candles."

Special Waxes for Hand-Molding

Molding wax is a combination of paraffin, stearin, perhaps a little beeswax, and/or colorant. You can purchase it ready-mixed, or make it yourself to use for overdipping.

Modeling wax is a mixture of equal amounts of bleached beeswax and paraffin with or without colorant. This mixture can be purchased ready-mixed, or you can make it at home.

Unusual Rolled Beeswax Candles

If you can find a good, inexpensive supply of beeswax from a beekeeper, you might want to experiment with rolling beeswax candles into unusual shapes. Experiment with cutting the sheet diagonally—this will produce a spiral effect in the finished candle. If you get beeswax sheets that have aged into a darker color along with newer ones of a lighter color, you can cut two together on the diagonal, one slightly larger than the other, which will give you the result of a striped spiral effect—interesting yet attractively understated. (See Chapter 6, "Handmade Rolled and Poured Candles" to refresh your memory about how to make rolled candles.)

Beaded Candles

The shape and size of paraffin wax beads makes them ideal for creating an unusual candle. Following the instructions for molded candles, first wick up your mold. Then seal the opening with mold seal. Fill the mold loosely with wax pellets. *Do not pack them tightly—you need the airspace.* The idea here is that when you pour the melted wax over the pellets it will penetrate the spaces between them.

Heat your wax mixture (use stearin for this) along with any other additives such as dye or scent (see Chapter 10, "Shape, Color, and Fragrance") until melted to the correct melting point for your wax formula.

Pour the melted mixture into your mold, tipping the mold if necessary so that the liquid wax will run into the crevices of the wax pellets in the mold. Let the wax settle a bit and then pour on more, if needed.

When sufficiently cooled, remove the mold seal and slide the candle out. (Don't forget to use mold release.) The effect of the inner beading is quite dramatic. For something really unusual, experiment with different colors.

ESSENTIALS

To make unusual candles, you needn't use or go to the trouble of dipping. Use the pour method and make many unusual candles just by choosing oddly shaped or interesting-looking containers. Try seashells (an abalone shell is spectacular!), discarded cans of any kind, glasses, vases, pots, pans, jars.

Surface Mottling

The simple addition of oil to a candle's wax will create an interesting textured surface. The mottling that results will produce a random design on the surface of the candle. Exactly what kind of mottling result you get will depend on the percentage and type of oil you use. The best oil for mottling a candle's surface is one that is light and odorless (although you can use scented oil). Mineral oil (usually sold in drugstores as a laxative) will work well, as will any vegetable oil.

To make a mottled-surface candle, add the oil to the melted wax just before you pour. For a translucent effect, add 1 to 2 percent of the wax's volume in oil. For crystalline shapes on the surface of the candle, increase the percentage of the oil in the wax's volume to 3 to 5 percent.

After you have poured the candle, *do not cool it in water*. It is the wax cooling slowly that allows the oil to create the mottling effect. The surface will appear to be irregular but actually it will be smooth. After you take the candle out of the mold, you need to wipe the oil off the surface with a soft and absorbent cloth. Wipe the mold clean as well. Polish the finished candle with nylon pantyhose.

Unusual Molds

You can buy any number of fancy molds in a vast range of shapes (see Chapter 7, "Molded Candles"). However, you can also make many unusual candles from improvised molds, such as terra cotta flowerpots. Conveniently, these already have a hole at the bottom for the wick! If you have any lying around the potting shed, wash and dry them thoroughly before using. Or, purchase new ones at your garden center. They come in a wide variety of sizes and shapes and are quite inexpensive. And, if you don't break them, they are infinitely reusable.

Remember that you have to fill the hole in the flowerpot with mold seal before you begin to pour the wax. Follow the basic directions for making molded candles on p. 118.

Holy Moly!

Once you begin to look around for molds in which you can make unusual candles, your imagination will be ignited. Not only flowerpots, but old tin cans, Bundt cake pans, coconut shells, seashells (available in bulk at craft stores)—practically anything that has a hollow center—can be used to make unusual candles.

Great Glassware

As I was working on this section, I received my monthly catalog from the Vermont Country Store, one of my favorite places to shop. They carry all sorts of old-fashioned items that have long since gone out of stock in most stores. On one page I found a huge collection of glassware that would be perfect for container candles.

There are old-time jelly glasses, such as restaurants used to use, in six different sizes, shapes, and colors—green and sapphire as well as clear. Tall, short, squat, footed, these are all inspiring. Another glassware offered is heavy-duty footed ware, which would stand up under a melting candle.

Yet a third variety perfect for container candles is another restaurant-quality, i.e., heat-tempered, glass made originally for use in diners. These come in three sizes: diner juice glass, diner beverage glass, and diner iced tea glass. Best of all, these glasses (sold in sets of six) run from $2.50 to $3.50 each.

Another item that intrigued me as a future container for candles is the "Jelly Glass Bowl," which holds 14 ounces. These come with plastic lids (great for gift giving—just put on the lid and tie a ribbon around it) and are listed as dishwasher-safe, which means candle-burning safe.

To reach the Vermont Country Store for a catalog, call (802) 362-8440, or visit their Web site at *www.vermontcountrystore.com.*

Unusual Candles Made with Large Molds

You can make unusual candles with large molds, such as milk cartons, or any other large mold, such as a food tin (large juice cans are good), waxed cracker boxes, etc.

Once you have finished your large molded candle, melt some wax and slowly pour it over the finished candle so that it drips down the sides. Let the first pouring cool a bit, and then pour some more, letting it drip over the first layer. You can do this as much as you like for whatever effect you want.

Multiwick Candles

These are quite unusual and fairly new to my knowledge. Today I see them advertised in many mail-order catalogs of the upscale variety—that is, the pricey ones! However, you can make multiwicked candles from large molded candles quite easily. Using the hardened-candle wicking process described on p. 127, simply poke two, three, or more holes in your molded large candle and run wicks through them, knotting each one securely at the bottom and trimming flat.

You can multi-wick a candle of any shape—square, rectangular, cylindrical, round; tall or short. These burn prettily, though at a bit quicker burn rate than a single wick candle. But, you will have used more wax on the large mold candle, so it makes up for the burn time rate. Multiwick candles are impressive when placed individually or in groups, and they are good for outdoor use when you want a lot of candlelight in a small space, such as on an outdoor dining table.

Chunk or Chip Candles

Another use for ice-cube trays is to make little chunks of wax, especially from leftover colored wax that you only have a little of. Once you've collected a bunch of different colored chunks, you can make some really unusual candles.

Chip candles

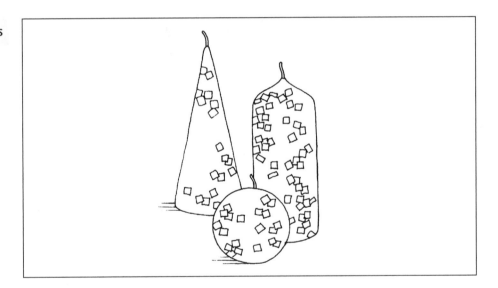

You can use plastic ice cube trays for saving leftover wax and making it into chunks. Just pour in what you have, a different color in each little section, and let harden. When you have a bunch of them, you can make chunk candles. You can also use candle ends you have saved for this purpose.

ESSENTIALS If you don't have candle leftovers, you can easily make chunks—just like making fudge. Pour your melted wax into a shallow pan, let it cool, and then cut it into chunks with your sharp knife. Proceed as above.

All you have to do is to put some chunks in a mold—milk cartons are great for this as are food cans—and pour clear melted wax over the chunks, filling in all the spaces. (This may take more than one pouring.)

Making a
chip candle

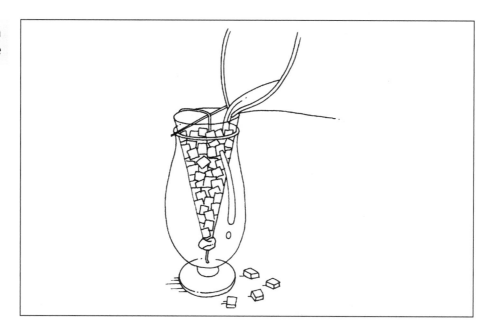

When you take the candle out of the mold, you'll be surprised at the effect you have achieved! There's no limit—use one color of chunks, or two, or a dozen. Indulge both your fantasy and your leftovers.

 For a marbled effect, pour a lighter colored wax over darker chunks. You might try white over black, for example. Pale green over dark green will give a Travertine marble effect. As always, you are advised to use your imagination and experiment.

Dripped Dipped Candles

Years ago in New York, rustic Italian restaurants, typically with red-checkered tablecloths, always had a candle on the table in a basket-covered wine bottle that had an enormous buildup of drippings from successive candles burned in it. You can get this unusual effect as well. To do this, deliberately use a wick that is too small for the candle's diameter. This will cause it to drip. Ordinarily, of course, you don't want a drippy candle. But if you are striving for an unusual effect, this is a great way to go.

After making the candle(s), dip each one successively into red, blue, and green wax—three dips each. In between each dip, cool the candle with a water bath. After the red, blue, and green dips, make four dips in yellow wax and then four dips in ivory wax. (Remember, you will need a different dipping can for each color. You can use fewer colors if you prefer to simplify this process.)

After all the colored dips, while the candle is still warm from the last dip, press all around it with your fingertips (use your thumbs) to make indentations. Give the candle a final cold water bath to cool it.

Lastly, after it is cold, take a sharp knife and core the base in a circle about 1" from the bottom. Pull off the colored part of the wax so that the original taper end will fit into the holder (use a wine bottle for the Italian-restaurant effect described above). Whatever holder you use will be permanently dripped with wax, so don't use your best sterling silver!

A simpler way of making this dripped dipped candle is by the same method as described above for the large molded candle. Simply pour the different colors of melted wax slowly over the candle (in its holder) and let them drip down the sides over each other. This is messier, but it requires much less wax.

CHAPTER 10

Shape, Color, and Fragrance

Wax is an extremely malleable and flexible substance. In the warm stage it can be hand-molded into an infinite variety of shapes. In the liquid stage, it can be poured into an equally infinite number of molds. In addition, wax can be carved into a multitude of shapes, limited only by the expertise of the candlemaker and his or her imagination and artistic sensibility.

Infinite Variety

Candle shapes are as varied as are the shapes of all natural and man-made objects—you can make a candle the shape of a tin can, or the shape of a banana. You can mold, carve, sculpt wax into figurines, flowers, fruits, and any number of other shapes to suit your fancy.

At Christmas, candlemakers make the usual decorations— Santa Clauses, Christmas trees, wreaths, baubles, etc. You can simulate just about anything with candle wax for just about any occasion or purpose you wish.

In this chapter, we are going to discuss what you can do with the *basic* shapes such as the cylinder, block, square, etc., and provide detailed instructions for making them. In addition, we are going to show you how to make some more complex—yet still fairly simple—shapes.

Wax Works

You can make candle shapes from all the methods of making candles that you have learned so far—dipping, molding, using sheet wax, etc. Of course, candles made in containers take on the shape of the container. Many objects used for making container candles will also serve as molds if you like a particular shape for that purpose.

Sheet wax is probably the simplest method for making a variety of shapes with little effort. Next in ease comes hand-molding.

Purchased sheets of embossed beeswax, for example, can be rolled into numerous shapes other than the plain taper or square, as we have already shown. (Refer back to the section on rolled beeswax candles in Chapter 6.)

Once you have made a plain rolled taper, you can bend and squeeze it into different shapes. You can also join two or more tapers together (see "Making Taper Trees from Danish Tapers," p. 168) to make interesting shapes. If you buy beeswax sheets in various colors, you can fold one or more sheets together so that your candle's shape displays the colors of the wax. For example, you can lay two different colored sheets of beeswax one on top of the other, and roll on the diagonal. Since beeswax is soft and sticky, it is easy to roll and mold into interesting shapes.

Gentle Beeswax

With beeswax sheets, you can stick to simple, basic shapes—such as the taper and spiral—or you can be as creative as you want. As beeswax is malleable at room temperature (in a fairly warm room), you can make these rolled candles easily and in many shapes—as complicated as you like. You can cut the sheets into strips of color and wind these around a basic taper to make parts of it thicker or thinner as well as adding different colors to the shape. With the same method, you can quite easily create spirals, diamonds, cones, pyramids, and other shapes.

To make a cone, simply roll the beeswax sheet into a cone shape. To make an *ice-cream cone* using a beeswax cone made from a sheet of beeswax, simply add a "scoop" of hand-molded wax that has been sculpted into a round shape. It needn't be smooth—just as a scoop of real ice cream is not perfectly round. This is a wonderful project to do with children, who get a big thrill out of lighting their "ice-cream cones." It's great for a child's birthday party, or as favors for any occasion. Even adults love getting an ice-cream cone candle!

Blending Waxes for Molding

If you require a certain melting point for wax and it is unavailable in a preformulated mix, you can combine the characteristics of two waxes by blending them. Blending two or more waxes together will ordinarily provide you with a combination of their individual characteristics. For example, if you blend equal amounts of 128° Fahrenheit melting point wax and 145° melting point wax, the end product will have approximately the same characteristics and melting point as 135° melting point wax would have. Another example is that if you blend microcrystalline wax with a low melting point wax, the resulting blend will be sticky and thus better suited for hand-forming.

Should you decide a blend is what you need, simply study the types of waxes until you find one with the characteristics you wish your base wax to exhibit. Add this wax to your base wax, experimenting with small batches until you achieve the right combination. The easiest way to do this is to blend several batches in different proportions at the same time. Then, after the blends (be sure to label each one with the proportions of what you used) have cooled and hardened, you can determine which is best for your purpose. Do keep records in your notebook if you choose to use this blending technique. There is, as always, much trial-and-error involved in home candlemaking, especially when you are making different shapes and getting creative.

ESSENTIALS Some fruit shapes are also very easy to make with hand-molding, such as apples, pears, oranges, and the like. Hand-molded wax lends itself to many applications in terms of making different shapes. We will discuss these more fully in the coming chapters on advanced candlemaking.

Basically Interesting

For now, let's stick with the basic shapes and show you how to extrapolate on these to make many different—though easy and simple—interesting shapes.

Simple Circles

As you already know, round tin cans come in all sizes. These make splendid molds for creating unusual shapes of candles. From a slender tomato-paste can to a 32-ounce fruit juice can, round shapes are many and varied. You can use simple round or cylindrical shapes to mold candles, then glue these candles together with wax glue (or by a little judicious melting or overdipping) to create interesting shapes. For example, I created a wedding-cake shape from baking pans—of exactly the same sort one would use to make a real wedding cake! It was a simple matter of making several round shapes in several heights of differing diameters and layering them. Such a shaped candle can be decorated in several ways—one of them, the dripping method, is discussed on p. 180. Other ways of decorating candles will be discussed in further chapters.

Square Deal

After cylinders, squares or rectangles are probably the most versatile basic shape from which to create other shapes. Like tin cans, square shapes can be obtained in many sizes and diameters, from half-pint whipping cream containers to half-gallon milk cartons. Food storage containers also come in square shapes—half-pint, pint, quart—that are useful for making this basic shape.

Square or rectangular candles can be put together to make new shapes, using a variety of sizes and candle glue. One extremely interesting—yet actually simple—idea that I created was a castle! A few large squares for the base, a few cylinders for the turrets were all that was needed.

Incidentally, cardboard tubes such as come inside rolls of paper towels, kitchen wraps, and toilet paper, make excellent shape-making molds and are useful in a variety of ways in combination. For example, my castle tower was "fortified" with some tall candles made in cardboard tubes.

Cones

After cylinders and squares/rectangles, the next easiest shape to create is a cone. This can be done either with a purchased mold (cone molds come in various sizes), or it can be improvised with cardboard.

To improvise a cone shape, take a piece of stiff but flexible cardboard (the kind that is used as stiffener for photographs in the mail is ideal) and cut it into a square. Measure each side carefully so that you have a perfect square, or your cone will be lopsided. Then, just roll the square of cardboard into a cone shape. Tape it together securely (plastic strapping tape is good for this). Cut the large end of the cone so that it is level and flat. Then cut the tip off of the narrow end and glue this end to a piece of hard cardboard. This will be the base support for the cone. Make a hole in the base cardboard large enough to hold the cone's tip. Before pouring in your wax, wipe the inside of the cone with a little dishwashing liquid to act as a mold release and to prevent the hot wax from penetrating the cardboard.

You can make any size cone you like. However, if you make large cones you may not be able to use the cardboard-base support described above. If the cone is large, you will need to stand it in a container of some sort—such as a large glass—for proper support. In any case, be sure you have glued the cardboard base securely so that the hot wax doesn't drip out of the bottom end of the cone resting in its support vessel.

Cone-shaped molds are great for making chunk candles, as described in Chapter 9, p. 178. They are particularly nice when made with multicolored chips (or chunks).

To make a nice flat base for your cone-shaped candle, warm a baking tray in the oven slightly and then set it on a heat-resistant surface. Put the candle's base on the tray and push down gently. The heat from the baking tray will melt the candle's base evenly.

Identical Twins

Another method that is quite easy is to make two half-candles from the same mold (or two identical molds, such as custard cups or half-round bowls).

Play Ball!

To make a round spherical candle, use two half-round glass bowls for molds into which to pour the wax. With this method, you can quite easily make holes for the wick: While the wax is set but still warm in each half, join the two halves with the wick (previously primed by dipping in hot wax and cooling) between them, tying a secure knot at the end you have designated to be the bottom. After this, you can overdip the candle to hide the seam and give it a hard finish. In this basic way, you can make two halves of practically any shape and join them together to get a new shape.

Eggs-actly!

Egg-shaped candles can be molded in a plastic egg that screws apart in the middle to be filled with candies. You can purchase this type of plastic egg in many sizes during the Easter season.

To use these plastic eggs as molds, first take one apart and coat its inner surfaces with mineral oil (which works well as a mold release agent). With the point of an ice pick, or skewer, or very sharp knife heated over a candle flame, poke a hole in the center of the small end of the plastic egg cup. The hole should be large enough to accommodate the end of a small funnel—such as is used to fill perfume bottles.

Screw the plastic egg back together and stand it upright in something that will support it securely—a custard cup is good, or a small bowl, depending on the size of the plastic egg. Melt wax as directed in Chapter 6 and pour the melted wax through the funnel to fill the shell. Remove the funnel. Tie a metal weight to one end of a cord wick and drop it through the hole in the top of the shell. The weight will drop the wick through to the bottom of the mold.

After completing this procedure, set the entire mold in its container in the refrigerator until it is thoroughly cold and hardened. This will take several hours, depending on the size of the mold. Remove from the refrigerator and run hot tap water over the shell for a few seconds before taking it apart. Unscrew the two halves of the plastic egg, pulling them apart gently to release the egg-shaped candle inside. Smooth out the seam with a craft knife or other sharp knife, or melt it smooth with the flat side of a heated knife. You can overdip your egg-shaped candles in Easter egg pastel-colored wax and simulate real Easter eggs. Or, you can leave the candles white and decorate by painting. (See Chapter 13, "Surface Techniques for Decorating Candles.")

Improvise

A quick look around your house—kitchen, bath, living room—will give you many ideas of how to create different shapes using improvised molds you already have on hand. Obviously, molded candles can only be released out of a shape that has a top as large as its bottom, or that comes apart. But, wonderfully shaped containers that can be used to make container candles are all around you. Bowls, glasses, jars, cups, antique baking pans, oddly shaped vessels, cut glass pitchers, copper bowls and pans— the list is seemingly endless.

While not exactly a shape, you can make interesting overall shaped designs from an arrangement of candles on a tray or platter. Using one shape—such as a cylinder or a block—in a variety of sizes (and/or colors), you can make attractive "candlescapes" that have form. Also, try mixing several different shapes—tall slender blocks with short, fat cylinders, for example. Or, mix cones with blocks and/or cylinders. These candlescapes can be monotone or multicolored, constructed of one shape or several shapes.

You can also make fun shapes from gelatin molds—the fancier the better! And don't forget muffin tins. You can use muffin tins as two-part molds for a unique shape with a narrow bottom and a narrow top and a bulge in the middle. Ice-cube tray–made chunks can be threaded on wicks to make lots of varying shapes, like a spiral staircase or a building-block type of structure. A bit of candle glue and your imagination is all you need!

SSENTIALS

You can make your own molds for different shapes of candles from practically anything. (See the sections on moldmaking in Chapter 7.) Many objects lend themselves to this process, such as melons and hard-shelled squash. And you can purchase a wide variety of ready-made molds.

Using Color and Fragrance

One of the great joys of modern-day candlemaking is the use of color and fragrance. How glad we must be that the old days of "necessity," of making tallow candles that smelled of the barnyard, or worse, are over and done with.

Though today there are many perfumes manufactured in the United States, these are almost all made not from flower essences, but from chemicals that mimic them exactly. This marvel of chemistry is not only what put the distinctive odor of roses or lavender in our perfumes, toilet waters, lotions, and shampoos—it is the same as what puts the smell of beefsteak into the vegetable oil used to make the French fries of fast-food chain burger purveyors.

FACTS

Today's home candlemaker has available to her or him such a wide variety of color and fragrance as to rival the master painters of the past and the great perfume makers of Arabia, who invented the process of distilling essential oils from plants and flowers. The French raised this to a fine art through their development of *enfleurage*, the meticulous and extremely complex process of pressing the essence out of flowers.

Luckily, the *real* thing is still available to us in essential oils, about which more will be said later in this chapter.

Delightful Shades

First, however, we will delve into the fascinating subject of color for your candles. Anyone who has shopped for candles has already seen how many color possibilities are available to the consumer. Most of the commercial colors are fairly standard: red, green, blue, pink, orange, purple. The higher-priced lines of candles offer many more colors in more subtle shades, and the recent spate of upscale candle shops, which produce mail-order catalogs, offer such a great range of beautiful and subtle colors as to almost defy belief. "All the colors of the rainbow" have been multiplied to the nth degree.

As a home candlemaker, you have as many possibilities for coloring your candles as does an artist for mixing his or her palette. This is the area of candlemaking that you can have the most fun with as you experiment with the almost endless possibilities. Often, serendipity takes a hand and you accomplish something that you hadn't started out to do! These "happy accidents" deserve recording in your notebook.

Serendipity

Betty Oppenheimer describes one such incident in her highly recommended book, *The Candlemaker's Companion*. In "My Rosemary Story," she tells of her unique experience:

> Like many other people, I love the scent of fresh rosemary and decided to try my hand at adding this delightful fragrance to a batch of candles. Once my wax was melted and 20° above its melting point, I added fresh sprigs from my garden and let the mixture steep for hours.
>
> My house was filled with the smell of the herb and I eagerly anticipated burning the tapers I made with the wax. Imagine my disappointment when I lit my first rosemary candle and discovered all its scent had dissipated in the infusion. However, the wax was a beautiful shade of sage green.
>
> Ah, well, you just never know until you try.

Try, Try Again

This charming story illustrates the always-prevalent trial-and-error component of candlemaking. It's what makes it such a challenge and such an entertainment! Without these little unpredictable delights (and, yes, sometimes disappointments), our home candlemaking might be dull instead of exciting. Who wants to always have a perfectly predictable result? There she was, looking for a particular scent and getting instead a gorgeous, subtle color. Now, I call that a happy accident! (And plus, sage is my own favorite color, and I appreciated the tip on how to achieve it.)

Professional Coloring

In commercial, factory-scale candlemaking operations, coloring is done with different methods than are available to the home candlecrafter. This is not a bad thing, as commercial operations use solvents. For example, much coloring in large-scale candlemaking is done with powdered dyes that are dissolved in xylene solvent. I've never come in contact with xylene solvent, but I'm sure I'd not like to have it around my house!

These dye powders are so concentrated that, in many instances, a mere pinch will color several pounds of wax. In addition, these commercial dyes are so finely ground that the workers must wear protective masks over their noses and mouths—or even a respirator—to prevent them from inhaling the dye dust. Therefore, they would be a real danger to the home candlemaker. Fortunately, they aren't available for public consumption.

Colorants at Home

On the other hand, aniline dyes are available, and this is what many professional candlemakers prefer for colorants. They are the best options for the home candlecrafter because they come already prepared as chips, disks, or even blocks. These can be dissolved in your melted wax. And, you can add color bit by bit (or chip by chip) so that you don't overdo and find yourself with a pot of wax of a more intense color than you had intended to create. Always err on the side of caution when adding color chips or disks to your melted wax.

You can purchase a product called "ultraviolet inhibitor," usually only through a candle-craft supplier rather than at your local craft shop, which helps to prevent candle colors from fading. My own opinion on the matter is that the fewer chemicals we come in contact with the better off we are!

And—I know this is getting repetitive but it cannot be emphasized too much—*keep records in your notebook.* You may one day stumble upon that absolutely perfect color and in your excitement make your candles but then fail to record exactly how many chips of which colors you used to what proportion of which waxes. Later on, when you want to duplicate that color, you won't remember exactly how you obtained it.

Not Fade Away . . .

It's important for you to realize that all colored candles will fade over time. Some colors will fade more readily than others. Darker, primary colors, like red, fade less than pastels like pink.

The best way to keep your candles from fading is to store them carefully wrapped, in a dark place, such as a drawer or closet, and always keep them away from direct sunlight. Since it is time that is the main culprit, it only makes sense to burn your candles before they begin to fade. If you allow them to age, they will fade—and candles aren't fine wine, which benefits by aging. They are of a certain fragility and delicacy, and you are making them to *use*, not to store away like heirloom lace. An unused candle may look attractive sitting on display for a while—but it will become dusty and attract dirt from the air, and its colors will fade eventually. So, candlemaker, burn your art! It's the only way to go.

Scents, too, will dissipate with age, so if you want that wonderful perfumed odor to permeate the room when you light up your candles for a soothing aromatherapy bath or for a festive party, use them while they are fresh.

Mix and Match

In using color chips or disks purchased from your supplier, you are not limited by the colors provided. You can blend and mix your own to achieve any shade you like. With a bit of practice and a color chart (available at art stores), you can create a veritable artist's palette.

Paint stores provide free color cards, which give you a visual indication of how much color to white (in this case, white wax) you need to get almost any shade of almost any color. These are excellent guides to have around. You can also use them to make notes on for future reference.

Remember that you are starting with white, not with color. So, for example, just a smidge of blue in white wax will give an Easter egg–blue pastel. A tiny bit of red added will result in a lovely lavender pastel. For full-blooded colors, such as bright orange, you want to blot out the white base with color.

You can purchase a whitener that will make the dyes opaque (or whiter), for use in making pastel-colored candles. When deciding how much dye of which color to use, remember to take into account the color of your wax and its opacity. Also bear in mind whether your candle is going to be made of translucent wax (usually pure paraffin). This will make a big difference to the final color when the candle is burned. Pastel *and* translucent is a lovely combination for a candle.

**SSENTIALS**

To test the color you have mixed, dip the end of a long, tall block of wax into the colored wax. Allow it to cool completely, then judge the final result. Always remember to add color only in small amounts. You can always increase the intensity.

Blending Basic Colors

Primary colors—red, yellow, blue—are blended to make secondary colors as shown:

red + yellow = orange
yellow + blue = green
blue + red = purple

You can vary the proportions of the primary colors to achieve different shades of the secondary colors, such as a lemon yellow, a mint green, or a lilac or lavender shade of purple. Adding a bit of black will darken the color, but be careful and go extra slowly with black or it can muddy the result.

A Guide to Mixing Colors

White—No color needed
Red—Red color chip

ESSENTIALS

Red seems to be the most powerful—and it can be overpowering—of dyes. Adding red to any mixture will often result in a red-brown color. Recycled blends of used colors of wax (candle ends, leftovers) that have red in them will ordinarily turn out with a reddish cast, even if red is not the largest proportion of color in your mixture.

Cherry red—Red color chip with a small bit of yellow
Pink—Small piece of red color chip; start with only a bit and then increase until you get the shade of pink you want
Wine red—Combine a red color chip, or a part of one, with a bit of blue; again, go slowly
Dusty rose—Start with half a red chip and a quarter of a blue chip; add more red if you want a rosier shade
Yellow—Yellow color chip
Lemon yellow—Start with a quarter of a chip and slowly add more bit by bit until you achieve the color you desire; a rich lemon might also benefit from just a touch of red, but only a hint
Orange—Use one yellow chip and one red chip; try this mixture first and then vary the proportion of yellow to red to achieve the exact shade of orange you want
Tangerine—Use the same formula as above, but increase the proportion of red to yellow—slowly
Blue—Blue color chip
Light blue—Small piece of blue color chip; add more until you achieve the desired result
Dark blue—Blue color chip with a very small piece of black
Green—One blue chip and one yellow chip

Light green—Use less color in the same proportion—half a yellow and half a blue; experiment until you get the shade you like (see "My Rosemary Story" above)

Mint green—Use part blue and part yellow in small amounts, starting with blue and adding yellow until you get the shade you had in mind

Turquoise—Use one blue chip and then add yellow slowly in small amounts until you achieve the shade desired

Purple—One blue chip and one red chip; check this shade and adjust the proportion of red and blue to achieve different hues of purple

Lavender or lilac—Use blue and red. Depending on the exact shade you are striving to achieve, start with either color and add the other until you have what you want.

Black—Black color chip

**SSENTIALS**

You probably won't want to make solid black candles very often, except for ritual purposes. Black is used in tiny amounts to darken other colors, but always use with care or you may ruin your batch.

Brown—Use yellow, blue, and red, in that order, starting with yellow and small amounts of blue and red

Honey—Use natural beeswax, or tint other waxes with yellow, adding just a small amount of blue and red. You can get many shades by using three colors, but go slowly.

Decorate, Don't Dye

If you are going to make a decorated candle, you won't need much dye. And, you can also conserve dye by overdipping. If you are going to overdip in color, you don't need the entire candle to be colored. The same applies to candles that are to be decorated. You may want an overdipped color behind your decorations, or you can just use white as a base.

A candle that is made to be decorated—either by painting, overdipping, adhering objects to its surface, and the like (candle decoration is discussed in detail in later chapters) is called a "core candle." Your core candle can be plain white—you can then color your wax paints in rich, bold colors, make vivid wax sheets for cutouts, and use bright colors for overdipping.

Using Leftover Colored Wax

Chances are you'll always have some colored wax left over. It takes a large amount of wax to make dipped candles, and if you dip in solid color, you'll have a lot left. No matter how experienced you are, it's nearly impossible to melt exactly the amount of wax you will need in a particular color. Still, it is best to make colored wax in the smallest quantity possible for your purposes. And, choose colors that are easily reusable—pink can be turned to rose or red, lavender or purple. On the other hand, five pounds of blazingly bright magenta isn't what you'd call versatile. Of course, if your leftover wax is white, you are home free.

Colorants not made for coloring candles often will clog up the wick's ability to burn its fuel. Using lipsticks, for example, isn't a good idea. Oil paints used for fine arts are not recommended. Any of these products can cause your candle to burn badly.

Making Sense of Scents

Originally, the only scented candles were those made of a wax that was naturally scented—beeswax smells of honey, and bayberry wax smells of, well, bayberries, a unique fragrance. Today's scented candles run the gamut of known fragrances—from floral to spicy. Among those available is everything from scents we associate with the flower garden to those that recall to us the smell of different foods—the fragrance of fruits such as citrus and homey cinnamon-and-apple smell of a freshly baked apple pie. With today's flourishing business in chemical fragrances (though some of these are declared to be "natural" on the labels of products that contain them, they are nonetheless derived by a chemical process), you can scent your home or office in many ways, ranging from the commercial "air freshener" products to completely natural herb and/or flower potpourris.

Candlemaking certainly takes advantage of the variety of scents available for use. Generally speaking, you can purchase a variety of common scents from your craft store. These are known in the trade as "industrial odorants," and are synthetic derivatives. Still, they smell good, and it's sometimes difficult to tell the difference between a "real" fragrance—one made from an actual flower, plant, or herb—and a synthetically produced scent.

The perfume industry is also a source of fragrances that can be used to scent candles. There are concentrates of basic fragrances available and some blends that are licensed. When using scents of any kind, be sure they are oil-based (wax is an oil). Alcohol-based scents will simply evaporate on contact with the hot wax.

Using Potpourri for Scenting Candles

One source of candlemaking techniques suggests using potpourri for scenting candles by rolling the still-warm candle in the potpourri so that a layer of the leaves, flower petals, or whatever the potpourri is composed of, adheres to the candle. Then, the candle is overdipped to fix the potpourri bits to its surface. The possible problem here is that as the candle burns it might burn the plant material, producing an odor other than what was intended. However, if the candle is of large diameter and the overdip is made from a hard wax, this probably will not happen.

Never use basic potpourri "refresher" oils in a candle-wax mixture. The oils will change the balance of the wax formulation. One method of adding fragrance to candles is to soak the wick in essential oil prior to pouring the wax.

Combining Color with Scent

Clearly there are many color-scent combinations. Some of these are quite obvious—white or ivory with vanilla, for example. To get you started, here are a few suggestions about combining colors with scents:

White—Gardenia, lily of the valley
Red or pink—Rose, tea rose, carnation, geranium
Yellow—Honeysuckle, lemon, freesia
Orange—Citrus
Blue—Hyacinth
Green—Mint, herbs like tarragon, dill, eucalyptus
Purple or lilac—Lavender, violets, hyacinth
Brown—Clove, cinnamon, spices

Knowledge of the physiological and psychological effects of natural fragrances is the basis of aromatherapy, and scented candles are often used for aromatherapy.

All About Essential Oils

With the increasing popularity of aromatherapy, with various types of aromatherapy candles available for purchase, the essential oils are being used more and more. These are completely natural and readily available locally and from many Web sites, as well as from various mail-order sources that sell herbs and other natural health products. They are well worth your attention and investigation, not only for the pleasant scents they can provide for your candles, but also for the therapeutic possibilities they offer.

Many excellent books are available on the fascinating subject of essential oils. You can obtain a detailed listing of essential oils, descriptions, Latin names, the part of the plant used, and the country where the oil is produced, at *www.halcyon.com/kway/details*. Another useful source of information is *www.aromaweb.com*. This site will provide information about where to buy essentials, allow you to look up books, contact experts, and gives lots of tips for beginners. The advice here is straightforward and no-nonsense—written by real people who know their stuff, not by manufacturers or someone trying to sell you something.

A History of Essential Oils

How, one might wonder, is it possible to extract those tiny droplets we call "essential oils" from the bulk of the plant material? And how can these extracted oils be stored?

Considering this secret was known some 5,000 years ago in Egypt, it seems quite odd that it has been so often "lost" through the ages and has had to be rediscovered.

Archaeologists discovered distillation devices in Mesopotamia, circa 5,000 B.C., and Egypt was using essential oils as early as 4,000 B.C. The most frequently used oils in that ancient era were distilled from cedar and other conifers, cinnamon, lily, dill, basil, and coriander—all plants still familiar to us today. Used for healing as well as cosmetic purposes—and for ritual ceremonies—essential oils were known in Babylon, India, and China. After their conquest of the Egyptian empire, the Romans incorporated the knowledge of essential oils into their culture.

However, there are no records suggesting that essential oils were used after the fall of the Roman Empire. They reappeared at the end of the tenth century in Arab countries where physicians used them to treat patients. It is believed that the famous Arabian physician who went by his European name of Avicenna (980–1037) rediscovered the method for extracting the precious oils from plants. Later, after their conquest of Spain, the Moors taught the art of extracting essential oils at universities in Spain, which they founded. However, with the ouster of the Arabs from Spain, essential oils once again fell into disuse.

Ironically, the first major indication of the antiseptic properties of essential oils in Europe came from the fact that perfumers—who handled the oils daily as part of their profession—were seemingly immune to the plague known as the "Black Death" and to the epidemics of cholera that periodically swept Europe during the Middle Ages. By the late seventeenth century, the oils were back in use, primarily for medicinal purposes.

Toward the end of the nineteenth century, scientific inquiries into the antibacterial properties of plants began to clarify the chemical composition and potential healing powers of essential oils, which work on a molecular level, benefiting the chemical makeup of our organisms. Alas, and as usual, instead of this discovery leading to an increase in the use of essential oils, scientists attempted to mimic their properties in order to create synthetic chemical substitutes.

It was the work of a French chemist, René-Maurice Gattefossé in the early 1900s that brought renewed interest to this form of healing. Considered the "father of modern aromatherapy," Dr. Gattefossé coined the term *aromatherapy* when he used it as the title of a book he published in 1937. He was especially interested in the medicinal aspects of essential oils.

During World War II, another French physician, Dr. Jean Valnet, who had been much impressed with Gattefossé's findings, used essential oils in the treatment of wounds received by soldiers in wartime Europe. He used the oils to disinfect and heal, and in turn published a book, translated into English as *The Practice of Aromatherapy: A Classic Compendium of Plant Medicines & Their Healing Properties.*

Fortunately, Dr. Valnet was interested in teaching other physicians the medical uses of essential oils and, as a result, there are today more than a thousand physicians in France who use essential oils in their practices.

During the 1920s, Italian scientists conducted experiments with the *psychological* effects of essential oils. Two of them, Dr. Renato Cayola and Dr. Giovanni Garri, published an article in 1922 discussing the effects of essential oils on the nervous system. They had not only observed the bacteria-destroying capacities of the oils, but they had studied their stimulating and calming effects as well.

Another Italian, Professor Paolo Rovesti, at the University of Milan, conducted research on the psychological effects of essential oils, treating patients afflicted with depression and hysteria. He recommended a variety of combinations of the oils—for example, for depression he recommended combining jasmine, sandalwood, orange blossom, verbena, and lemon oil.

How Essential Oils Work

Today, people all over the world are paying attention to the healing effects of essential oils, and scientists are continuing to conduct research in an attempt to understand more about the effects of these amazing aromas on the human mind, body, and psychology.

Essential oils are extracted from the aromatic essences of certain plants, trees, fruits, flowers, herbs, and spices. Natural volatile oils, they have identifiable chemical and medicinal properties. At this point, over 150 have been extracted—and each has its own definitive scent and unique healing properties. Oils are produced from a wide range of plants—from the exotic jasmine to the garden-variety parsley. For optimum benefit, the oils must be extracted from natural raw ingredients with attention to purity. They must be stored in dark, tightly-stoppered glass bottles and kept away from light and heat in order to maintain their potency. They can be used individually or in combination.

Essential oils affect people through the sense of smell, which is the most potent of all the senses because the information is delivered straight to the hypothalamus. As moods, motivation, and creativity all stem from the hypothalamus, odors affect all of these processes. Think of a disgusting odor and how it can put you off at dinner—or think of a fragrance that brings back a pleasant memory of a loved one, and you'll get the idea of how intimately intertwined scents are with our emotions, memories, and ideas.

Despite considerable research, the chemistry of essential oils is not fully understood. Each oil—by current count—contains at least 100 different constituents, which are chemically classified. Not only that, scientists think there may be many other chemical compounds in essential oils, yet to be identified.

Thus, the oils and their actions are extremely complex. Not only are all of them antiseptic, but each also possesses individual properties. The collective qualities of each oil give it a dominant characteristic—stimulating, calming, energizing, relaxing. Essential oils have obvious psychological effects, and they also have notable physiological effects, which means that within the body they are able to operate in three ways: pharmacologically, physiologically, and psychologically. From the pharmacological perspective, the oils act like medicine by reacting with body chemistry, but with a slower and more sympathetic effect—and with fewer side effects.

ALERT

Handle essential oils carefully! Do not get essential oils directly on your skin. If accidentally ingested, get immediate medical help. Do not get essential oils in the eyes. Keep all oils away from children.

Some oils, like lavender, are known as *adaptogens*. As the name implies, these oils adapt to whatever condition needs assistance. In addition, certain oils have a particular affinity for different body parts— spice oils, for example, tend to benefit the digestive system. Finally, the psychological effect of essential oils is triggered by the connection the aromatic molecules make with the brain.

Those to Leave Alone

Not all natural plants and essential oils are beneficial. The following essential oils should *never* be used:

Bitter almond	Mustard	Tansy
Boldo leaf	Pennyroyal	Thuja
Calamus	Rue	Wintergreen
Horseradish	Sassafras	Wornseed
Jaborandi leaf	Savin	Wormwood
Mugwort	Southernwood	Yellow camphor

Source: *The Complete Book of Essential Oils and Aromatherapy* by Valerie Ann Worwood

Using Essential Oils to Scent Candles

Essential oils are volatile, which means that merely adding an essential oil to your wax mixture may not produce the strength of fragrance you expect when the candle is burning. One way to use essential oils to scent your candles is to soak the wick in the oil before pouring in the wax. Another is to add a drop or two of the oil to the pool of melted wax after the candle has been burning for a while. This is the same principle as the aromatherapy "diffuser," which is a small cup or indentation under which a small candle is lit, such as a votive or tealight. The heat from the candle releases the constituents of the oil into the air where they produce the results through the olfactory system.

Commercially prepared candle scents contain fixatives and stabilizers to make the fragrance last while the candle burns. Most of these products are synthetic, and so the person in search of a natural alternative usually turns to the essential oils, or to herbs and flowers from the garden.

One candlemaker suggests experimenting with the ingredients commonly found in your home: vanilla beans, scented bath oils, or any other scented oil-based product. Often these oils are made with a small percentage of essential oil in what is known as a "carrier base," which could be vegetable oil or mineral oil—a neutral oil. You can also purchase various oils made from spices—cloves, cinnamon, and so on, at your pharmacy for use as candle scents. Just remember the scent must be *oil-based* or it will be useless.

SSENTIALS

If you're interested in mixing scents to achieve unusual duplications of such things as baby powder and apple strudel, check *www.candlemaking.org.uk/scentrecipes.html* for a list of such inviting scent combinations as pink champagne and blueberry muffins!

As a general formula for using essential oils to scent candle wax, start out with half a teaspoon of essential oil to one pound of wax. Never use more than 3 percent of oil by weight, unless you are deliberately trying to mottle the candle's surface. (See "Surface Mottling" on p. 175.)

Here are some representative examples of the uses of essential oils to make scented candles:

Lime blossom	=	Energy
Lemongrass	=	Love
Lavender	=	Stress relief
Sweet citrus	=	Rejuvenation
Tangerine and lavender	=	Well-being
Patchoili and cedarwood	=	Sensuality
Wood spice	=	Tranquility
Chamomile	=	Comfort

Herbal Scents

In addition to essential oils, you can try adding herbal scents, using the leaves or powders you have in your kitchen—any dried herbs can be used to scent wax. (You should realize, however, that they don't always work: see "My Rosemary Story" on p. 190 for an interesting anecdote on what happened with one such experiment.)

To use dried herbs for scenting candles, allow the herbs to steep in the melted wax for several minutes. Then, either filter them out (with cheesecloth) or leave them in to create an interesting visual effect. Remember, however, that any plant material within the candle runs the risk of being burned as the candle burns—and it might not smell so good! You can also use the method described above for using potpourri with dried herbs.

Here are some herbal/spice suggestions: allspice, caraway, cinnamon, cloves, coriander, fennel, ginger, mint, nutmeg, rosemary, tarragon, thyme, vanilla. You may also use pure oils of citrus—oil of lemon, oil of orange, and so on. These oils can be added directly to the melted wax. As is usual with candlemaking, you have to be willing to experiment and exercise your creativity—and keep records.

CHAPTER 11
Advanced Creative Methods

Now that you understand the basics of candlemaking, you're ready to move on to some advanced creative methods of making, shaping, and coloring candles. This is where the creativity really begins!

Making Braided Tapers

Chances are you already know how to make braids—either you've plaited your own hair or your daughter's, or a friend's. Still, the fashion for braided hair has long waned and if you *don't* know how to make braids, you'll have to learn in order to make these interestingly shaped braided candles from tapers.

You can practice with your own hair—if it's long—or find a friend with long hair to practice on. Hair is a lot easier to braid than wax, because it's soft and flexible. You can also practice with fairly thick string. As usual, practice makes perfect.

Once you've mastered the art of braiding, or making plaits, you're ready to add that skill to your repertoire of candlemaking tricks. Be prepared for some spectacular results once you've mastered the knack of braiding wicks.

ESSENTIALS

Although you *can* master the art of candle braiding single-handedly, plaiting regular size tapers is much easier with two people than just one. So, find a friend—preferably a fellow candlemaker, or, take on an apprentice and teach!

Plaited candles are extremely attractive and well worth the trouble, but don't try to learn how to plait using candles! It's a wise move to make a few simple attempts at plaiting, or braiding, three waxed wicks together. Start with plain cords, then work with cords dipped in a few coatings of wax (vestas), and then move on to progressively thicker tapers until you are confident you can handle the regular size tapers.

Be prepared for this to feel a bit clumsy at first (unless you've done a lot of hair braiding!), but don't let that discourage you from perfecting the skill. It's truly worth the effort for the artistic results you can obtain by plaiting tapers. And you automatically get a multiwick candle as there are three wicks to light!

Obviously, you need to work while the tapers are still warm so that they will be flexible. And the thinner your taper, the easier the braiding will be. Warm vestas are great to practice the braiding of tapers as you work your way up to the thicker, normal size, tapers. However, plaited, thick tapers in three colors are the ultimate goal of this technique. I've seen some that were real works of art! However, it's best to start with modest objectives—just to learn the skill.

Instructions for Plaited Candles

To begin to plait candles, you will need scissors, two pairs of freshly made dipped tapers (if you make them in pairs; otherwise, three tapers), a hook at a convenient working height (you may need to practice to figure out just where to place the hook), and a lot of patience. The candles should be approximately ½" in diameter and about 10" tall. You can also work with taller candles, up to 12". Use what you regularly make.

If your candles become too cool and begin to stiffen while you are braiding, keep your blow-dryer handy and use it (on warm setting) to keep them soft and pliable. Just don't use too much heat—you don't want melted tapers!

If you are using pairs of tapers, separate one set and put one of the two candles aside for another use. Hang the second pair by its wick over the hook; tie the wick of the third candle to the hook. Make sure the tops of all three candles are at the same level.

Plait the three candles together. (Remember, we said you'd have to practice!) To facilitate the braiding, squeeze the bottom ends together smoothly and flatten the base with your hands so that it can support the finished candle without tipping over. You can use the method of melting the bottom of the finished candle to get a smooth, flat surface that is described on p. 100.

Once you've got the three candles braided together, hang them up on the hook and allow to cool and dry for at least one hour. Overnight is even better.

Twisted Tapers

Another creative technique—less difficult than braiding but with a similar result—is to twist two warm tapers together after they have been dipped. (You aren't required to twist the pair that was made together, so you can use two differently colored candles.) To do this, simply take the two tapers in your hands and twist them like you'd wring out a washcloth, but gently.

Once you've twisted the pair of candles, you can then overdip them, either for color or to give a more finished look to your now double-wicked taper. Twisted tapers give a sophisticated look to a table set for a dinner party—especially if the candles are color-keyed to your décor or theme.

ESSENTIALS

Candlemaker Betty Oppenheimer, author of *The Candlemaker's Companion*, says that she finds twisted tapers "particularly beautiful in beeswax." And, since beeswax when warm is quite sticky, twisted beeswax tapers would stick together nicely. It's worth a try!

When you finish the twisted candle, remember to slice off the bottoms to make a flat surface. Twisted tapers will require a larger candleholder than regular tapers. These can often be improvised. If the candleholder isn't snug enough, melt a little wax into the bottom of it to help the twisted taper adhere securely.

Alternatively, you can squeeze the bottom ends tightly together so the finished candle will fit into a regular sized holder. Or, you can start with thinner tapers.

Winding Waxed Wicks

Another advanced technique that gives interesting results is that of winding the waxed wick around something. Use the method for making vestas (see p. 170), and a long wick—the length will depend on the object around which you plan to wind the wick. You can premeasure it with plain string.

To practice this method, you are going to wind the waxed wick around an object—any simple shaped object will do, such as a plastic pharmacy bottle (the kind pills are sold in). First practice with a piece of cord dipped in wax a few times. Don't waste wick material before you have acquired the skill to wind the waxed wick neatly and attractively.

For practice, the important thing is to take care to wind the waxed cord symmetrically, either with the rings overlapping or touching each other. You can remelt your practice wax after you've finished your session with it.

The Real Thing

To be honest, it's not easy to make a truly attractive job of winding a waxed wick (which is what a taper basically is), but it is possible to achieve some excellent results with this technique. To prepare the waxed wick for winding, use the "drawing" method (see p. 55). The wick should be slender, and about 40" long. After each wax bath, hang it straight (a nail is good) until the wax hardens. Repeat the procedure until you have a slender taper.

Once you have finished winding the wick around the object (small blocks of wood work well as do slender tubes of glass or small, smooth drinking glasses), remove the core form, allowing a small length of the taper to protrude at the top for lighting. You can burn your tapers made from winding wax as you would use any other candle.

FACTS

There are beautiful winding tapers from the early nineteenth century that have been preserved as works of art. Some are extremely intricate, often made on carved blocks of wood as showpieces. The women who made them (housewives for the most part) were proud of their work, much as quilters of the same period displayed their best designs but did not use them. These elegant tapers were never lit. In a way, that's a good thing, or we would not have such examples to admire today.

Making Spiraled Tapers

Spiral twisted candles are extremely attractive on the dinner table and not too difficult to make, once you get the hang of it. This is a marvelous and fairly easy advanced technique for shaping tapers. The only equipment you need is a rolling pin and a flat hard surface for rolling (a cutting board, for example), a knife, and a freshly dipped, warm taper about 1" in diameter and 10" tall.

Lay the taper on the board and roll it out just as you would dough for biscuits or pie crust. Flatten the candle *from the top end*, leaving an inch or so at the bottom unrolled, to fit into the candleholder. If the candle should crack while you are rolling, it has cooled too much. You need to work fairly quickly with this technique. If you do get a crack, re-dip the candle (having kept your wax pot handy) for two or three seconds in 160° wax to soften it. If it merely begins to stiffen but hasn't yet cracked, you can soften it with your blow-dryer.

Once you have it flattened, hold the taper upside down, holding it at the base with one hand. Place the flattened end (now on the bottom) between the thumb and forefinger of your other hand. Sliding the candle upwards between your fingers, turn it into a spiral as you lift. You can make a wide twist, or you can repeat the process for a tighter twist. This technique sounds easier than it actually is, but you can practice first on a plain candle that you can easily remelt before going on to work with colored candles.

Advanced Creative Techniques with Color

Color can be used creatively in many ways that allow you to express your creative nature, be decorative, have fun, or even use up your leftover colored wax. Color doesn't have to be simple, although certainly beautifully colored tapers and pillars are wonderful to have around and to burn for any occasion—or none at all, just to fit or lift your mood.

The Pour-In/Pour-Out Method for Molds

This interesting technique is the polar opposite of overdipping. It might be called "innerdipping." What you do here is pour wax into a mold, and then pour it right back out, leaving a thin coating on the inside of the mold. As you do this, layers of color are built up on each other *inside the mold*, which means inside the finished candle.

There are many ways you can utilize this method, with different colors and different waxes. Remember that the last pour forms the core of the candle. You will need a fairly strong color to show through the outer layer, and a fairly thin outer layer of harder wax. Of course, you don't need to limit yourself to two colors, but it's a good idea to begin learning the technique using the simpler method.

Using paraffin for the outer layer provides a translucent effect so the inner core of color glows through. Because paraffin is softer than waxes with additives, mind the temperature of the inner wax to avoid a meltdown. (If the colors do bleed together, however, it could give an interesting effect.

When dying the wax for the last pour, you should use approximately four times the amount of dye that you would use for overdipping, unless you want a pale-on-pale effect. Generally speaking, the stronger colors work best here.

Be Flexible

As for molds, any kind of mold will do, but flexible molds give the best results because with them the color will be thicker in some areas of the candle than others (say, with a figurine). This thick-thin distribution of color through the finished candle creates nice variations of show-through. Beginners are advised to stick to simple shapes. Cylindrical and block shaped molds work great for making pour-in/pour-out color show-through candles. Or, try a star shaped mold for something a bit more fancy.

Here's How . . .

Here's the "how to" of the pour-in/pour-out method. You'll need a mold. Any kind will do, but flexible may be best. You'll need enough wax to fill the mold twice—once for each color.

1. Wick the mold according to the instructions on p. 122, or by whatever method a special mold might require.
2. Fill the mold with wax heated to 180° Fahrenheit and let it cool long enough for an eighth of an inch layer to form inside the mold.
3. Pour off the wax that is still liquid and wait about ten minutes for the inner layer to solidify.
4. Fill the mold with the colored wax that will form the core of the candle, heated to 180°. Allow the second pour to cool for two hours.
5. Poke holes in the wax (as described on p. 124) to eliminate air bubbles and then add more melted wax to fill in the gaps.
6. Allow the candle to cool inside the mold for two hours before removing it. Don't forget to use a mold release agent suitable to the type of wax you are using for the first pour, or the outer layer.

ESSENTIALS

If the outer layer doesn't seem quite thick enough, you can strengthen the finished pour-in/pour-out candle by overdipping it in clear wax. Finish up with a plunge into cold water to make the candle shine, and polish with nylon pantyhose or a soft buffing cloth.

CHAPTER 12

Holidays and Special Occasions

Naturally, you will have many private special occasions that you can celebrate with your candle-making skills—births, weddings, etc. And there are so many joyous holidays throughout the year that can be enhanced by the presence of warm candlelight. This chapter will give you some suggestions for making all of your holidays and special occasions *really* special with your own handmade candles.

Gift-Giving

Candles are always welcome gifts—especially when you have made them yourself. Giving your art away is gratifying when you know how much pleasure you are providing for a friend or loved one.

Theme gifts are always appropriate. These can be based on specific holidays or religious celebrations, or made in a person's favorite color. For example, when I redecorated my home in sage and peach, I received a dozen lovely handmade tapers, six of each color that exactly matched my décor! Be aware that candlemakers have their personal trade secrets—when I exclaimed over the colors and said, "How did you get those colors?" the answer was along the lines of, "Oh, I just fooled around until I got it right."

If you are giving candles as holiday presents, you can make candle sets appropriate for whichever one you are honoring. Giving your handmade candles in the correct colors and holders and quantities to light for each night of these oncoming holidays is an especially thoughtful gift. The recipient will appreciate an early arrival of such a gift in order to plan their celebration with family and friends, using your gift as a showpiece.

FACTS

Traditionally, New Englanders believe that a gift bayberry candle, burned down to the end on New Year's Eve, will bring the recipient many benefits in the coming year. They say, "A bayberry candle burned to the socket, puts luck in the home, food in the larder, and gold in the pocket."

Candle-Wrapping Tips

For a single candle, taper or pillar, simply roll it in a sheet of tissue paper and twist the ends of the tissue, securing with a ribbon tie (or a twist tie). To wrap pairs, wrap one first, overlapping it with paper to protect from scratching, and then lay the other in the paper and wrap, twist, and tie. You can do this with multiples, too.

SSENTIALS
See-through wrapping is particular nice for candles. You can use cellophane or plastic food wrap for bundles of tapers, tying a ribbon around the heavier bottom end. A strip of interesting fabric that doesn't clash with the candle's color can also bind several candles together for an attractively presented gift.

Constructive Covering

You can also use construction paper to make a holder for the candles. Cut a section about half the height of your candles. Roll it first around each candle, making a tube, and then continue rolling around the others so that in the end each candle is nestled in its own protected enclosure. Wrap the end of the paper totally around the package. Tape and tie with a decorative ribbon and bow.

Yule Rules!

The magic of glowing candlelight really lights up the festive celebrations of our holidays. Candlelight is always welcome, but some holidays just wouldn't be what they are supposed to be without candles to help us celebrate. The season that first comes to mind when we think of candles is Yule time. Whether you are celebrating Christmas, Hanukkah, Kwanzaa, Las Posadas, or Ya Dhiu, it's the season of the Winter Solstice, or Yule.

The Winter Solstice is the point in the calendar year when night is longest and day is shortest; after the Winter Solstice the days begin gradually to lengthen. With its bold red and green traditional colors taken from nature's holly berries and evergreen trees repeated in our candles and decorating schemes for the home, schools, offices, and public spaces, it's a time of celebrating the victory of light over darkness.

Yule is the perfect time to deck your own personal halls with an abundance of handmade candles intertwined with the brightly colored decorations traditionally hung from our Christmas trees and with branches of evergreens from the woods and fields, or your own backyard.

Making candles for Yule time couldn't be easier—and it's festive and fun, something the whole family can enjoy. Even small children can help make a seasonal candle by doing the polishing or gathering small branches and berries for the decorating. Kids usually have lots of good ideas about decorating—and they like to feel a part of things, so it's always a treat for them to help you with your candlemaking, just as they like to help with baking and decorating special cookies for the holidays.

Everybody can have a hand in the decorating—a toddler can put a candle in a holder and a teen can be a real help. Every age in between can play a part—each child can be assigned a special candle of his or her own, for example, to light and take care of.

Hearts and Candles

Though the banks don't close and the mail still gets delivered—as it must!— Valentine's Day is a holiday that almost everyone holds dear. Who doesn't like sending and receiving Valentines and Valentine gifts? And what better gift for a Valentine than a candle you made yourself? It says "love" with all its heart—especially if it's a heart-shaped pink candle!

SSENTIALS

If you don't have heart-shaped cookie cutters, you can cut out heart shapes by hand. They may not be perfect—but love is known for its imperfections. You can overdip your hand-cut heart shapes to cover up the rough edges.

Making heart-shaped candles is a snap. All you need is wax, a shallow baking pan, a chip of red colorant (for both red and pink colors), and a heart-shaped cookie cutter—or a bunch of different sizes of heart-shaped cookie cutters.

How to Make Heart-Shaped Candles

To make your heart-shaped candles you will need shallow baking trays (one for each color heart you want to make), some heart-shaped cookie cutters, a few ounces of wax, a red color chip, a melting pot and double-boiler system, a 1" primed wick for each heart candle, and a skewer or wicking needle.

Before you start, decide how many hearts you want of each color (red, pink, white) and in which sizes. You will need cutters for each tray of color. If you don't have enough cutters, make one tray at a time, remelting the wax in between pourings.

1. Set up your double-boiler system.
2. Put out your baking trays.
3. Melt the wax to 180° Fahrenheit.
4. If you want some white hearts, make them first. Pour a thin layer of wax (¼") on the bottom of each tray. Press the molds into the bottom layer to set them and then gently fill the molds with the hot wax.
5. Next, add enough of the red color chip to color your wax the pink you prefer. Pour a tray of pink wax as directed above—first set the molds, then fill.
6. Then, add more of the red color chip to color the remaining wax red. Pour a tray of red wax, set molds, and fill them.
7. After filling each mold, push a hole into its center and insert the wick.
8. Add a bit more wax to each mold to smooth the surface (remember that wax shrinks as it hardens), being careful to keep the wick centered.
9. After the candles have completely cooled, remove the molds from the tray(s) and push the heart shapes out. You now have heart-shaped candles!

SSENTIALS

If you are going to stack your heart-shaped candles, do not wick them individually. Wick the finished hearts according to the directions for wicking stacked candles.

There are several ways you can use heart-shaped candles. You can make them into "floaters," or candles designed to float in a shallow bowl of water (see Chapter 17, "Novelty Candles"). Another option is to make a stacked candle with hearts. For a stacked candle, you can use different size hearts and/or different colored hearts—red and pink, for example. And don't forget twisted tapers for Valentine's day (see p. 208) Twisted tapers are lovely in any combination of red, pink, and white. Spirals (p. 210) are another good idea for your Valentine's Day dinner table.

Candy Is Dandy

You can simulate chocolate candies in wax quite easily and give your Valentine a gift box of "chocolate" candles. This is a really nice touch for the candle-lover you love.

To make wax chocolates, simply color your wax chocolate brown and use the ice-tray molding method described on p. 178. Wick each "candy" as described above by poking a hole and inserting a short length of primed wick into each section of the ice-cube tray mold. While you are at it, make some for yourself, too. These make cunning place-markers on the dinner table. Or offer each guest a chocolate candle candy as a take-home favor. If you want to get fancy about it, wrap each one in gold foil!

Spring!

Spring! What a welcome change for candlemakers. In the same way that flora and fauna change in their annual cycles, with the colors of flowers and fruits and vegetables marking different seasons, so candles can be used as part of holiday displays year round.

Easter presents the home candlemaker with a wonderful opportunity to create egg-shaped, pastel-colored candles for decorations and gift-giving. (See "Eggs-actly!" in Chapter 10.) Bunny-shaped molds can be purchased or hand-molded. Flowers can be shaped from pliable wax (see Chapter 17, "Novelty Candles"). A myriad of lovely colors that mimic the flowers of spring can be created in candle wax.

FACTS

Easter is the feast in which candles have the greatest meaning for Christians. During the period known as Lent, the symbol of the victory of light over darkness is demonstrated during the Easter Vigil, with the lighting of the Paschal Candle. Those participating in the Easter Vigil renew their baptismal vows while holding candles that have been lighted from the flame of the Paschal Candle.

Easter brings a feeling of joy and optimism and a sense of the renewal of earth life's yearly cycle. Spring evenings during the season of Easter bloom with the magic of candlelight.

The Fourth of July

Decorating for the American national holiday isn't much of a challenge—it's the good old red, white, and blue motif. Red and blue are primary colors, so they always go well together, even if the bands aren't playing or the parades marching. But, when the summer's high point comes around and there are lots of outdoor activities, the bright colors of our nation's flag can be displayed in your candles, indoors and out.

Not only does this color scheme set off a patriotic vibration, it suits the bold colors of summer and contrasts with summer's bright colors in the natural world.

SSENTIALS

If you've mastered the art of braiding tapers, the Fourth of July is the perfect time to show off your skill. Red-white-and-blue braided tapers are the perfect decoration for a Fourth of July celebration.

Red-white-and-blue candles can be created several ways. Layered cylinders and blocks work well, especially for outdoor dining when you want long-burning candles. Using milk-carton molds for Fourth of July motif candles is easy: just pour in equal amounts of the three colors in any order.

Groupings of single-colored candles in each of the three colors work well too. Try a group of different size pillars set on a tray—equal numbers of the three colors, or in any proportion and arrangement you choose. One friend made a flag out of multiple same-size blocks, using Danish tapers for the stars. When lit, it was stunning.

Halloween Candles

When fall rolls around and all the countryside changes color to shades of orange, gold, reddish-brown, and pumpkin, it's a good time to begin thinking of making special candles for Halloween. What could be more appropriate in the prime season of the jack-o'-lanterns?

No doubt you've already made your share of carved faces out of pumpkins and put a single store-bought candle inside to make the cutouts leer menacingly—or with a friendly grin. You can be as creative as you like with pumpkin carving, and make a variety of Halloween lanterns. You can make star-shaped cutouts, create unusual designs of incised lines in geometric or freeform shapes, make leaf shapes, etc. Just be sure to use a sharp blade (a lino or woodcutting tool is good) to carve the designs. And, make holes so that the candle inside can get sufficient oxygen to burn well.

SSENTIALS

You need not limit yourself to the common orange pumpkin. You can use all sorts of hard-shelled winter squash, such as acorn and butternut. These hard-shelled vegetables will also work as molds to give you gourd-shaped candles to burn during this season. (See Chapter 7, "Molded Candles.")

For other types of candles—pillars, tapers, molded—your color scheme for Halloween is predetermined—make half-orange and half-black layered candles; twist one black and one orange taper together; or make pillars and blocks in black and orange and arrange them in groups here and there.

If you want to delight a child, make a hand-molded ghost shape out of white wax, forming it around a wick. Paint on black eyes. Or, take a large blob of orange wax and hand-mold a pumpkin shape; carve the child's initials into the warm wax.

Put branches of autumn leaves around the candles for further decoration, and when Halloween is over and Thanksgiving is coming round, make your candles in the shades of russet, bronze, brown, and gold that nature provides in the gloriously colored dying leaves of the autumn foliage.

Making Candles for Thanksgiving

The annual feast of Thanksgiving doesn't have any specific color scheme, but it does have its theme: thankfulness. As you make candles for your holiday table, give thanks for the abundance you enjoy. Not the least of our blessings these days is the luxury of making our own sweet-smelling and beautifully colored candles as a joyful hobby, not an onerous chore.

Candle Etiquette

When setting your Thanksgiving table (or any other dining occasion), place candles and centerpieces about two inches below the eye level of your guests. A candle flame flickering between your gaze and the person opposite is annoying, and certainly not conducive to delightful conversation.

Burn the tips of new candles down an inch or so before using them on the dinner table, to take off the sense of "newness." When having guests for dinner, light the candles immediately *before* seating the guests. Allow them to continue burning until the dinner is over and everyone stands.

Here are some other guidelines to keep in mind when preparing candles for a dining occasion:

- Tall, slim candles are best for elegant dining.
- Short, wide pillars/blocks are good for casual dining.
- Arrange candles with different heights and shapes around the room on windowsills, sidetables, and fireplace mantles.
- Light candles at dusk, or on overcast days to dispel gloom.

New Baby

Oh, what a joyful event it is in any family's life when new life graces the circle! You can make a perpetual birthday candle for the happy new parents. This is very easy and will be appreciated for *years* as the child grows.

Begin with a tall white pillar candle—10" or so. Mark the surface at ½" intervals for the eighteen years it will take for the new baby to reach legal maturity. You can do this with a small pen and a ruler as a guide. Make a tiny pinprick in the candle at each division so you will know where to paint the yearly separations.

Beginning at the top with "1," continue downward to the base until you reach "18." You will have about an inch of candle left at the base. Decorate the candle at each point of division by painting on a line and add some other surface decorations, or sheet wax appliqués.

SSENTIALS

The perpetual birthday candle described above is a perfect gift for a baby shower. But, you can also use some other candle ideas, such as aromatherapy scented candles to soothe, relax, or invigorate the mother-to-be during her pregnancy.

Include in your gift basket for the new baby and his or her parents a note on how to use the candle. It will burn for about 1 hour for each yearly division. As the child grows old enough to understand the candle's purpose, he or she will delight in this visual evidence of growth—and look forward to the lighting of the birthday candle each year. Of course, you can also include regular birthday candles for the celebration of the first birthday—which comes all too soon for most parents!

Romantic Weddings

The romance of candlelight and weddings is a given. What would one be without the other? Whether it's a huge formal wedding with all the trimmings or a small, private affair, candles will enhance the proceedings and make the bride and groom—and everyone else—feel special on that meaningful occasion.

Depending on the time of day chosen for the ceremony and the reception, candles can be utilized in a number of different ways. If, for example, the wedding is a daytime affair followed by a luncheon reception, suitably decorated candles can be placed on every table as place-markers.

ESSENTIALS

To remove bits of wax residue from votive cups, place them in the freezer overnight. Because wax shrinks when it freezes, it will then be easy to remove. Another nonstick idea is to coat the inside of votive cups with pan spray, which also will prevent wax from sticking.

The wedding that is followed by an evening reception provides the best venue for using candles, which can be displayed throughout the reception area, be it a great hall or a private living room. Popular colors include, of course, white and ivory, surrounded with lilies and stephanotis or other white-flowered sprays of the season.

For a different note, try using pastel colors—perhaps to match the bridesmaids' dresses. If the bride has chosen a specific color scheme for her wedding party's gowns, that can be repeated in the candles used both for the ceremony and the reception. These can be combined with the flowers chosen for the bride's and her bridesmaids' bouquets.

Or, for an autumn wedding, choose rich, deep colors—like burgundy and russet—and mix these with the colors of the season. Whichever color scheme is chosen, all types of candles work well, depending on the type of wedding.

Post-Wedding Candles

A nice note for the newly married couple is to save a pair or two of elegant dipped tapers from the wedding candles for after the ball is over. A thoughtful "morning after" gift of their special wedding candles will remind them that it's important to take time out for a candlelit dinner just for two to keep the spark of romance alive after their return to normal—hectic and busy—life. There's no better way to strike a romantic note—just make sure to include matches!

And don't forget about engagement parties and wedding anniversary celebrations. These too will be enhanced with thoughtfully chosen candle arrangements.

Birthdays

Blowing out candles on the birthday cake and making a wish is a time-honored tradition, and it's just as important for adults who are growing older as it is for children. Handmade birthday candles are a real treat—I've described some variations on these earlier but you can devise your own as well. And after the little candles are blown out and removed for serving the cake, how festive it is to have made some other candles with which to adorn the birthday table.

Another idea for a birthday party is cupcake candles (see Chapter 17, "Novelty Candles"). These little wax cakes aren't for eating, but you can make them look like the real thing.

Cone-shaped candles can be made to look just like party hats, especially using the method for making chunk candles (see p. 178 in Chapter 9). You can stick some colorful tinsel around the top to complete the effect. (Be sure to remove the tinsel before lighting the candle: it's only window dressing.)

Zodiac Candles

Making a candle for the birthday person's sign of the zodiac is especially thoughtful. A simple large pillar is best. Although there are no hard and fast rules, each of the signs of the zodiac is related to specific colors. Here's a list:

Aries	(March 21–April l9)	red/cardinal/fire
Taurus	(April 20–May 20)	green/fixed/earth
Gemini	(May 21–June 20)	yellow/mutable/air
Cancer	(June 21–July 22)	blue/cardinal/water
Leo	(July 23–August 22)	orange/fixed/fire
Virgo	(August 23–September 22)	brown/mutable/earth
Libra	(September 23–October 22)	ivory/cardinal/air
Scorpio	(October 23–November 21)	purple/fixed/water
Sagittarius	(November 22–December 21)	burnt orange/mutable/fire
Capricorn	(December 22–January 19)	russet/cardinal/earth
Aquarius	(January 20–February 18)	dark blue/fixed/air
Pisces	(February 19–March 20)	lilac/mutable/water

Wax glue is a soft, sticky wax that is available in solid form for attaching pieces of wax together and also to stick decorations to candles. Use it to glue a small zodiacal symbol (make sure it is nonflammable) to the candle, incise the symbol with a knife, or just paint on the name of the sign. (Also see Chapter 13, "Surface Techniques for Decorating Candles.")

FACTS

The planet Mars, ruler of the astrological sign of Aries, is known as the "fire god." He is visible to us as a red sphere in the night sky, the only such tinted planet. When Mars is active in a person's chart, they are imbued with the energy of Fire, an element of vital importance to human life.

Candle Centerpieces for Special Occasions

Mirrored tiles make great bases for candles in holders, for they reflect light. You can use all sorts of decorative embellishments to surround a candle on a mirror tile—greens, ribbons, net, confetti, potpourri. Flowers can be fresh, dried, or artificial.

To make a centerpiece with a mirror tile, simply place greens or stems of flowers diagonally across the square of tile. Add ornaments of your choice in the spaces between the greens/flowers, or fill in with more flowers. Add two votive candles in tall glass cups on either side of the diagonal of greens and flowers. As a final touch, sprinkle confetti or glitter on the mirror tile.

For simple elegance, place a spray of long stemmed flowers such as roses or calla lilies, tied with a ribbon bow, across the mirror tile. Add two tall tapers on either side of the flower spray.

For a more casual presentation, put a pillar or block candle in a hurricane lamp holder on a platter and lay greens around the base of the candleholder. Scatter a few flowers or berries, or autumn leaves, amongst the greens.

CHAPTER 13
Surface Techniques for Decorating Candles

Materials for decorating the surfaces of candles can be found all around you—in the garden, sewing room, even in the supermarket. Further, you aren't limited to adding extra materials to the candle's surface—you can alter, improve, or decorate it with paint; make impressions on the candle's surface; or add more wax to the candle's surface in a variety of ways to create different effects.

Candle-Painting

Painting the surface of a candle may be the easiest method for surface decorating, especially for the beginner. You paint a candle just as you paint on a piece of paper. The types of paints to use are water-based—tempera or acrylic—because they adhere to the candle's surface best. Oil-based paints will slide off.

Tempera paint is available from arts stores; your craft shop may carry it as well. As you can mix your own colors quite easily, you need only purchase the basic primary colors: red, blue, yellow; and white and black. (Refer back to "A Guide to Mixing Colors," p. 194.) From these five colors you can mix almost any color you can think of, except gold and silver, which are also available. Pens that are filled with gold and silver inks are excellent for fine-line drawing on candles.

Inspiration for painted candles abounds. You can paint an abstract design of your own making; geometric shapes such as triangles, squares, stars, etc.; or flower shapes in different colors. Decorating candles with painting is easy and fun, and leaves your imagination lots of room to be creative.

Paint with Wax

Not only can you paint your candles with poster paint or acrylic, you can overpaint them with another wax in as many colors as you like. To make painting wax, simply mix one part paraffin with 3½ parts of turpentine, following the instructions below:

1. Melt the paraffin and add the turpentine.
2. Permit the mixture to stand for a few days, stirring three times daily to help the turpentine evaporate. The result is a pasty wax pliable enough to use for painting.
3. Add color to your painting wax, using a different dish or container for each color you plan to use. If the wax is too stiff, put the containers in a pan of water and warm until the colored wax is pliable enough to use with a brush. Use artist's paintbrushes for wax painting, but

don't expect to use them for any other purpose. I advise buying inexpensive sets of brushes and disposing of them.

4. Once you have painted your candles, be sure to leave them untouched in a protected place while they dry.

5. When the candles are thoroughly dry, overdip them in clear wax—quickly—for a final finishing touch.

You Don't Have to Be an Artist!

Decorating candles with paint is fun. You don't have to know how to draw. You can make interesting squiggles—sort of doodling in paint. Or, hold the paintbrush in one hand and the candle in the other and twirl the candle around, making a spiral design! Use your imagination—be creative.

Stenciling Candles

Stenciling is perhaps the easiest way to decorate a plain pillar or block candle to give it an elegant, interesting finish. Stenciling utilizes only the stencil and the paint, requiring no other tools but your brush. Stencils can be purchased in a variety of designs—usually from stores that sell wallpaper and interior decorating supplies. Or, you can make your own stencils.

Making Stencils

Remember how you learned to cut out a snowflake in first grade? You folded a piece of paper a few times and snipped here and there. Then, when you unfolded it you were astonished at the snowflake you had created. Making stencils is the same, only in reverse. You cut out a pattern from the paper using the same technique as with the snowflake. When making your own stencils, remember to use a heavy enough paper to wrap around the candle tightly. You don't want the paint to seep through the stencil or slip underneath the template.

For example, first fold a sheet of 8½" × 11" typing paper in half across the short length. Next, snip three long cuts into the fold. Then, refold the paper about ½" from the cuts and make a few wedge-shaped snips in that fold. When you open it, you will have a simple pattern of leaves and diamond shapes. You can expand on this idea indefinitely and make shapes as intricate as you like.

Or, you can draw a pattern on the paper (or trace one from a picture) and cut it out with an Exacto knife. Using lace doilies or pieces of lace is yet another of the many options.

For a lacy edge on your candle, take a strip of lace and wrap it around the bottom edge. Tape the lace firmly in place with masking tape and spray paint over it. Leave the candle to dry thoroughly and then remove the lace "stencil" and the masking tape.

Once you have your stencil and your candle ready to go, wrap the stencil around the candle carefully and either tape it tightly or hold it with one hand, depending on the shape of the stencil. You might work better with both hands free to secure the candle and paint without worrying about the stencil slipping loose.

When you have your stencil securely in place, either brush or rub the paint into the open spaces. Usually the surface will be done with one coat, depending on the type of paint you are using.

One candlemaker uses spray paint to stencil candles. If you choose this medium, either do it outside or make sure there is plenty of ventilation. And be sure to protect all surfaces. Spray paint can go all over the place.

If you want a buildup of paint—such as with a silver or gold decoration—then you must apply several coats. Some paints are naturally thick and pasty, while others are thinner. For a flowing effect—such as calligraphy—use thinner paint. For a dimensional effect, use thicker paint.

A Neat Trick

You can create a stenciled effect without a stencil! This is a very easy technique for painting a design on the surface of a finished candle. Its only drawback is that you are limited to geometrical shapes, but you can make many beautiful designs with them. The secret? Masking tape!

Use artist's masking tape—the kind that peels off easily, leaving no marks. Simply put tape on your candle, paint or spray-paint (you don't have to bother about being neat or staying within the lines, as with a stencil). Peel off the tape and—bingo! You have a really neat design.

You can use this easy technique to create stripes, either vertical or horizontal. The horizontal stripes will give the effect of a layered poured candle—but with much less effort.

For example, you could make a stunning black and white striped candle by using a white base candle (pillar or block) and black paint. First, wrap the masking tape around the candle carefully to make as many stripes of whatever width you like. Then, spray the candle black. When you peel off the tape after the paint dries, you will have a bold design. Of course, you can do this with any colors, bright or pastel. This is a great way to experiment with using color without much effort or expense. And, if you don't like the result, just scrape the paint off and remelt the candle for another use.

In addition to making horizontal and vertical stripes with the masking tape method, you can lay the tape in such a way that only tiny spaces are left—you can make squares, diamonds, triangles, and other geometric shapes just by the way you place the tape. For a checkered effect, first make vertical stripes and then make horizontal stripes. This will give you small squares that will result in a checkered design. You can even paint over more than once using tape. Once again, use your imagination and experiment! You'll be surprised at what creative results you can achieve on a plain candle's surface.

Other Surface Decorations

Another easy way to decorate the surface of your finished candle is to stick things on it, such as beads or small shells. You can do this while

Using wax to attach decorations

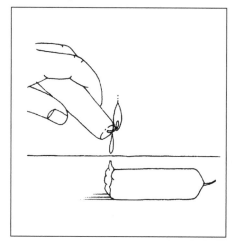

the candle is warm, either right after you make it, or by overdipping it in another coat of wax.

An easy way to attach decoration to a candle is to use wax from another candle. To do this, simply lay the candle on its side. Holding the second candle over the first, allow the wax to drip in the desired area. Quickly attach your decoration while the wax is still warm.

Try simply rolling newly overdipped candles in tiny beads, or glitter, or even sesame or poppy seeds. You can also use colored bits known as jimmies, which are made for decorating cookies and ice cream. Just make sure you are using a candle with a large enough diameter so that as it burns it does not melt the outer layer.

And, of course, *never* use anything flammable to decorate the surface of any candle.

ESSENTIALS Have you ever made a pomander by sticking an orange or an apple all over with cloves? You can do the same with a still-warm candle. Just press whole cloves into the sides all the way around, about halfway up the candle. You can do this with cinnamon sticks, too. The result will be pretty and fragrant!

Making Textured Candles

You can create a raised, or embossed, pattern on sheet wax and then use the sheet wax to decorate the surface of your candle. All you need is a raised (relief) pattern. It could be anything. For example, I have a wine bottle with a bunch of grapes on it that is perfect for this technique. Once you begin looking around for possibilities you'll find they are abundant. The end result is a sheet of wax with an embossed design on one side, flat on the other.

To make embossed sheet wax, first coat the object with the design with mineral oil or petroleum jelly or pan spray. Then, cover it with silicone caulk. Let the caulk dry thoroughly. Carefully peel it off the original mold. You will have an embossing form. Either press just-made, warm sheets of wax into the mold, or fill it with wax like any other mold. Once you have your embossed wax, adhere it to the surface of the candle with wax glue, or wrap the wax sheet around the candle.

Decorating with Wax Scraps

Remember how, when you were a kid and your mother made piecrust, she would cut the scraps up into leaf or flower shapes to decorate the top of the pie? Maybe your mother didn't do that—but it's a common pastry technique you can transfer to the surface decoration of candles. As we have noted, there are many parallels to cooking and candlemaking. This wax-on-wax method is easy and utilizes bits of wax you have left over from the wax sheets or pots of melted waxes of various colors.

If the scraps have cooled, you can warm them up again with a blow-dryer. When the pieces are pliable enough, you can cut them into interesting shapes—leaves, flowers, stars, half-moons, etc.—and glue these to the candle's surface, using wax glue or simply taking advantage of the malleability of warm wax surfaces (beeswax will stick by itself). With scraps, you can create a vine climbing up the candle, or a spray of flowers with leaves and a stem.

Child's Play

If you have children about, you can let them have strips of wax that they can wind around the candle, making stripes. This is a fun way to let children help make holiday candles—using basic white pillars, you can make pans of colored wax to cut into strips for decorating in the colors appropriate to the holiday. Or make a batch of different colors and let the kids use their imaginations to make striped candles of many colors. Peppermint candy sticks can be simulated with this method by wrapping strips of red around a tall, slim, white pillar candle. As you can easily see, the possibilities are endless.

Kitchen Magic

Using sheet wax, you can cut shapes with cookie cutters and stick them on your candle's surface as described above, with wax glue or with warm wax. Sets of cookie cutters in a multitude of shapes are available at kitchenware departments, or through mail-order catalogs. Depending on the size of your base candle, you can use regular cutters, or you can get mini-cutters, which are great for surface decoration of tapers and smaller pillars and blocks. A heart shape, for example, can be bent to make angel wings. Small heart shapes can be stuck on the candle all over for a romantic effect. Try a red candle with pink hearts, or the reverse.

Cookie cutter cutouts from sheet wax can be lots of fun for decorating your candles, and very easy. You can cover the entire surface of the candle with add-ons, or make one striking addition—like a medallion. Use this method when you have children helping you. They love to cut out the wax and stick the shapes on the candles. So what if some are a little crooked? It only adds to the charm!

Or, if you'd like to combine more than one surface decoration method in a clever way, use paints to decorate the cutouts you have attached to your candles.

Adding Texture to Finished Candles

In addition to painting, stenciling, and wax-on-wax methods, you can decorate a finished candle by adding texture—and color. Here's an example for a two-tone textured candle:

You will need: a finished pillar candle; your candle dipping setup; 4 pounds paraffin wax; ¾ ounce microsoft additive; wax paint in a color of your choice—gold is nice; and a zest peeler (the kitchen tool used to remove peel from lemons and oranges).

Before starting this project, decide what colors you want to combine. What you are going to do is use the zester to create little fine ridges in the overdipped candle; then, you are going to rub the wax paint into the ridges, giving a two-color textured effect.

There are any number of effective color combinations for this technique—gold paint over an ivory candle; silver paint over a black candle; purple paint over a turquoise candle; blue over white; green over blue; orange over yellow; and so on.

The Process

First, overdip the finished candle in the color you have chosen, three times. Then plunge it into cold water for a moment. Remove the candle and let the wax cool a little, so that it is still warm to the touch. Pressing the zester firmly against the candle, draw it downward from top to bottom, which will score the wax in fine lines. Repeat until you have made score lines all around the candle.

Allow the candle to dry. Then, using your finger dipped into the paint, gently rub the paint onto the raised lines on one half of the candle, while you hold the other side. Let the paint dry and then do the other half. Let it dry completely before lighting.

You need not limit yourself to one color on the outer surface of the candle. You can use the same technique to make a candle of many colors. Just dip a finger into one pot of paint and rub on the color down a length, an inch or more wide. Do the same with a second color, a third, a fourth. Remember, however, to do only one side of the candle at a time so that you can hold the other half in your hand, or you will get a smeared mess.

Carved Candles

Another technique for altering the surface of a candle is cutting into it, or carving. This can be as simple or as complicated as you desire. For a marbleized effect, just take a vegetable peeler and peel away some of the outer layer of a white candle overdipped in a color, revealing the white beneath. Or, dip several layers of color on one candle and then cut notches into the candle to reveal each layer.

Red and Green Marbleized Candle

1. Dip a white candle into red wax once.
2. Dip the same candle into white wax three times.
3. Dip the candle into green wax three times.
4. Dip the candle into red wax once more.

Allow the candle to cool slightly between dippings. While the candle is still warm, make small indentations in it with your thumbs all around its surface. With a vegetable peeler (it should be good and sharp) begin to peel or shave off the candle, just as you would peel a potato. Work evenly up and down the sides of the candle, or around it if you are making a ball-shaped candle. Continue carving until you have reached the effect you like, exposing some of the underlayers of color. (This may take quite a bit of carving/shaving.)

Once you are satisfied with the result, re-dip the candle in clear wax at 185° Fahrenheit and watch carefully as the rough edges melt off. As the candle is immersed in the hot wax, more of the underlayers will show. When you've got the look you like, remove the candle from the hot wax and plunge it into cold water to achieve a shiny surface.

You can use this "dip and carve" technique on a candle of any shape. It is especially nice on balls and pillars. Tapers are too slender to benefit by this method, but they can be carved as well.

Carving Tools

You can carve candles with your fingernails, a nail, knives, palette knives, chopsticks, a linoleum cutter, various kitchen implements (a cake tester is great!), or a special carving tool—anything that will cut or shave away bits of the candle's surface to reveal some of the color(s) underneath. Razor blades should be used carefully so as not to cut too deeply into the candle and weaken it, especially with tapers.

Carving with Heat

You can achieve some interesting effects by carving with a heated, sharp-pointed object, such as a nail or an ice pick. Using a candle flame as your heat source, heat the nail's point and begin to make lines, swirls, or any other pattern you like in the wax as it melts around the heated point. Don't dig in too deeply and work slowly at first. You can always go back and make the indentations deeper. Once you are used to this technique, you can quite successfully draw designs—such as vines and flowers as well as spirals and swirls—into the candle's surface.

You can also use other kitchen tools—spoons, forks, knives, etc.— for heat carving. A spoon, for example, when heated will make round indentations, or you can use it to create smooth channels up and down, or around, the candle. A fork can be used to add texture as can a serrated knife-edge. Also, you can use your fingers to pinch up little raised shapes in the soft wax around the heated tool.

Surface Decorating Methods

To expand your creative surface decoration repertoire, try any or all of these approaches:

1. Overdip in clear wax to smooth out any blemishes.
2. Overdip in a different color. You can change the color completely by using a strongly colored overdipping wax.
3. Pour different colors of melted wax over the finished candle. (See "Dripped Dipped Candles," p. 180.)
4. Splash the candle with crystalline wax. As it cools, it forms little crystals. This is a very effective means of decorating a single-colored candle.
5. Overdipping in ice water. If you dip the freshly made candle into ice water (not just cold water for shine), a square crystal formation will

appear on the outer surface of the candle. This effect makes for attractive decoration.

6. Using a round-headed (ball-peen) hammer, you can make indentations around the surface of an overdipped white candle that will result in white rings decorating the surface, around little dents. This can be very pretty.

7. Ordinarily, the ideal is a smooth, shiny candle, but for a rustic effect you can sandpaper the surface. Fine sandpaper will give a nice finish (just like it does on wood). Coarse sandpaper will provide a "country" look. This is especially charming when you are setting a country theme dinner table—with baskets, checkered tablecloth and napkins, homey decorations, and plain wholesome food.

8. You can embed objects in your candle two ways. Either roll the warm candle in a pan of small objects, as described above, or use wax glue. Both methods work well, but wax glue is recommended for embedding larger, heavier objects—such as tiny washers or large beads. Candles with objects embedded in them can be overdipped into clear wax to help the objects adhere to the surface. Just make it a quick dip so you don't cover up the decorations!

Decorating Supplies

- **Candle Varnish**—This is a special varnish made for candles. It gives a hard surface and a brilliant shine. Paint candle varnish using a soft brush.

- **Gold and Silver Wax**—For holiday candles and special occasions, gold and silver wax is wonderful. It can be rubbed on the candle's surface in various ways and is easy to use. (See "Adding Texture to Finished Candles," p. 234.)

- **Poster Paints (tempera)**—These water-based paints are perfect for painting the surface of candles. If you mix them with a bit of dishwashing detergent, they will be easier to apply and adhere better. Best of all, cleanup is easily achieved with plain water.

- **Felt-Tipped Pens**—Some felt-tipped and metallic ink pens will work well on candles; others will not. This is an area in which you will need to experiment.

Mixing Methods

Once you have mastered the basic techniques of candlemaking and examined the many possibilities for decorating your candles, the results you can achieve are varied and endless. From elegant gold-ridged pillars to rustic heavily textured blocks, you can make candles in interesting shapes and colors, and add patterns to the surface.

You don't even have to make your own candles to decorate them! You can use store-bought candles as a base for your decorations and still have something uniquely yours. No matter which methods you choose, you can create artistic and beautiful, creative and satisfying candles of your own. Using just a few simple methods, you can bring the light of candles and the magic of lovely ornamentation to any occasion and make even an ordinary weeknight dinner a festive celebration.

As a bonus, all of the methods described in this chapter can be combined with each other for different and stunning effects. For example, you can paint *and* embed a candle. You can add texture *and* pattern to a candle. As usual with home candlemaking, the only limit is your imagination!

Starry Sky Candle

To make a wonderful star-studded candle representing the night sky, make or buy a white candle—any shape will do, but a spherical shape would work best. Get a box of the little stars that teachers paste on children's school charts when they have been good or done an assignment well. Affix the little stars all over your candle. The glue-backed stars may stick by themselves, depending on the wax formula in the candle, or you may need to adhere them by either softening the candle or using wax glue. Once you have glued all the stars on your candle, spray-paint it a dark blue. When the paint is dry, peel off the little stars and there you'll see a replica of the night sky! (Need I tell you an astrologer thought this one up?)

CHAPTER 14

Appliquéd and Inlaid Candles

For the creative candlemaker, the freshly made candle is but a base of operations, the raw material for the candle-to-be. Candle finishing can be plain and simple—like the cold water bath for sheen, and nylon pantyhose for polish—but there are so many decorating options, why would you stop with that? This chapter takes the already discussed methods a step further down the road toward real artistry.

Using Pressed Flowers and Grasses

In order to use plant materials for appliquéing, they must first be dried. To dry leaves, grasses, flowers, herbs, etc., lay them flat between two sheets of tissue paper inside the middle pages of a heavy book.

You should prepare your dried flowers, grasses, herbs, or other plant material at least ten days or so before you plan to use them. You might gather wild grasses from your backyard or use flower petals or whole flowers from your garden or the florist shop.

ESSENTIALS

Be aware that some flowers will take longer to dry than others. In general, grasses and petals will dry in a week to ten days. Whole flowers like geraniums, alyssum, and pansies may take as long as three weeks to dry properly. These, however, are excellent choices for appliquéing on candles.

Candles of almost any shape can be appliquéd successfully. However, choose shapes that will complement the plant material. Long grasses would look best on a tall, slender pillar or block candle. A single pansy might be perfect on a globe-shaped candle. You might use a spray of leaves to decorate a tall pillar, and leave room at the top for a flower.

Pressed flowers—and other plant material—work especially well in "church candles," which are made with beeswax. They not only burn longer, but because beeswax is naturally sticky, it is easier to attach the flowers and leaves to it.

QUESTIONS?

What is the appliqué technique in candlemaking?
The appliqué technique is attaching relatively flat plant material to the candle's surface. Alternatively, you can attach shapes made from thin sheets of wax cut into various shapes such as stars, flowers, hearts, and the like.

As for choosing colors, it is best to stick to white or pale candles, which set off the colors of the dried grasses or flower petals. For example, if you are going to use dark green grasses, they would look nice against a light green background. Purple pansies would be outstanding against a pale lilac background.

Variations on a Theme

You can use three variations of the "adhere and overdip" technique with natural material such as flowers, leaves, herbs, grasses, and the like.

1. Using straight pins, pin the surface decorations to the candle, sticking the pins in straight; then overdip. (These pins will be removed later; keep reading.)
2. Dip the plant material itself into melted wax and stick it onto the candle while the wax coating is still hot.
3. Use the rounded backside of a heated spoon to warm the candle's surface. To do this, heat the spoon (you can lean it against the back of an electric iron or dip it in boiling water) and press it against the plant material laid on the candle. This will soften the wax under the dried plant stuff, melting it into the candle.

Here's How . . .

Once you have attached your dried flowers or grasses to the candle, overdip the entire candle in clear wax at 205° Fahreinheit for three seconds.

Do not use stearic acid in the wax you use for overdipping! It will make the outer coating of wax on the candle opaque, and thus obscure the decorations.

Remove candle from overdipping wax and while the surface is still warm, with your fingers or a spoon or the flat of a knife, press all the ends and stems of the plant fibers firmly into the candle's surface. Make sure everything adheres flat and nothing is sticking out. If you used pins, remove them.

Return the candle to the overdipping wax can and immerse it for two seconds. Then plunge the candle into cold water.

Wax Appliqué Method

You can make any number of interesting shapes from wax to use as an appliqué. Before starting out on such a project, make a collection of wax shapes in various sizes, shapes, and colors. Then, when you are ready to decorate your candle, you'll have the materials at hand.

Shapely Wax

Here's how to make wax shapes:

Prepare shallow baking pans (such as cookie sheets with rims), one for each color you want. Next, melt enough wax to form a ¼" coating on each sheet. (You can measure this in water first.)

Melt your wax in the usual way and pour out just enough to cover the bottom of the baking sheet. When wax is set but still warm, cut out shapes, using cookie cutters. While the wax is still warm, remove the shapes and press them with your fingers into formed shapes, such as flowers or angel wings made from a heart shape. Or, simply leave the cut out shapes in the pan to cool and use them as they are.

Adhere the wax cutouts to the candle either with wax glue or by using the hot spoon method described in the previous section. Attach the shape onto the candle where you have melted the surface wax.

When you have applied all the shapes to your candle—it's a good idea to draw out your design beforehand—follow the instructions for overdipping. Be sure to overdip *quickly* so that your wax shapes don't melt off!

Waxing Real Flowers

You can dip fresh flowers into pure paraffin wax and use them for appliqué. They are most charming when applied to the surface of large candles, especially pillars. Many flower blossoms can be used with this technique— roses, lilies, pansies, sweet peas, geraniums, and daisies, for instance.

To dip a flower in wax, you can run a florist's wire (used to hold long-stemmed flowers upright) through the center of the flower and hold it by the wire's end. Or, you can hold the flower by its stem (use long tweezers if the stem is fairly short).

Be sure to have all of your wax melting paraphernalia in order and ready to go before you cut the fresh flowers or take them out of their water. If the flowers have been sitting in a vase of water, take care to dry their stems on paper towels so as not to get water in your melted wax.

When you are set up, dip a flower once. While it is warm, reshape it with your fingers to its original form. Lay the dipped flower on a lined tray and spoon melted wax over it to achieve a second coating. As these fresh flowers coated with wax are exceptionally fragile and delicate, you must take great care when adhering them to your candle.

Openwork Appliqué

You can achieve a wonderful effect by pasting openwork such as lace or paper doilies on candles. Any kind of paper cutouts will work, and you can design your own with ease. Just draw (or trace) a pattern on a piece of paper and cut out the segments with an Exacto knife or a razor blade. You can attach the paperwork to the candle with wax glue, hot wax, library paste, or spray adhesive.

It's best to use this technique on large pillar candles so that there is no danger of the paper catching fire. When the candle burns down, the light will shine through the pattern of the lace or cutout paper. The well formed by the melted wax in a pillar is far enough away from the outer shell of the candle to prevent a mishap. Nonetheless, never forget the cardinal rule of burning candles: NEVER, EVER LEAVE A BURNING CANDLE UNATTENDED!

Inlays

Strictly speaking, inlaying is not a true finishing technique. As we said earlier, inlays are an advanced form of embedding—the difference being that the attaching is done from the *inside* of the candle, rather than from the outside. The final effect, however, is of a surface technique; therefore, we include this method here.

Basically, to make an inlay you stick either chunks or pieces of candle wax, or some non-wax object, such as slices of dried fruit, to the inside of the candle mold before filling it up with wax. This is a variation of the pour-in/pour-out method, except that in between pourings you embed things in the outer layer of wax you made with the first pour. (See "The Pour-In/Pour-Out Method for Molds," p. 211.)

When the candle is removed from the mold, what you have stuck in the wax inside the mold is revealed as "inlays," or contrasting visual objects inside the candle itself. This is a fascinating technique to work with and can produce many interesting and artistic results. There is practically no limit to what you can use for inlays—as long as what you use is not flammable. You can, as just noted, use chunks of other candles (more about this in a moment), slices of dried fruit (details will follow as well), or such things as nuts, nutshells, seashells, whole spices, beads, and baubles.

Bull's Eye!

David Constable, in his book *Candlemaking*, offers a design he calls a "bull's eye." It is quite attractive and easily done. According to Constable, "The bull's-eye candle is an attractive design, with a slightly spooky effect when lit that children seem to love."

To make Constable's bull's-eye candle, you need the usual equipment for candlemaking, plus an electric iron or mineral spirits. In addition, you will need three dipping cans for three different colors.

First, take a colored dipped taper candle. Overdip three additional colors onto the candle. (See the sections on overdipping in Chapter 8.) The final diameter of the taper should be 1½". The best length is about 6" or a bit more.

After the overdipped candle has cooled completely, slice it into 1" pieces horizontally, like you'd slice an orange or lemon. Next, using wax glue, stick one slice to each of two opposite faces of a square mold (4"–6" square). Wick mold per instructions in Chapter 7.

Pour the melted wax into the mold following basic instructions for making molded candles. Wait forty minutes before poking holes in the surface and adding additional wax. Allow the wax in the mold to cool completely, then remove from the mold. Smooth the sides of the candle against a warm electric iron, or polish with mineral spirits. Buff with a wet tissue.

This is truly an extraordinary candle, and David Constable is to be congratulated on its unique design. Do try making one—you'll love it and so will the kids!

Using the same idea, you can make all sorts of variations on this theme. For example, you can get a stained-glass effect by using square slices of candle set in a square mold. Or, you could use diamond shapes, or triangles, or any other shape instead of the round "bull's eye." Here we go again—experiment . . . use your imagination . . . have fun!

Inlay with Dried Fruits

This design is from another candlemaking wizard, Sue Spears, author of *Candlemaking in a Weekend*. Though the result is spectacular, the process is simplicity itself. There's a catch here, however. Unlike the inlaid candle described above, Ms. Spears's design is actually a candleholder made of wax—or a candle within a candle. It's also a variation of the pour-in/pour-out method already described.

Here's how she describes the "Lantern Candle with Dried Fruits": "A wonderful, everlasting gift, this unique wax lantern would make a welcome decoration in any home. The warm colors of the dried fruit embedded in the sides glow warmly when a candle is placed inside the lantern and lit." And she is absolutely right!

Here's How . . .

As Ms. Spears is British, I've modified her fruit selection just a bit to accommodate what is readily available in American supermarkets. To wit, you'll need an orange, a lemon, a lime, a peach, and a kiwi fruit.

Cut each of the fruits into thin slices. Place all on a cookie sheet in a warm oven (150° Fahrenheit) for one to two hours, or until the fruit is dehydrated.

Using a rectangular mold—half a half-gallon milk carton is good—melt clear paraffin (about 2 pounds) and pour it into the mold. When the wax has cooled sufficiently for a layer about ¼" thick to have formed on the top, cut out the top layer using an Exacto or craft knife, lift it out of the container with a spatula, and set aside.

Pour out the molten wax still inside and reserve. You should have an inner layer thick enough to embed the dried fruit slices firmly. You must work quickly with this method, as the wax is already partially hardened. Press slices of the dried fruit into the wax covering the sides of the molds. You needn't be particular about the order or the design as whatever you do will look spectacular! Do try, however, to use different pieces of fruit next to each other rather than piling up one kind in a single area.

Once you have embedded the fruit slices, remelt your wax, including the slice from the top, and repour. Pour to about ½" from the top edge of the inner layer. Allow to set as before, and again cut out the top, partially hardened layer so that you can again pour out the still molten wax. You will have sealed the dried fruit in between two layers of wax—which is what makes this a permanent decorative holder rather than a mere candle.

To use your "lantern," place a votive candle or a tealight in a glass holder into the center of the lantern and light. Then, just stand back and admire your work!

ESSENTIALS

You can make the fruit-embedded inlay into a regular candle if you like. Just follow the instructions for making the bull's-eye candle on p. 246. Alternatively, you can turn the bull's-eye candle into a lantern. Both methods are interchangeable and useful fodder for your imagination.

Variations on the Theme

Either of the above methods can be used for inlaying other objects, such as seashells or dried herbs, leaves, flowers, and other plant material. You can even use pebbles or small garden stones for an outdoorsy look. Try wood bark for a rustic effect, or use vegetables such as zucchini, tomatoes, cucumbers, and parsley sprigs for a vegetarian surprise.

CHAPTER 15

Making Decorative Shapes with Molds

The molding technique dates from the fifteenth century. The first molds were of carved wood and many exist in European museums. In those days, only tallow candles could be made in the wooden molds. Beeswax was too sticky to be removed from the mold—they didn't have mold release agent. Today's modern technology has provided us with molds in many materials.

Build It Yourself

Most of the molds already discussed have been of the simple variety—milk cartons, food tins, etc. But you can create many decorative shapes with molds, as well. The rule of thumb here is: if it can hold boiling water without collapsing, you can use it for a candle mold.

Pyramid candle

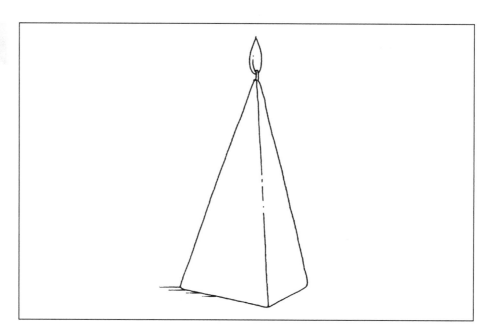

Textured Cardboard Molds

Corrugated cardboard—the kind with ridges exposed on one side that is flexible enough to roll or bend—is an excellent material for homemade molds in decorative shapes. The cardboard can be shaped into many forms—from a simple pillar to a pyramid and anything else you can devise.

A second advantage to corrugated cardboard molds, in addition to making decorative shapes, is that you automatically get a beautiful texture on the outside of your candle made in the cardboard mold. And, releasing the candle from the mold couldn't be easier: just peel off the tape and take the cardboard off the hardened candle.

To make molds from corrugated cardboard, decide first on the shape of the candle. Then, cut the cardboard accordingly. For a conical shape, you only need a square that you will roll into a cone. (See the section on cone-shaped candles in Chapter 10.) For more complex shapes, you will need to draw out your design on paper, and cut and fold it into the shape you desire before you make the cardboard mold. Once you have designed the shape you want, simply transfer the design to the cardboard, and cut and fold it, taping all edges securely with plastic tape so that no wax will dribble out when you pour.

Making a
pyramid mold

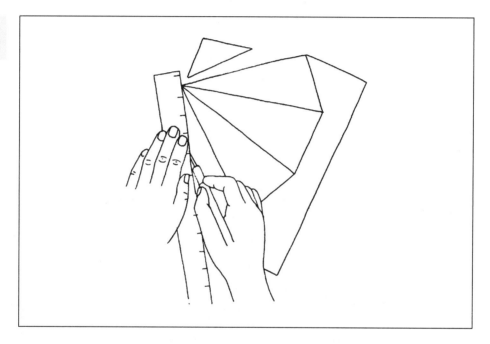

One challenge you will probably encounter if you use cardboard molds is stabilizing the wick, which needs to be centered. See "Wicks," p. 70, for how to handle wicking in molds. Also, you must be careful to seal the "top" end—it's going to be the bottom of the candle but it is also the hole through which you are going to pour your wax. Once you have overcome these difficulties with a bit of practice, you can really go to town making decorative shapes from corrugated cardboard.

Using a cardboard mold

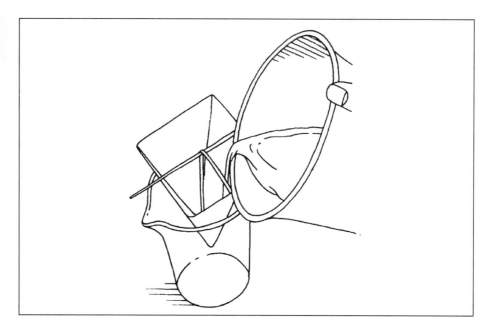

Easy Spheres

A spherical (ball) mold can easily be made by slicing an old tennis ball in half. Punch a hole in the center of one half for pouring in the wax—this will be the bottom half. In the other half, using your ice pick, make a small hole for the wick. Tape the two pieces securely together and wick and pour as usual. Ball candles are great fun and versatile—you can stick several of them together with wax glue and expand your repertory of candle shapes. And, you can stack them for an interesting decorative shape. If stacking the ball candles, don't wick them in the mold: use the wicking hardened wax method.

Copycat Molds

Once you have made a few molds yourself and your confidence is high, you can begin making your own decorative molds from instant molding compounds. (The method for making a molded shape is described on p. 128.) Here is how:

1. The object to be molded is coated with release agent.
2. It is then covered with the mold material, either poured or painted on.
3. The mold is allowed to dry thoroughly.
4. It is then peeled off the object whose shape you are duplicating and used the same way as a rubber mold.

Once you master this technique—and it does take a lot of practice—you will see unlimited possibilities before you for creating decorative candle shapes with molds. You can copy china dogs, a bust of Beethoven, an interesting wine bottle, or your own—or a friend's—hand or foot! As a bonus, you can reuse the molds that you create from interesting originals.

Casting Candles

"Casting" means using a *temporary* form as a mold. This can be sand, aluminum foil, or even a balloon. This is a neat method to use for molding decorative shapes. It's easy, inexpensive, versatile, fun, and provides plenty of latitude for the creative spirit. Molds for casting are used once and then discarded. But, since the material is so cheap, this isn't a problem as it would be with an expensive fancy mold. Casting candles is a marvelous method, and it may quickly become a favorite once you've tried it out. The casting method allows you to experiment with and explore the wonderful plasticity of wax.

Casting works on a simple principle: the shape you make with the casting material is the shape the candle will have when it hardens. You can take a sheet of heavy-duty aluminum foil and squish it into a crinkly shape. Pour the wax into it, peel off the foil, and you have created a superb decorative shape that could not be achieved any other way!

You could form a star shape from foil—or a half-moon, or anything that strikes your fancy—and cast a candle in that shape. Nothing could be easier or more conducive to creativity. A roll of foil, a pot of hot wax, a bit of wick—and you are making decorative shapes all over the place.

Wicking Cast Candle Shapes

Because of their freeform quality, candles made by the casting method may not lend themselves to regular wicking methods used for molds and other types of candles. This, however, need not deter you. There are two ways of wicking a cast candle:

- Use the method for wicking a hardened candle.
- Insert a cored wick when the candle is partly hard.

Casting Sand Candles

Sand candles . . . represent creative candlemaking at its very best—creating beautiful candles from shapeless sand and raw wax. For sheer flickering, glowing beauty, nothing can compare with a sand candle as the light soaks through the outer layer of sand. Try one and I think you will agree with me.

—David Constable, *Candlemaking*.

This is a favorite of the young and almost anybody else who enjoys the beach or who likes playing with sand. With sand candles, the sand not only serves as the mold shape, it also becomes a component of the candle itself by forming a crust on the outside. Essentially, sand candles are very simple—an impression is formed in wet sand and this is the mold from which the candle is made.

Kids love to make sand candles. However, because the wax must be hotter than usual to adhere to the sand (145° Fahrenheit or higher), adult supervision is vital. Keep safety paramount.

Because of the higher melt point required, candlemaker Betty Oppenheimer recommends melting the wax over direct heat instead of the usual double-boiler method. If you choose to do this, the safest way is in a concealed-element heater, such as an electric Crock-Pot or cooker.

If you are at the beach, you can melt the wax over your campfire—but do be extremely careful and *never* leave a pot of melting wax unattended on a stove or an open campfire. Remember that wax, being a fuel, is highly flammable. Don't ever take any chances.

And always keep items for extinguishing fire close at hand; baking soda, wet towels, and a large pot lid are acceptable options. On the beach, you could have a bucket of wet sand ready in case of accident. You know the old adage: an ounce of prevention . . .

Sand Candles 1, 2, 3

To cast candles in sand you will need the following:

1. Sand
2. Cored or primed wick
3. Wax with a high melting point
4. Color chips for wax, optional
5. Scent oil, optional
6. Large basin to hold sand
7. Direct heat source
8. Thermometer
9. Large wooden spoon
10. Skewer or ice pick

Scoop sand from a beach if you have one nearby, or buy it from a building supply outlet or garden store. Different grades of sand produce different textures, from very fine to extra coarse. Match the type of sand you use to the nature of the shape you are making. For example, if you are making a star you might want very fine sand to complement its celestial shape, but if you are making a gourd shape, choose a coarse sand for a rustic, country look.

Once you have assembled your cast candle–making items, you are ready to begin. There are three components to successful sand-casting: (1) temperature of your wax; (2) compactness of the wet sand; (3) ratio of sand to water. The first step is to wet the sand. (Beach sand may already be wet enough.) To do this, fill the basin with sand, leaving some room for mixing, and add water. Mix or stir (use your hands or a trowel) until the sand is wet enough to hold a shape when you squeeze a handful. It must be well compacted.

The next step is to dig a hole in the sand in the shape you want to make. For example, if you want a bowl shape, impress a bowl into the wet sand. A gelatin or baking mold in a fancy shape, such as a fish, bunny, or other decorative shape, can be used successfully if your sand is properly compacted.

SSENTIALS

You can add legs to your animal sand candle's shape—an "art form" popular in the 1970s—by inserting a stick or dowel into the sand to form three long holes into which the wax will run.

Have your primed or cored wick ready and cut it to the length needed. Use multiple wicks for larger candles.

Pour your hot wax (at a temperature of 275° Fahrenheit) into the sand-shape (having first removed the object with which you formed the shape). When pouring, go slowly, because the sand is absorbing some of the wax. As the wax fills the shape you have created, it will seep into the surrounding sand, making a shell. For this first pouring, use uncolored wax. If you want a colored candle, allow the wax to cool before adding the color chip: very hot wax muddies color. Add scent if you are using it. Pour again until the mold is filled, holding the spoon under the stream of wax so that the wax does not splatter. Try to disturb the sand as little as possible when pouring the wax into the shape.

When the cast shape is full, wait until a thin layer has solidified on top. Then, insert the wick straight down through the wax to the sand, keeping it carefully centered.

Once you have inserted the wick, set the basin of sand in a protected place where it will not be disturbed (you don't want your candle spilled) and allow it to cool for several hours. Carefully dig the cast shape up from under the bottom and brush off the excess sand. Congratulate yourself! You have just produced a unique work of art.

Colored Sand

Craft shops sell beautifully colored sand—but it's expensive to use except for small shapes. You can use this brilliantly colored sand in clear glass containers of any shape suitable for a container candle. It is also used without wax to make decoratively colored layered objects.

Freeform Sand Candles

By mixing sand with wallpaper glue, you can get a "dough" made of sand that will hold together while you shape it into freeform decorative shapes. Proportions of sand to glue will vary with the type of sand, so you'll have to experiment. Just add the glue to sand and mix until it is of a consistency similar to bread dough. Then, make shapes with your hands. This is just like kneading. You can press the dough into a bowl, an ashtray, a shell, or any other shallow vessel to get a basic shape. Manipulating it with your fingers—just as you would pastry dough—will result in interesting textures as well as a decorative shape. Allow the sand/glue container to dry for forty-eight hours before filling with wax and wicking as with sand candles.

CHAPTER 16

Decorative Candleholders and Containers

There is an enormous variety of decorative candlesticks and candleholders available through shops and using household and garden objects, improvisation, found items, odd things picked up at yard and garage sales. Simple, fancy, romantic, ornate, period, modern—you can choose your candle accessories both to coordinate with any theme you like and to please your pocketbook.

Candleholders Galore!

Candles can be placed in just about anything that is nonflammable and hollow. Candleholders can be placed upright or hung from wires, used in groups or as a singular, attention-getting object. Decorative holders can be manufactured from all sorts of materials—crystal, glass, tin, silver, wood—or they can be created from nature's own organic materials. One of the most fun parts of making and using candles is putting them in decorative holders either for a singular effect—such as a fat pillar in an old ship's lantern—or for a thematic effect—like using a variety of hollowed out gourds for a fall event.

Everyday objects can be transformed into decorative candleholders—an old square cheese grater set over a block candle gives the same effect as manufactured pierced-metal holder—little points of light peek out at you winningly.

I've used all sorts of food jars, jelly glasses, wine bottles, stemware, punched-tin cans, canisters, candy jars—the list goes on. As usual in the matter of candles, your imagination is your best guide—just add your taste or decorating scheme and think creatively.

 **SSENTIALS**

Try using several cups and saucers of different patterns as candleholders on an end table for a party. Often, you can find a single cup-and-saucer set at garage sales, or in thrift shops and flea markets. When you visit such places, try to be on the lookout for objects that are suitable for using as decorative candleholders.

Many items you have in your house right now can be used as candleholders. Pieces of crystal and cut glass ornaments will make an impressive display for that special dinner party or important occasion. You may have some odd pieces of china lying about—mismatched or one-of-a-kind china makes splendid decorative candleholders.

Shimmering Glassware

Candles placed in ornamental glassware create a shimmering atmosphere that positively glistens with brightness and offers an invitation to partake in a joyful celebration. So-called "depression glass" is one of my favorites. This type of glassware, which includes drinking glasses, bowls, and dinnerware (plates, cups and saucers, etc.) is extraordinarily effective when used to hold candles. You may be able to find beautifully tinted stemmed glasses. Another lovely pattern especially suited for candles is "bubble glass," a pale blue color covered with little bumps, or bubbles. Much depression glass is green, and there are pressed-glass pieces of beautiful designs.

A collection of inexpensive embossed clear tumblers—whether a matched set or a motley crew—makes a stunning display either for colored votive candles or for white pillars, depending on your decorating scheme. Use tealights in smaller glasses for a sparkling miniature effect.

Build Your Collection

If you like to collect bottles, jars, and bowls, as I do, you already have a plentiful supply of material for creating decorative candleholders. Group several bottles together—these are especially interesting if all the bottles are differently colored and of different shapes—and put candles in them according to the type of bottle. For example, a tall wine bottle is nice for a taper, while a short, fat bottle cries out for a pillar. If you have made tapers of differing thickness, you can fit them into different sized bottle openings. Such a collection of bottle candleholders looks wonderful on a broad windowsill or a sideboard.

ESSENTIALS

Be on the lookout for old and/or oddly shaped bottles when you travel. In New York, I've found marvelous ones lying on the street as discards that I've "rescued" and given new life as decorative candleholders. Others' trash can be your gain when improvising candleholders!

A bottle collection will work best if you display a range of colors of glass with candles in colors that draw the whole together. Wine bottles are wonderful to collect. They come in a wide variety of colors—from light and dark greens to light and dark browns. And they vary greatly in shape and size.

Vases of all sorts also make interesting candleholders. What can hold flowers generally can be pressed into use to hold candles. A crystal bud vase is perfect for a slim taper. A flared Chinese patterned yellow-and-blue vase of mine works splendidly with a narrow pillar. A deep vase of clear glass is perfect as a decorative holder for a large pillar—especially for outdoor use.

Wax Will Bowl You Over

Wax is one of the most versatile of mediums for the creative person. It has literally dozens of possibilities. One of the most interesting is *wax bowls* (or other vessel shapes) to use as candleholders for your handmade candles. Here's a basic method for making bowls from wax— once you've mastered it you can go to make other shapes using whatever containers you have around the house, or even purchasing special or unusual shapes to expand your repertoire. Almost any mold can be used to make a bowl.

Here's how you make a wax bowl:

Step 1. Using *interior* wax, heat approximately ¼ pound over low heat, stirring constantly. If you like, add a small color chip to the melted wax and stir until color is evenly distributed. (See color chart on p. 194.)

Step 2. Choose a shallow or medium bowl, like a soup or salad bowl, approximately 3" to 4" at the base and a wider top. Pour a small amount of the heated wax into the bowl and gently swirl it to cover the entire surface of the bowl, until all the wax in the bowl is used.

Step 3. Repeat the above step several times, until you have used all the wax in the pot. (You will have to keep your wax at a melting heat.) This process builds up a shell of wax inside the bowl.

Step 4. While the wax in the bowl is hardening, prepare a pan of water with ice cubes in it that is deep enough to hold the bowl without submerging it. Immerse the finished bowl into the ice water—the wax shell will pop right out when you invert the bowl.

Step 5. Using a paper towel, blot the wax shell dry gently. If you wish to decorate it, do it at this stage by painting a design on it. (Refer back to Chapter 13 for surface decoration techniques.)

Step 6. When your bowl is finished, you can seal the decorations by dipping the bowl one half at a time into clear wax, or spray it with acrylic fixative.

Wax bowls are easy to hang for outdoor use on the deck or patio, and are great for a barbecue or other party *al fresco.* To hang your wax bowls, use only silicone wire, which is available at hardware stores and electrical shops.

SSENTIALS

Your candle bowls make attractive holders for floating candles and are versatile when used as part of larger decorative schemes, such as centerpieces. You can make different colored bowls for a two or three color plan (such as red, white, and blue for the Fourth of July).

Nature's Bounty

Nature provides a multiplicity of possibilities for creating decorative candleholders—especially during the autumn season. Of course, everyone knows about using pumpkins for decorative candleholders— and about their wonderful versatility and the opportunities they provide for creativity. But other squash and gourds can be used to terrific effect as well. For example, a small green-striped squash with a scalloped edge paired with a candle that has been surface-decorated with leaves offers a lovely display.

ESSENTIALS

Gourd/squash decorative candleholders are simple to make: just hollow out the center with a paring knife or an apple corer to fit the size of your candle and insert the candle. For a finishing touch, tie with a raffia bow or set on a bed of loose grasses and autumn leaves.

Dry, inedible gourds in an astounding variety of sizes, shapes, colors, and textures are available in the fall from farmers' markets and in supermarkets. These are inexpensive and can be reused more than once. Try a selection of several of these gourds fitted with candles that complement their shapes and colors as a centerpiece for your Thanksgiving table, or any other autumn dining event.

This approach can be used with many other vegetables and fruits. A large red apple with a red candle makes a merry display in the winter months. In spring and summer, other bounty from the garden can be used—zucchini, yellow squash, cabbages, to name a few possibilities.

A Nutty Tropical Candleholder

Halved coconuts make excellent candleholders—great for a beach party. Simply saw the coconut in half, remove the meat (freeze for later eating), and smooth the edges with sandpaper. For a more decorative, or elegant, effect, paint the insides with high-gloss lacquer, or with gold or silver. Enhance your coconut candleholder display with a few other items from nature—sand, leaves, herbs, spices. For a genuinely tropical effect, part the leaves of a pineapple (careful—they are spiked) and insert a taper in the center, fixing it in place with wax glue. Soon you'll have the makings of a Hawaiian luau.

SSENTIALS Thick church candles work best with organic holders—they burn longer and adhere better. Or you can use a bit of wax glue to fix ordinary tapers in place. Always pare off some of the vegetable on the bottom so the candle sits flat.

Punched-Tin Holders

Simple patterns punched into tin cans make beautiful decorative candleholders. You can use a cheese grater as a punched-tin candleholder, as mentioned above, simply by placing it over a candle sitting on a flat surface, such as a plate or tile. Punched holders can be purchased—they are extremely popular in Mexico, and shops specializing in Mexican imports are likely to sell them. I have a spectacular example of this art in the shape of a large fish.

You can also make your own punched-tin candleholders from tin cans. If you wish, you can just punch holes at random—this is the easiest way to make a punched-tin holder. Or, you can create a pattern to follow by using a template or stencil.

To make a punched-tin candleholder, fill the washed and dried can with wax first. Using a steel punch or an ice pick and a hammer, punch holes in the can. The wax inside will prevent the can from denting. If you are using a pattern, wrap the stencil around the can and tape it securely so it does not slip as you punch. This takes quite a bit of skill and I personally think a random pattern is equally effective and attractive. The result will be the same: little pinpoints of light coming through the tin can placed over the lighted candle provide an air of mystery and romance.

Be careful when using your tin holder: When a candle is burning inside it, it will become very hot.

Dull sharp edges with a file before filling the can with wax. After punching, open the end of the can and push the wax through with the lid. Dip the can in boiling water to remove leftover wax (don't pour the water down the drain) and wipe it dry inside.

Potted Candles

In addition to items you might have around the house, you will find inspiration for decorative candleholders in the garden and potting shed. Terra cotta pots for plants make perfect candleholders for all types of candles. You can use them as they are—old or new—just wash and dry. Or, you can spray-paint them solid colors or in bold and dramatic contrasting colors. If you want a rustic effect, paint a terra cotta pot with yogurt and let it sit outside for a few days. Soon, it will be covered with living green moss!

Other garden appurtenances make splendid candleholders—a sprinkler frog, for example. Hanging baskets made of metal can also be used decoratively with candles, as can various patio plant containers. Galvanized trays are splendid for a display of different heights of pillars.

CHAPTER 17
Novelty Candles

Novelty candles are shaped candles—they can be formed into replicas of such things as fruits and flowers, animals, figurines, and so on. Or, they can be freeform irregular shapes. Novelty candles are the ideal for both casual and important occasions or just one of those lazy days when you have the time and inclination to let your creative imagination roam in the wonderful medium of candle wax.

The Novelty Challenge

Novelty candles are made by molding, sculpting, carving, and/or pouring. Sculpted and/or molded forms can be made and decorated just about any way you like. You can create novelty candles of your own original designs by combining the various techniques discussed in this book.

Making novelty candles will greatly expand your repertoire of creative candlemaking. These fairly simple techniques can be used to enhance a simple dipped candle or poured pillar. You can even put a beard on Santa!

Many novelty candles are extremely complicated and challenging to accomplish. Many are designed by professional candle designers, and only experienced candlecrafters attempt them. As one progresses through the various stages of learning the craft of candlemaking, gaining expertise in the methods available, novelty candles are tempting to try. If you have an adventurous spirit and aren't afraid of the new and daring, a novelty candle project may be just the thing.

Floating Candles

For the amateur or intermediate candlemaker, floaters are a good place to begin making novelty candles. Candles floating in a bowl or basin of water—or on a pool or pond—are extremely attractive. As the water under the candles undulates, the candle flames flicker like fireflies on the wing.

You can also place floating candles in a large bowl and use it as a centerpiece for a dinner party. A friend I know floats candles in the sink of the guest bathroom when she gives a party. (Since guests can't wash their hands, she puts out a pack of premoistened wipe towels.)

Floating candles are different and unusual; luckily, they are relatively easy to make. As with other candles, you can color floaters to complement the color scheme of your décor for that special dinner occasion, or any other event. Floating candles also make lovely gifts.

Simple Floating Candles

By their nature, most floating candles are small, even tiny. They are enchanting when grouped together in a large bowl where they have the drawing power of a candy shop. Small floaters can be made in metal petit four tins or other small cups. A madeline pan—in which the French shell-shaped cookies are baked—makes an ideal mold for floating candles.

The petit four tins come in attractive fluted shapes, which give the candles a scalloped edge and a flowery look.

The rule for using tin baking pans with small cups is that the pan must have a smooth surface and the cups must be wider at the top than at the base. Otherwise, the candles won't release from the molds easily.

Other molds for small floating candles that feature patterned or embossed details that will transfer to the candles' surface can be discovered if you keep your eyes open.

Here's How . . .

To make small floating candles in cup molds:

1. Set up your double-boiler system and melt the stearin.
2. Add color with a dye chip and stir until well blended.
3. Add paraffin and heat to 180° Fahrenheit.
4. Pour the wax carefully into the molds. After the wax is poured, gently tap the sides of the pan with the edge of a knife to eliminate any air bubbles.
5. Put the mold in a shallow tray of cool water to help the wax solidify. If you are using individual cups (such as fluted aluminum muffin-pan liners), you may have to weight them down so they don't float in the water bath prematurely!
6. Once the wax has begun to set, make a small well in the center of each candle with a chopstick or pencil. Add a bit more melted wax to fill in the depression.
7. When the wax has hardened to the firm-but-still-soft stage, push a length of primed wick into the center of each candle
8. Allow the wicked candles to cool completely. As they cool and the wax shrinks, you can then easily pop them out of their molds.

In a Nutshell

Walnut shell halves make lovely floating candles. Fill them with wax and tiny cored wicks. You can then float them in a bowl of water, or the bathroom sink if you are giving a party, or even in a punch bowl (remove prior to serving). These tiny floaters can even light up a pond or swimming pool.

Making Floating Flowers

Creating floating flowers is more complicated than making simple floating candles. Still, it is fun to do and you can create beautiful floating candles with this method. Essentially, you hand-mold sheet wax into shapes that are layered to create the flower effect. This is really an exciting method. Since wax is a very versatile, flexible medium, there is practically no limit to what you can achieve. After you have developed the skill of sculpting/hand-molding, you can transform sheets of wax into many beautiful and thrilling forms.

SSENTIALS

You can also sculpt (or hand-mold) other shapes—such as leaves and feathers—that will float on water. Once you have mastered the following technique for making flowers, you can let your imagination lead you on to greater heights of novelty candlemaking achievements.

The Process

To make floating flower candles you will need:

1. Your usual melting/candlemaking equipment: double-boiler or concealed-element heater, thermometer, ladle
2. Three melting cans, one for each color
3. Three 8" × 8" square cake pans
4. Cake pan
5. Aluminum foil
6. Pastry cutter or palette knife
7. Paraffin wax and beeswax— ½ pound of each
8. Cored wick
9. Pan spray or vegetable oil
10. Color chips—one red, one green

Note: This project requires thicker sheets of wax than usual. Therefore, pour the wax about ¼" deep into each pan, one color per pan.

To begin, melt the wax and divide it equally among the three cans. Add a bit of the red chip to one can to make a pink color; add enough red to the second can to make a deep rose color; color the third green to represent leaves.

Pour each color into one of the cake pans as noted above. Allow to cool for about 10 minutes, to a pliable stage.

Using the pastry cutter or palette knife, cut petal shapes of different sizes. Have 4" lengths of wick ready.

Cut several petals out of both the pink and rose sheets and cut some leaf shapes out of the green wax.

With your fingers, shape and curve the cutouts upward, like a flower forms petals. It takes a little while to get the feel for this, but once you feel the pliability of the wax under your fingers you'll enjoy it immensely. It is a wonderful tactile experience as well as a visually pleasing artistic endeavor.

Using the green leaf shapes as the bottom layer, squeeze them around the wick, allowing ½" of wick to stick out the bottom. Start adding the rose petals in layers, using wax glue or warming the wax so it will be sticky (the beeswax helps here). As you work, bend the wax petals to mimic the upward curve of flower petals. You will need to work quickly—and keep your blow-dryer handy to warm the wax if it cools and becomes brittle. Keep adding petals, with the pink layer on top, until you have enough to make a sturdy candle that is evenly spaced and won't tip over when it is put on the water. Make sure your base is relatively flat.

Once you have finished, tuck any remaining wick at the bottom into the green wax so that it won't absorb water.

Continue with this process until you have made flowers out of all the wax. Depending on the size flowers you make, this recipe will give you six to eight floating flower candles. You can scent the wax at the melted stage if you want a particular flower fragrance.

Daisy, Daisy

You can make another interesting flower floating candle by using three daisy-shaped cutters in small, medium, and large. Cut out the shapes in appropriately colored wax and hand-mold them so that the sides turn upwards. Then put the shapes on top of one another, largest on the bottom, medium in the middle, smallest on top. Wick according to the wicking hardened wax method.

By the Beautiful Sea

Many lovely novelty candles can be made using seashells, either as molds or containers. For example, try filling a conch shell with paraffin—it makes a beautiful light as the candle flame glows in its softly pink–colored interior.

FACTS

Seashells in general make great candle molds or holders. If you make candles in small, shallow seashells, you can float them. A wide variety of shells are available in many shapes and sizes. I buy them prepacked at my craft store and then sort through for the most beautiful or useful. There are usually many unusual shells in a package as well as some plain scallop shells. These scallop shells are especially terrific for floating candles.

To make a scallop or another small seashell candle, first wash and thoroughly dry the shells. In order to stabilize the shells while filling them with the molten wax, place them on a bed of sand, salt, or rice in a shallow baking pan.

For wicking, use purchased tealights. Remove the tin casing from each tealight and gently pull on the metal tab at the bottom to remove the wick. Place a wick with its metal tab attached in each shell, standing upright in the center.

Melt paraffin. For small amounts, you can cut the paraffin into 1" blocks and melt it in a measuring cup in a microwave oven. Heat on high for about six minutes, or use the conventional double-boiler method. Using a pot holder or mitt, remove the melted wax from the microwave and gently pour it into the shell, taking care not to disturb the wick. Allow to cool thoroughly before lighting.

SSENTIALS   Seashell candles are wonderful reminders of happy times spent on the beach—especially in the dead of winter when snow lies on the ground! When you visit a beach, keep in mind the many possibilities of seashell candles and gather a few shells for your winter's candlemaking activities.

Whipped Wax

Another exciting way to make novelty candles is with whipped wax. Believe it or not, wax can be whipped just like heavy cream! It can be whipped to resemble snow, whipped cream, ice cream, or the foam on a head of cold beer. If you've ever frosted a cake with whipped cream, sculpting and forming peaks and valleys, you'll be delighted with the qualities of whipped wax.

As liquid wax cools, it can be whipped to a froth, like egg whites. An old-fashioned egg-beater is the best tool to use, but a fork will work too. As whipped wax holds its shape at room temperature, you can sculpt it into many unusual shapes. In addition, whipped wax has a built-in surface texture that is attractive.

Basic Method for Whipping Wax

Different candlemakers use different wax formulas for whipped wax. Some use pure paraffin. Candlemaker Betty Oppenheimer suggests a different approach. In her book, *The Candlemaker's Companion*, she advises using one of the following two formulas to make whipped wax:

A. One pound paraffin; 1 tablespoon cornstarch
B. One pound beeswax; 1 teaspoon turpentine

My suggestion is that you begin with straight paraffin and see how you like the technique and what results you get. Then, experiment with Ms. Oppenheimer's formulas. As always, take notes.

Make an Ice-cream Cone with Whipped Wax

To make an ice-cream cone candle, see the directions for rolling a cone out of beeswax on p. 183. Whip melted wax as described above, until a thin skin has formed. Then, spoon it into the cone and shape it as you like—one dollop for a single–scoop cone, two dollops for a double–scoop; or, make a Dairy Queen–type cone.

Applying whipped wax

Meringue-Topped Wax Pie

You can replicate your favorite meringue-topped pie with whipped wax. Or, make wax tart candles in small pans. If you want a pie, first make a poured candle in a deep-dish pie pan. While it is still warm, cover the "pie" with the whipped wax using a spatula (reserved especially for working with wax). Swirl it attractively and then add multiple wicks. This is a dessert that will amaze and delight your friends!

ESSENTIALS

With a little imagination and a warm candle for a base, you can create a glass-of-beer candle or an ice-cream sundae candle, just by adding whipped wax on top. For the glass of beer, use a large pillar candle. For the ice-cream sundae, use a cone shape with a disk for a base.

Quick and Easy Molded Candle

What You Need

- ❏ An empty cardboard milk carton
- ❏ Scissors
- ❏ A piece of string
- ❏ A pencil
- ❏ Two tin cans—1 large, 1 small
- ❏ Paraffin
- ❏ Crayons (whatever color you like)
- ❏ A hot plate (or you can use a stove)
- ❏ An oven mitt

What You Do

1. Using the scissors, cut the milk carton down to the size you desire. This will be the mold for your candle, so make it the height you want the candle to be. It helps if you use a ruler and measure up from the bottom, draw a straight line around the carton, and then cut.

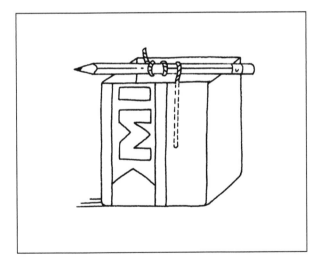

2. Starting at one end of the pencil, wind the string until you get to the middle. Let the remaining string hang down from the middle. Lay the pencil across the top of the carton. The string should hang down, nearly reaching the bottom of the carton. The string will serve as your wick.

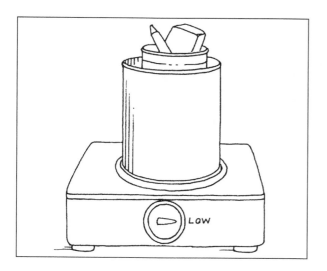

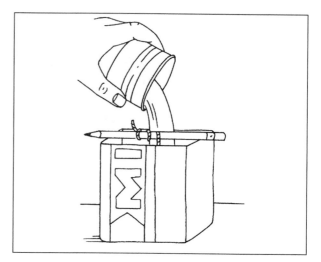

3. Set your hot plate for low heat. Fill the large tin can half full with water and place it on the hot plate. Place a block of paraffin and a crayon into the small tin can. Place the small tin can inside the large one and allow the paraffin and crayon to melt.

4. When you have a melted mixture of paraffin and crayon, turn the hot plate off. Use an oven mitt to remove the small tin can. Be careful because this will be extremely hot. Pour the melted paraffin into the milk carton slowly, being careful to not move the string around too much. Fill the carton to about an inch from the top.

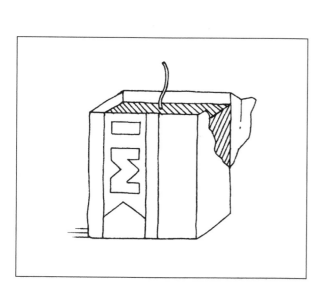

5. Now just sit back and let it cool. Once it has hardened, tear off the milk carton and unwrap the string from the pencil. Voilà! You have just made a molded candle.

APPENDIX B

Quick and Easy Seashell Candle

What You Need

- ❏ At least one seashell
- ❏ A small bowl
- ❏ Sand (or you can use rice)
- ❏ Tealight
- ❏ Paraffin

- ❏ A knife
- ❏ A glass measuring cup
- ❏ A microwave
- ❏ An oven mitt

What You Do

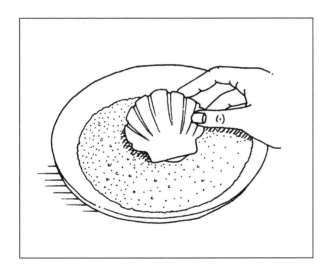

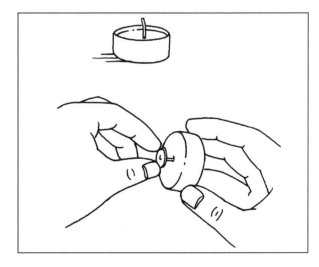

1. Fill the small bowl with sand. Situate the seashell in the middle of the sand so that it doesn't move around easily. You will get the best results if the seashell has been washed and dried thoroughly.

2. Remove the outer casing from the tealight. Next you will remove the metal plate from the bottom of the tealight. Do so gently because the metal plate is attached to the wick and you will want both of these to remain intact.

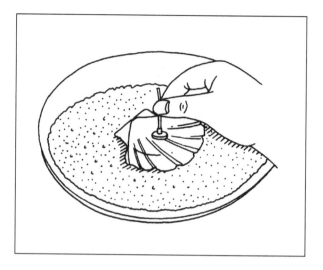

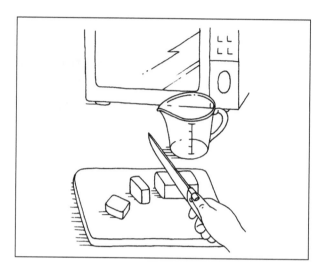

3. Set the metal plate and wick in the middle of the seashell. Make sure it is standing upright—a wick on its side isn't going to do you much good.

4. Using the knife, cut the block of paraffin into cubes (make them small so they can melt easily). Put the cubes into the glass measuring cup and place in the microwave. Heat on high for approximately six minutes or until the paraffin is completely melted.

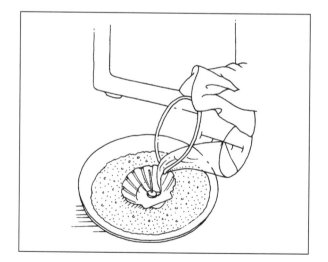

5. Using the oven mitt, remove the measuring cup from the microwave. Slowly pour the melted paraffin into the seashell, being careful not to upset the wick. Set aside and allow to cool.

Quick and Easy Sand Candle

What You Need

- ❏ Three small bowls
- ❏ Three-quarters of a cup of salt
- ❏ Food coloring, three different colors
- ❏ A spoon
- ❏ A small glass jar (baby food jars work well)

- ❏ Paraffin
- ❏ A double-boiler
- ❏ An empty can
- ❏ An oven mitt
- ❏ Candlewick (approximately 2" long)

What You Do

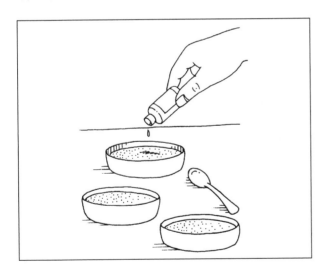

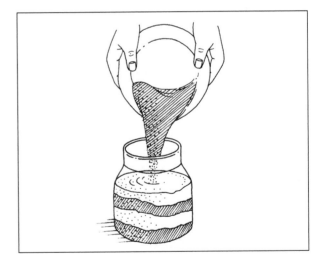

1. Add ¼ cup of salt to each of the three bowls. Then add a few drops of food coloring to each of the bowls of salt (one color per bowl). Using the spoon, mix the salt and food coloring.

2. Pour the salt into the glass jar, layering the colors. Leave approximately an inch of space at the top. Do not shake.

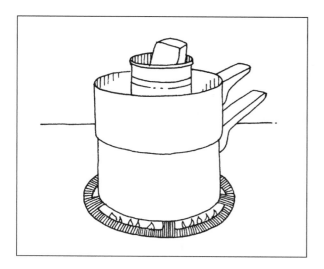

3. Place a block of paraffin into the empty can. Fill both the top and bottom of the double-boiler half-full with water and place on low heat. Put the can with the paraffin into the top of the double-boiler. Heat until the paraffin has melted.

4. Remove the paraffin from the double-boiler using an oven mitt. (Careful, this will be very hot!) Slowly pour the melted paraffin into the glass jar on top of the layered sand.

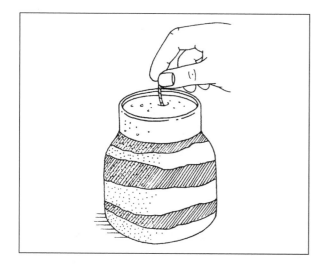

5. While the paraffin is still hot, place the wick down into the center of the paraffin. You will want to leave approximately an inch of the wick sticking out at the top. Set aside and allow to cool.

Index

A

Acorn candleholders, 220
Acrylic paints, 228
Adaptogens, 202
Additives, 102, 103–4
Advent, and candles, 34
Agricultural Extension Office, 173
Almy & Brown, 24
Almy, Brown & Slater, 24
Ambergis, 22
American Society for Testing and Materials (ASTM), 27
Animal fat, 7, 8
Appliquéd candles, 241–45
    techniques for, 242–45
    variations of, 243
Archaeological finds, 3, 4, 5
Arkwright, Richard, 24
Aromatherapy, 45, 200
Assistance online, 128
Astrological charts, 41
Automatic wicking, 127–28

Avicenna, 199
Awaken to Your Spiritual Self, 43, 47

B

Bain marie, 79
Ball-shaped candles, 186
Baumer, Francis X., 26
Bayberry candles, 18, 23, 26, 214
Bayberry wax, 63–64
Beaded candles, 174–75, 232
Beef fat, 8
Beehives, 67, 160
Beekeepers, 67
Bees, 65, 66, 158
Beeswax, 65–67
    as an additive, 121
    dipping, 158–59
    for molding, 183
    overdipping, 161
    production of, 158

types of, 66
Beeswax candles, 3, 7, 8–9
    Catholic Church and, 8, 26, 33
    popularity of, 27, 63
Beeswax dipped candle, 158–59
Beeswax sheets
    keeping warm, 95, 99
    storing, 67
    types of, 94
Biblical writings, and candles, 4, 37
Birthday candles
    drawing method, 169–70
    as gifts, 222–25
    length of, 170
    making, 101–2
    wicks for, 169–70
Blackfriars Theatre, 10
Blending colors, 193
Bottles, 81–82, 261, 262
Bowls, making, 262–63
Braided tapers, 206–7

Braided wicks, 12, 25, 71–72, 75
Brinsley, Richard, 11
Broaches for dipping, 24–25
Brown, Nicholas, 22
Brown, Obediah, 22
Build of Tallow Chandlers, 16
Bull's-eye candles, 246–47
Bunyan, John, 38
Burn rate, 74
Burn treatment, 87–88
Burning candles properly, 52–53
Burning point, 86
Butternut candleholders, 220

C

Cachalots, 14, 21
Cake pans, 82
Campbell, Joseph, 37
Candela, 49
Candelilla wax, 64
Candere, 49
"Candies", from wax, 218
Candle accessory, 62
Candle bowls, 262–63
Candle Care Kit, 158
Candle centerpieces, 221–22, 225–26, 264
Candle clock, 7, 166
Candle colors, 58–59. See also Colorful candles
Candle drips, 52
Candle etiquette, 221–22
Candle-gazing mediation, 45
Candle industry, 50–51
Candle labeling, 27

Candle-molding machinery, 10, 12
Candle molds. See Molds
Candle painting, 228–29, 235
Candle pouring, 54, 102–3, 211–12
Candle safety, 28, 157. See also Safety precautions
Candle shapes
    ideas for, 187–88
    with molds, 249–58
    types of, 56–58, 181–87
Candle varnish, 238
Candlefish, 5, 18
Candleholders
    ideas for, 260
    types of, 5, 8, 62, 259–66
Candlemaker's Companion, The, 190, 208, 273
Candlemakers, 8, 20
Candlemaking
    as art, 28
    in Colonial times, 18–21
    contemporary candles, 167
    creative candles, 167
    do's and don'ts, 90–91
    equipment for, 76–86
    hints, 103
    history of, 1–16
    in the home, 19, 23
    importance of, 19–20
    improvements in, 12–13, 24, 27
    kids and, 97, 155–56, 216, 233–34
    methods of, 54–56
    in pioneer states, 23

    as sacred art, 29–48
    safety precautions, 86–91
    testing candles, 60
Candlemaking, 246, 254
Candlemaking in a Weekend, 247
Candlemaking kits, 167
Candlemaking machinery, 16
Candlers, 20
Candles, 26, 33
    Advent and, 34
    biblical references to, 37
    burning tip of, 221
    Catholic Church and, 8
    Christianity and, 33–34
    decorating with, 221–22, 225–26, 264
    description of, 62
    for gift giving, 46, 214–15, 222–25
    Jewish symbolism, 35
    literary references to, 38–39
    magic of, 2–3, 41–43
    as main light source, 4, 9, 25
    Mass and, 34
    mythology and, 30–32
    rituals and, 39–41, 43–48
    safety of, 28
    for special occasions, 44, 213–26
    storing, 53–54
    styles of, 27
    as symbols of age, 37–38
    as symbols of the soul, 34–35
    as symbols of virtue, 36–37
    testing, 60
    unique styles, 165–80

Candlescapes, 188
Candlesnuffer, 76
Candlesnuffing, 76
Candlewicks. *See* Wicks
Cardboard molds, 250–52
Carnauba wax, 26, 64
Carnavon, George, 3
Carter, Howard, 3
Carved candles, 235–37
Carving tools, 236–37
Casting candles, 54, 253–57
Casting sand candles, 254–57
   colors for, 257
   materials for, 255
   steps for, 256–57
Catholic Church, and beeswax
   candles, 8, 26, 33
Cayola, Renato, 200
Centerpieces, 221–22, 225–26,
   264
Chandeliers, 11
Chandlers, 8, 20
Chestnut Street Opera House,
   15
Chevreul, Michel Eugène, 13
Chip candles, 178–79
Christianity, and candles,
   33–34
Christmas candles, 215–16
Chunk candles, 178–79
Circular candles, 184
Clay candleholders, 3, 5
Clay molds, 130, 132–33
Cleanup, 89–90
Clothing, and wax removal,
   91–92, 157–58
Coconut candleholders, 264

*Colonial Craftsmen and the
   Beginnings of American
   Industry*, 19
Colonial period, 18–21
Colorants, 191–92, 196
   for dipped candles, 145–46
   technical papers on, 113
Colorful candles
   blending colors, 112, 193
   color significance, 41, 58–59
   colorants for, 191–92
   decorating, 195–96
   fading, 192
   leftover wax, 196
   matching colors, 192–93
   mixing colors, 192–95
   pouring technique, 113
   professional coloring, 190–91
   scents and, 198
   shades for, 189–90
   styles of, 27
   techniques for, 188–95,
      210–12
Combustion qualities, 53
Commercial molds, 116, 117
*Complete Book of Essential
   Oils and Aromatherapy, The*,
   202
Complex molds, 136–37
Concealed element method, 78,
   80
Cone-shaped candles, 185–86
Constable, David, 246, 254
Container candles, 56
   making, 109–10
   materials for, 109–10
   repouring process, 112

steps for, 110–13
   types of, 259–66
Containers
   selecting, 106–9
   types of, 105, 259–66
Contemporary candlemaking,
   167
Cookie cutter shapes, 216, 234,
   244
Cookie sheets, 82
Cored wicks, 72, 111
Cotton, for candlewicks, 24
Cratering, 152
Creative candlemaking, 167,
   205–12
Crompton, Samuel, 24
Cutout tapers, 168–69
Cutting surface, 84
Cutting tools, 84

D

Daily rituals, 39–41, 43–48
Danish tapers, 167–68
Dante, 38
Decorated candles, 195–96,
   227–39
Decorative candleholders,
   259–66
Decorative shapes
   ideas for, 187–88
   with molds, 249–58
   types of, 181–87
Diagonal rolled candles, 100
Dipped candles, 139–63
   beeswax candles, 158–59
   burning safety, 157

Dipped candles—*continued*
  colorants for, 145–46
  cratering, 152
  drying, 150
  frame for, 55, 150, 154
  guttering, 151
  history of, 21, 140–41
  kids and, 155–56
  layering effect, 147–48, 153
  making, 144–47
  materials for, 142–43
  notes on, 149, 153–54
  overdipping, 160–63
  production of, 24–25
  quantities of, 154–55
  reverse dipping, 149
  sputtering, 152
  steps for, 146–47
  surface defects, 153
  teacher tips, 156
  technical papers on, 146
  technique for, 55, 142–44
  temperature for, 145, 149
  troubleshooting, 149–54
  wax formulas, 143–44, 146
  wicks for, 140, 144–45, 150–51
Dipping candles, 7–8
Dipping frame, 55, 150, 154
Disposable molds, 116, 117,
  127–28, 275
Double-boilers, 78, 79
Douter, 76
Dowels, 85
Drafting, 129–30
Drafts, 74–75
Drawing method, 55, 169–70,
  209

Dried fruit inlays, 247–48
Dripping candles, 52, 180
Drummond, Thomas, 15
Drury Lane Theatre, 11
Drying dipped candles, 150
Drying flowers, 242
Dublin, Ireland, 15–16

E

Easter candles, 218–19
Egg-shaped candles, 187
Electricity, 26, 28
*Encyclopedia of Wicca and
  Witchcraft*, 41, 42
English Tallow Chandlers, 8
Essential oils, 198–204
  avoiding, 202
  healing effects of, 201–2
  history of, 199–200
  precautions, 202
  for scenting candles, 202–4
Extinguishing candles, 53, 76
Extruded candles, 56

F

Felt-tipped pens, 238
Filled candle, 62
Fire-retardant wicks, 75
Flames, 2–3, 52–53
Flammable materials, 106
Flash point, 86
Flat candles, 100
Flexible molds, 211
Floating candles, 218, 268–70
  in cup molds, 269

  in nutshells, 270
  wicks for, 72
Floating flowers, 270–72
  materials for, 270
  steps for, 271
Flower appliqués, 244–45
Flower inlays, 248
Flowers, drying, 242
Forgotten Household Crafts, 18
Foundation sheets, 67
Fourth of July candles, 219–20
Franklin, Benjamin, 20
Franklin, Josiah, 20
Freeform sand candles, 257
Freestanding candles, 62
Fruit candleholders, 264
Fruit inlays, 247–48
Fruit-shaped candles, 184
Furtenbach, Joseph, 10–11

G

Garri, Giovanni, 200
Garrick, David, 11
Gaslight, 14–15
Gattefossé, René-Maurice, 200
Gift candles, 46, 214–15
Glass cutter, 82
Glass molds, 118
"Glass-of-beer" candle, 274
Glassware, 81–82, 105–8, 111,
  176–77, 261–62
Glitter candles, 232
Glow-through candles, 171–72
Gold wax, 238
Gourd candleholders, 220, 264
Greaseproof paper, 84

Greek goddesses, 31–32
Greek gods, 30–32
Greek titans, 30–32
Grimassi, Raven, 41
Guttering, 151

H

Halloween candles, 220–21
Hammer, 85
Hand-molded candles, 172–74
Hanukkah candles, 215
Hargreaves, James, 24
Healing Mind, Body, Spirit, 47
Healing, with candles, 48
Heart-shaped candles, 216–18,
    244
Heat carving, 237
Herb inlays, 248
Herbal scents, 204
Holiday candles, 44, 213–26
Home & Farm Manual, The, 25
Honeycomb rolled candles, 94

I

"Ice-cream cone" candle, 274
"Ice-cream sundae" candle, 274
Ice cube trays, 108
Identical candles, 186
Inlaid candles, 245–48
Inserts, 81

J

Jars, 105, 107–8, 261
Jelly glasses, 176–77

Jewish candle symbolism, 35
Jewish Shabbat ceremony, 35

K

Kids, and candlemaking, 97,
    155–56, 216, 233–34, 254
Kosher candles, 70
Kwanzaa candles, 215

L

Lacy candles, 230
Ladle, 84
Lalors Candles, 16
Lanterns, 9
Lard candles, 21
Las Posadas candles, 215
Latex molds, 117–18, 130–31,
    134–36
Lavender, 45
Layering effect, 147–48, 153
Leaf inlays, 248
Leftover colored wax, 196
Leftover wax
    storing, 70, 88
    uses for, 88, 233
Light, and darkness, 36
Limelight, 15
Literary references to candles,
    38–39
Lyceum Theatre, 15

M

Marbleized candles, 179, 236
Mass, and candles, 34

Matches, 11–12
Matches, of wax, 170–71
Measuring cups, 83
Meditation, 45
Melting point, 110, 112
Melting vessel, 79–81
Menorah, 35
Meringue-topped wax "pie", 274
Metal containers, 106, 260, 265
Metal molds, 117
Microcrystallines, 104
Milton, John, 38
Mineral wax, 26
Mixing colors, 194–95
Modeling wax, 174
Mold-release agent, 82, 119, 120,
    133
Mold seal, 117
Molded candles, 54–55, 115–38,
    275–76
Molding process, 119–23
    adding wick, 122
    easy techniques, 275–76
    filling, 120–21
    finishing the candle, 124–27
    materials for, 118–19
    polishing technique, 126–27
    pour-in/pour-out method, 211
    removing candle, 125–26,
        136
    repouring, 124
    shrinkage, 123, 125
    sticking, 126
    temperature for, 121–22
    wicks for, 118, 120
Molding terminology, 117–18
Molding wax, 174

Moldmaking
  complex shapes, 136–37
  craft of, 128–29
  drafting, 129–30
  latex molds, 134–36
  materials for, 130–32
  objects for, 136–37
  plaster bandage molds,
    137–38
  problems with, 129–30
  steps for, 129–32
  two-piece molds, 132–34
  undercutting, 129–30
Molds
  in Colonial times, 19
  commercial styles, 116, 117
  for decorative shapes, 249–58
  disposable molds, 116, 117,
    127–28, 275
  in early days, 8, 9–10
  flexible materials, 211
  large containers, 177
  types of, 81
  unique ideas, 176–77
Mordanting process, 13, 71
Morgan, Joseph, 13
Mottling, 175–76
Muffin tins, 109, 269
Multiwick candles, 177–78
Murdock, William, 14
Mutton fat, 8
Mythology, 30–32

N

National Candle Association, 27,
  50, 51, 113, 128

Nature's candleholders, 263–64
New baby candles, 222–23
Note taking, 59–60, 149, 153–54
Novelty candles, 57, 267–74
Nutshell candles, 270

O

Oils, from marine life, 5, 13, 21
Oleic acid, 13
Online assistance, 128
Openwork appliqués, 245
Oppenheimer, Betty, 208, 273
Orange shells, 109
Oven mitts, 83
Overdipping
  with clear wax, 125, 162
  with colored wax, 146, 163
  method for, 160–63
  precautions, 243
Oxygen deprivation, 74–75

P

Paint scraper, 85
Painting candles, 228–29, 235
Paper towels, 84
Paraffin candles, 13, 20, 27, 63
Paraffin wax, 68–69
  additives for, 102, 103–4
  at grocery stores, 68, 104
  labeling, 104
  suppliers of, 69
  types of, 69
Paschal Candle, 33, 219
Patriotic candles, 219–20
Pen drawings, 228

Pens, 228, 238
Pewter candleholders, 8
Pillar candles, 56
Pillowcase, 85
Pioneer candlemaking, 23
Plain rolled candles, 94
Plaited candles, 207
Plaster bandage molds, 137–38
Plaster molds, 131
Plastic bags, 86
Plastic molds, 117
Pliers, 85
Pliny, 5
Polishing cloths, 126–27
Polysulfide molds, 131
Polyurethane molds, 131
Pomander candle, 232
Pork fat, 8
Poster paints, 228, 238
Pot holders, 83
Potpourri scents, 197–98
Pots, for candlemaking, 79–81
Pots, stirring, 104
Potted candles, 266
Pour-in/pour-out mold method,
  211–12
Poured candles, 54, 102–3
Practice of Aromatherapy, The,
  200
Preserving jars, 105, 107–8, 261
Pressed candles, 56
Pressed-flower appliqués, 242–43
Primary colors, 193
Problems
  dipped candles, 149–54
  molded candles, 129–30
  uneven candles, 100

Progressive candles, 166
Providence, Rhode Island, 24
Pumpkin candleholders, 220–21
Punched-tin candleholders, 260, 265
Putting out candles, 53

R

Racks for dipping, 24–25
Rainbow glow candles, 172
Rathborne, Henry Burnley, 16
Rathborne's Candles, 15–16
Recipe box, 77
Recycling wax, 70
Refresher oils, 197
Release agent, 82, 119, 120, 133
Repouring process, 112, 124
Reverse dipping, 149
Rigid plastic molds, 117, 119
Ritual candle sets, 46
Rituals, and candles, 39–41, 43–48
Rolled beeswax candles, 174
Rolled candles, 54, 94–95
    making, 97–100
    materials for, 97
    steps for, 98–100
    wicks for, 98
Rolled taper candles, 100
Roman wick candles, 4
Romans, 32
Rovesti, Paolo, 200
Rubber molds, 117–18, 131
Rubber rules, 119–20

Rulers, 83
Rush dips, 4–6, 141
Rushlights, 4–6

S

Sacred candlelight, 39–41
Sacred space, 44, 45
Safe workplace, 88–90
Safety equipment, 87
Safety of candles, 28, 157
Safety precautions, 28, 86–91, 155, 157, 254, 255
Sand candles, 254–57
    colors for, 257
    easy techniques, 279–80
    materials for, 255
    steps for, 256–57
    types of sand, 255
Scale, 82–83
Scented candles
    colors and, 198
    in early days, 7, 18, 23
    essential oils, 202–4
    fading, 192
    fragrances, 188–89, 196–97
    herbal scents, 204
    potpourri, 197–98
    trial-and-error, 190
    types of, 27
Screwdriver, 85
Seashell candles, 232, 272–73, 277–78
Seashell inlays, 248
Serlio, 11
Seymour, John, 18
Shakespeare, William, 38

Shapes
    ideas for, 187–88
    with molds, 249–58
    types of, 55–58, 181–87
Shelley, Percy Bysshe, 31
Ship chandler, 20
Shopkeepers, 20
Shrinkage of wax, 112, 123, 125
Silver candleholders, 8
Silver wax, 238
Slater, Samuel, 24
Slow cookers, 78, 80
Smith & Hawken, 18
Snuffer, 76
Snuffing, 12, 25, 76
Soap Boilers, 16
Soapstone candleholders, 5
Spears, Sue, 247
Special-occasion candles, 44, 213–26
Sperm whale, 14, 21
Spermaceti candle factory, 22
Spermaceti candles, 14, 21–22
Sphere molds, 252
Spherical candles, 186
Spiraled tapers, 210
Sputtering, 152
Square-shaped candles, 56, 185
Square-shaped rolled candles, 101
Squash candleholders, 220, 264
Stacking candles, 217
Stagelighting, 10–11
Standard International Candle unit, 22
Starry sky candle, 239
Stearic acid, 13, 243

Stearin
   introduction of, 25–26
   invention of, 8, 13
   for molded candles, 27, 103,
     104, 119
   precautions, 243
   substitute for, 25
Stenciled candles, 229–31
Stenciled effects, 231
Stencils, 229–30
Stirrers, 104–5
Stirring pots, 104
Storing candles, 53–54
Storing wax, 70, 80
Straightedge, 83–84
Streetlights, 9
Sulfur matches, 12
Surface decorating techniques,
   227–39
   methods for, 237–39
   supplies for, 238
Surface defects, 153
Surface mottling, 175–76
Syracuse, New York, 26

T

Table settings, 221–22, 225–26,
   264
Tallow, 8
Tallow chandler, 20
Tallow-tree, 7
Taper candles, 57, 62
   braiding, 206–7
   carving, 100
   plaiting, 207
   spiraling, 210

   twisting, 208
   types of, 167–69
Taper trees, 168
Tealight candles, 57, 62, 103
Technical assistance online,
   128
Tempera, 228, 238
Temperature
   burning point, 86
   for container candles, 110, 112
   controlling, 145
   for dipped beeswax candles,
     159
   for dipped candles, 149
   explanation of, 78
   melting point, 110, 112
   for molded candles, 121–22
Terminology, 62–63
Test candles, 60
Textured candles, 232–34
Textured cardboard molds,
   250–52
Thanksgiving candles, 221–22,
   264
Theaters, and candles, 10–11
Theaters, and gaslight, 15
Thermometers, 78, 110
Timekeeping, and candles, 7,
   166
Tin molds, 19, 109, 269
Tinderboxes, 11–12
Troubleshooting problems
   dipped candles, 149–54
   molded candles, 129–30
   uneven candles, 100
Trying pots, 20–21
Tunis, Edwin, 19

Twisted tapers, 208
Two-piece molds, 132–34

U

Ultraviolet inhibitor, 191
Undercutting, 129–30
Uneven candles, 100
United Company of Spermaceti
   Candlers, 22
Unusual candles, 165–80
Unusual molds, 176–77
Utensils, 81–86
Utensils, cleaning, 90

V

Valnet, Jean, 200
Vases, 262
Vegetable candleholders, 264
Vegetable waxes, 7, 70
Ventilation, 132
Vermont Country Store, 18, 157,
   176
Vessels, for candlemaking, 79–81
Vesta's temple, 32, 33
Vestal virgins, 32
Vestas, 170–71
Visualization, with candles,
   46–47
Votive candles, 57–58, 62–63,
   103, 223

W

Water-based paints, 228
Water container, 84

Wax
  cutting, 244
  description of, 63
  for hand molding, 174
  melting, 78–80
  for molding, 182–84
  recycling, 70
  removing, 52, 91–92, 157–58
  shrinkage, 112, 123, 125
  storing, 70, 80
  suppliers of, 69
  types of, 63–64, 110
Wax appliqué method, 244
Wax Away, 157
Wax bowls, 262–63
Wax "candies", 218
Wax chandler, 20
Wax flowers, 244–45
Wax formulas, 143–44, 146
Wax holder, 85
Wax Light Makers, 16
Wax matches, 170–71
Wax myrtle candles, 23
Wax paints, 228–29
Wax "pie", 274
Wax removal, from cloth, 52
Wax removal, from clothing,
  91–92, 157–58
Wax removal, from surfaces,
  157–58

Wax Remover, 158
Wax scraps, 70, 88, 196, 233
Wax sheets
  creative ideas for, 96
  fun with, 96
  keeping warm, 95, 99
  kids and, 97
  making, 95–96
  types of, 94
Wedding candles, 223–24
Weights, 85–86
Whale oil, 5, 13, 21
Whipped wax, 273–74
Wick candles, 4, 12
Wick preparation, 120
Wick priming, 73–74
Wicking needles, 73, 85
Wicking tool, 85
Wicks
  automatic wicking, 127–28
  braiding, 12, 25, 71–72, 75
  burn rate, 73
  burning tip of, 221
  checking, 73
  classification of, 72
  description of, 63
  development of, 24
  fire-retardant fibers, 75
  guttering, 151
  for molds, 120, 122

  not burning, 152
  selecting, 71–72
  suppliers of, 72
  sustainers, 72–73
  trimming, 12, 25
  types of, 70–72, 75
  winding, 208–9
Winson, Frederick, 15
Wooden molds, 10
Work surface, 80, 84, 88–90
Worwood, Valerie Ann, 202
Wrapping candles, 214–15

Y

Ya Dhiu candles, 215
Yeats, W. B., 39
Your Psychic Potential, 47
Yule candles, 215–16

Z

Zodiac candles, 224–25

THE EVERYTHING SERIES!

BUSINESS

Everything® **Business Planning Book**
Everything® **Coaching and Mentoring Book**
Everything® **Fundraising Book**
Everything® **Home-Based Business Book**
Everything® **Leadership Book**
Everything® **Managing People Book**
Everything® **Network Marketing Book**
Everything® **Online Business Book**
Everything® **Project Management Book**
Everything® **Selling Book**
Everything® **Start Your Own Business Book**
Everything® **Time Management Book**

COMPUTERS

Everything® **Build Your Own Home Page Book**
Everything® **Computer Book**
Everything® **Internet Book**
Everything® **Microsoft® Word 2000 Book**

COOKBOOKS

Everything® **Barbecue Cookbook**
Everything® **Bartender's Book, $9.95**
Everything® **Chinese Cookbook**
Everything® **Chocolate Cookbook**
Everything® **Cookbook**
Everything® **Dessert Cookbook**
Everything® **Diabetes Cookbook**
Everything® **Indian Cookbook**
Everything® **Low-Carb Cookbook**
Everything® **Low-Fat High-Flavor Cookbook**

Everything® **Low-Salt Cookbook**
Everything® **Mediterranean Cookbook**
Everything® **Mexican Cookbook**
Everything® **One-Pot Cookbook**
Everything® **Pasta Book**
Everything® **Quick Meals Cookbook**
Everything® **Slow Cooker Cookbook**
Everything® **Soup Cookbook**
Everything® **Thai Cookbook**
Everything® **Vegetarian Cookbook**
Everything® **Wine Book**

HEALTH

Everything® **Alzheimer's Book**
Everything® **Anti-Aging Book**
Everything® **Diabetes Book**
Everything® **Dieting Book**
Everything® **Herbal Remedies Book**
Everything® **Hypnosis Book**
Everything® **Massage Book**
Everything® **Menopause Book**
Everything® **Nutrition Book**
Everything® **Reflexology Book**
Everything® **Reiki Book**
Everything® **Stress Management Book**
Everything® **Vitamins, Minerals, and Nutritional Supplements Book**

HISTORY

Everything® **American Government Book**
Everything® **American History Book**
Everything® **Civil War Book**
Everything® **Irish History & Heritage Book**

Everything® **Mafia Book**
Everything® **Middle East Book**
Everything® **World War II Book**

HOBBIES & GAMES

Everything® **Bridge Book**
Everything® **Candlemaking Book**
Everything® **Casino Gambling Book**
Everything® **Chess Basics Book**
Everything® **Collectibles Book**
Everything® **Crossword and Puzzle Book**
Everything® **Digital Photography Book**
Everything® **Easy Crosswords Book**
Everything® **Family Tree Book**
Everything® **Games Book**
Everything® **Knitting Book**
Everything® **Magic Book**
Everything® **Motorcycle Book**
Everything® **Online Genealogy Book**
Everything® **Photography Book**
Everything® **Pool & Billiards Book**
Everything® **Quilting Book**
Everything® **Scrapbooking Book**
Everything® **Sewing Book**
Everything® **Soapmaking Book**

HOME IMPROVEMENT

Everything® **Feng Shui Book**
Everything® **Feng Shui Decluttering Book, $9.95 (15.95 CAN)**
Everything® **Fix-It Book**
Everything® **Gardening Book**
Everything® **Homebuilding Book**

All Everything® books are priced at $12.95 or $14.95, unless otherwise stated. Prices subject to change without notice.
Canadian prices range from $11.95–$31.95, and are subject to change without notice.

Everything® **Home Decorating Book**
Everything® **Landscaping Book**
Everything® **Lawn Care Book**
Everything® **Organize Your Home Book**

EVERYTHING® KIDS' BOOKS

All titles are $6.95

Everything® **Kids' Baseball Book, 3rd Ed.** ($10.95 CAN)
Everything® **Kids' Bible Trivia Book** ($10.95 CAN)
Everything® **Kids' Bugs Book** ($10.95 CAN)
Everything® **Kids' Christmas Puzzle & Activity Book** ($10.95 CAN)
Everything® **Kids' Cookbook** ($10.95 CAN)
Everything® **Kids' Halloween Puzzle & Activity Book** ($10.95 CAN)
Everything® **Kids' Joke Book** ($10.95 CAN)
Everything® **Kids' Math Puzzles Book** ($10.95 CAN)
Everything® **Kids' Mazes Book** ($10.95 CAN)
Everything® **Kids' Money Book** ($11.95 CAN)
Everything® **Kids' Monsters Book** ($10.95 CAN)
Everything® **Kids' Nature Book** ($11.95 CAN)
Everything® **Kids' Puzzle Book** ($10.95 CAN)
Everything® **Kids' Riddles & Brain Teasers Book** ($10.95 CAN)
Everything® **Kids' Science Experiments Book** ($10.95 CAN)
Everything® **Kids' Soccer Book** ($10.95 CAN)
Everything® **Kids' Travel Activity Book** ($10.95 CAN)

KIDS' STORY BOOKS

Everything® **Bedtime Story Book**
Everything® **Bible Stories Book**
Everything® **Fairy Tales Book**
Everything® **Mother Goose Book**

LANGUAGE

Everything® **Inglés Book**
Everything® **Learning French Book**
Everything® **Learning German Book**
Everything® **Learning Italian Book**
Everything® **Learning Latin Book**
Everything® **Learning Spanish Book**
Everything® **Sign Language Book**
Everything® **Spanish Phrase Book, $9.95** ($15.95 CAN)

MUSIC

Everything® **Drums Book (with CD), $19.95** ($31.95 CAN)
Everything® **Guitar Book**
Everything® **Playing Piano and Keyboards Book**
Everything® **Rock & Blues Guitar Book (with CD), $19.95** ($31.95 CAN)
Everything® **Songwriting Book**

NEW AGE

Everything® **Astrology Book**
Everything® **Divining the Future Book**
Everything® **Dreams Book**
Everything® **Ghost Book**
Everything® **Love Signs Book, $9.95** ($15.95 CAN)
Everything® **Meditation Book**
Everything® **Numerology Book**
Everything® **Palmistry Book**
Everything® **Psychic Book**
Everything® **Spells & Charms Book**
Everything® **Tarot Book**
Everything® **Wicca and Witchcraft Book**

PARENTING

Everything® **Baby Names Book**
Everything® **Baby Shower Book**
Everything® **Baby's First Food Book**
Everything® **Baby's First Year Book**
Everything® **Breastfeeding Book**

Everything® **Father-to-Be Book**
Everything® **Get Ready for Baby Book**
Everything® **Getting Pregnant Book**
Everything® **Homeschooling Book**
Everything® **Parent's Guide to Children with Autism**
Everything® **Parent's Guide to Positive Discipline**
Everything® **Parent's Guide to Raising a Successful Child**
Everything® **Parenting a Teenager Book**
Everything® **Potty Training Book, $9.95** ($15.95 CAN)
Everything® **Pregnancy Book, 2nd Ed.**
Everything® **Pregnancy Fitness Book**
Everything® **Pregnancy Organizer, $15.00** ($22.95 CAN)
Everything® **Toddler Book**
Everything® **Tween Book**

PERSONAL FINANCE

Everything® **Budgeting Book**
Everything® **Get Out of Debt Book**
Everything® **Get Rich Book**
Everything® **Homebuying Book, 2nd Ed.**
Everything® **Homeselling Book**
Everything® **Investing Book**
Everything® **Money Book**
Everything® **Mutual Funds Book**
Everything® **Online Investing Book**
Everything® **Personal Finance Book**
Everything® **Personal Finance in Your 20s & 30s Book**
Everything® **Wills & Estate Planning Book**

PETS

Everything® **Cat Book**
Everything® **Dog Book**
Everything® **Dog Training and Tricks Book**
Everything® **Golden Retriever Book**
Everything® **Horse Book**
Everything® **Labrador Retriever Book**
Everything® **Puppy Book**
Everything® **Tropical Fish Book**

All Everything® books are priced at $12.95 or $14.95, unless otherwise stated. Prices subject to change without notice.
Canadian prices range from $11.95–$31.95, and are subject to change without notice.

REFERENCE

Everything® **Astronomy Book**
Everything® **Car Care Book**
Everything® **Christmas Book, $15.00**
 ($21.95 CAN)
Everything® **Classical Mythology Book**
Everything® **Einstein Book**
Everything® **Etiquette Book**
Everything® **Great Thinkers Book**
Everything® **Philosophy Book**
Everything® **Psychology Book**
Everything® **Shakespeare Book**
Everything® **Tall Tales, Legends, &**
 Other Outrageous
 Lies Book
Everything® **Toasts Book**
Everything® **Trivia Book**
Everything® **Weather Book**

RELIGION

Everything® **Angels Book**
Everything® **Bible Book**
Everything® **Buddhism Book**
Everything® **Catholicism Book**
Everything® **Christianity Book**
Everything® **Jewish History &**
 Heritage Book
Everything® **Judaism Book**
Everything® **Prayer Book**
Everything® **Saints Book**
Everything® **Understanding Islam**
 Book
Everything® **World's Religions Book**
Everything® **Zen Book**

SCHOOL & CAREERS

Everything® **After College Book**
Everything® **Alternative Careers Book**
Everything® **College Survival Book**
Everything® **Cover Letter Book**
Everything® **Get-a-Job Book**
Everything® **Hot Careers Book**

Everything® **Job Interview Book**
Everything® **New Teacher Book**
Everything® **Online Job Search Book**
Everything® **Resume Book, 2nd Ed.**
Everything® **Study Book**

SELF-HELP/ RELATIONSHIPS

Everything® **Dating Book**
Everything® **Divorce Book**
Everything® **Great Marriage Book**
Everything® **Great Sex Book**
Everything® **Kama Sutra Book**
Everything® **Romance Book**
Everything® **Self-Esteem Book**
Everything® **Success Book**

SPORTS & FITNESS

Everything® **Body Shaping Book**
Everything® **Fishing Book**
Everything® **Fly-Fishing Book**
Everything® **Golf Book**
Everything® **Golf Instruction Book**
Everything® **Knots Book**
Everything® **Pilates Book**
Everything® **Running Book**
Everything® **Sailing Book, 2nd Ed.**
Everything® **T'ai Chi and QiGong Book**
Everything® **Total Fitness Book**
Everything® **Weight Training Book**
Everything® **Yoga Book**

TRAVEL

Everything® **Family Guide to Hawaii**
Everything® **Guide to Las Vegas**
Everything® **Guide to New England**
Everything® **Guide to New York City**
Everything® **Guide to Washington D.C.**
Everything® **Travel Guide to The**
 Disneyland Resort®,
 California Adventure®,

Universal Studios®, and
 the Anaheim Area
Everything® **Travel Guide to the Walt**
 Disney World Resort®,
 Universal Studios®, and
 Greater Orlando, 3rd Ed.

WEDDINGS

Everything® **Bachelorette Party Book,**
 $9.95 ($15.95 CAN)
Everything® **Bridesmaid Book, $9.95**
 ($15.95 CAN)
Everything® **Creative Wedding Ideas**
 Book
Everything® **Elopement Book, $9.95**
 ($15.95 CAN)
Everything® **Groom Book**
Everything® **Jewish Wedding Book**
Everything® **Wedding Book, 2nd Ed.**
Everything® **Wedding Checklist,**
 $7.95 ($11.95 CAN)
Everything® **Wedding Etiquette Book,**
 $7.95 ($11.95 CAN)
Everything® **Wedding Organizer,**
 $15.00 ($22.95 CAN)
Everything® **Wedding Shower Book,**
 $7.95 ($12.95 CAN)
Everything® **Wedding Vows Book,**
 $7.95 ($11.95 CAN)
Everything® **Weddings on a Budget**
 Book, $9.95 ($15.95 CAN)

WRITING

Everything® **Creative Writing Book**
Everything® **Get Published Book**
Everything® **Grammar and Style Book**
Everything® **Grant Writing Book**
Everything® **Guide to Writing**
 Children's Books
Everything® **Screenwriting Book**
Everything® **Writing Well Book**

Available wherever books are sold!
To order, call 800-872-5627, or visit us at everything.com

Everything® and everything.com® are registered trademarks of F+W Publications, Inc.